Political Economy of Brazil

Political Economy of Brazil

Recent Economic Performance

Edited by

Philip Arestis and Alfredo Saad-Filho

palgrave
macmillan

First published 2007 by
PALGRAVE MACMILLAN
Houndmills, Basingstoke, Hampshire RG21 6XS and
175 Fifth Avenue, New York, N.Y. 10010
Companies and representatives throughout the world

PALGRAVE MACMILLAN is the global academic imprint of the Palgrave
Macmillan division of St. Martin's Press, LLC and of Palgrave Macmillan Ltd.
Macmillan® is a registered trademark in the United States, United Kingdom
and other countries. Palgrave is a registered trademark in the European Union
and other countries.

ISBN-13: 978-0-230-54277-8   hardback
ISBN-10: 0-230-54277-8   hardback

This book is printed on paper suitable for recycling and made from fully
managed and sustained forest sources. Logging, pulping and manufacturing
processes are expected to conform to the environmental regulations of the
country of origin.

A catalogue record for this book is available from the British Library.

A catalog record for this book is available from the Library of Congress.

10   9   8   7   6   5   4   3   2   1
16   15   14   13   12   11   10   09   08   07

Printed and bound in Great Britain by
Antony Rowe Ltd, Chippenham and Eastbourne

Contents

List of Tables

List of Figures

Notes on Contributors

Alvaro Angeriz is at the University of Cambridge, UK.

Philip Arestis is at the University of Cambridge, UK.

Tirthankar Chakravarty is at the University of Cambridge, UK.

Marco Crocco is Associate Professor at the Department of Economics and Center for Regional Development and Planning (CEDEPLAR) UFMG, and is a CNPq researcher.

Fernando J. Cardim de Carvalho is Professor of Economics at the Institute of Economics at the Federal University of Rio de Janeiro, Brazil.

Luiz Fernando de Paula is at the University of the State of Rio de Janeiro, Brazil, and CNPq.

Fernando Ferrari Filho is Full Professor of Economics at the Federal University of Rio Grande do Sul, Brazil, and a Researcher at CNPq.

Paulo Gaya is Master in Public Administration at the Brazilian School of Public and Business Administration (EBAPE/FGV) and is an analyst at the Brazilian Central Bank.

Frederico G. Jayme Jr is Associate Professor at the Department of Economics and Center for Regional Development and Planning (CEDEPLAR) UFMG and is a CNPq Researcher.

Lecio Morais is at Câmara dos Deputados, Brasília – DF, Brazil.

Alcino Ferreira Câmara Neto is Dean of the Law and Economics Center, Federal University of Rio de Janeiro, Brazil.

Leda Maria Paulani is at the Economics Department at the University of São Paulo, Brazil.

Alfredo Saad-Filho is at the Department of Development Studies, SOAS, University of London, UK.

João Sicsú is Associate Professor at the Universidade Federal do Rio de Janeiro, Brazil.

Rogério Sobreira is Associate Professor of Economics and Finance at the Brazilian School of Public and Business Administration, Getulio Vargas Foundation (EBAPE/FGV), Brazil. He is also a Member of the Money and Financial Markets Study Group at the Institute of Economics, Federal University of Rio de Janeiro (IE-UFRJ), Brazil, and a Researcher at Pronex (FAPERJ/MCT).

Matías Vernengo is Assistant Professor of Economics at the University of Utah, USA.

Carlos Vidotto is Associate Professor at the Universidade Federal Fluminense, Brazil.

1
Introduction

Philip Arestis and Alfredo Saad-Filho

The title of the book is in fact very revealing. It intends to cover recent political economy developments in Brazil by concentrating on its recent economic performance. The period we intend to cover in the following 11 chapters in this volume focuses crucially on the first period in office of President Luiz Inácio Lula da Silva, that is, 2002, when he was elected, to October 2006, when the election took place in Brazil and the President was re-elected. It is therefore very fitting to begin the volume with a chapter that attempts to discuss how Brazil came about accepting and embracing the political economy dimension of President Lula.

Alfredo Saad-Filho in Chapter 2, 'Neoliberalism, Democracy and Economic Policy in Brazil', offers the political economy dimension to which we have just alluded. It is an interpretation of three cycles of the Brazilian left in the post-war era, and it concentrates crucially on the President Lula's first period in office. The first (anarcho-communist) cycle lasted between the early years of the twentieth century and 1935. The second was led by the Communist Party of Brazil (PCB) in the middle years of the century. The third was led by the Workers' Party (PT). This cycle, lasting between the mid-1970s and the presidential election of Luiz Inácio Lula da Silva, in 2002, is examined in detail. The rise of the PT was supported by two platforms: demands for a socialist democracy, and the interests of the organized (formal) working class. Both platforms collapsed in rapid succession in the mid-1980s; the former because of the transition to political democracy, and the latter because of the economic and social changes wrought by neoliberalism. The PT responded to their collapse by shifting to the political centre. Lula's presidential election was the culmination of this strategy. It was based on a disparate alliance of social groups with limited objectives in common, and it required the abandonment of the PT's left-wing political programme. The chapter examines the performance of Lula's first administration (2002–06), and the ensuing crisis of the Brazilian left, and argues that this crisis defies rapid resolution.

In Chapter 3, Fernando Cardim de Carvalho discusses 'Lula's Government in Brazil: A New Left or the Old Populism?'. The election of Brazilian President

Luiz Inacio Lula da Silva in 2002 was surrounded by a diffuse but very strong expectation of change. Lula's voters expected him to take the necessary steps to resume economic growth, after almost 25 years of semi-stagnation, and to take steps to achieve some measure of income and wealth redistribution. A few segments of his electorate seemed to expect him to move even beyond these goals, to promote some form of radical structural change in Brazilian society, although different groups could entertain different ideas as to which structural reforms should be given priority. However, Lula's first administration was characterized by an over-cautious behaviour, maintaining, and in fact intensifying, Cardoso's monetary and fiscal policies. But Lula's attitude was ambiguous enough to allow his followers to feed the expectation that these were transitional policies. However, as President Lula's first term in office ended, one could see that those expectations were misguided. Conservative economic and social policies were adopted throughout the period and Lula did not seem to understand the alternative policies he could have followed. The chapter identifies and evaluates the policies implemented by Lula, which, although achieving some modest redistribution of income, were still responsible for keeping the Brazilian economy in the same stagnation state it had known for almost 30 years.

Leda Maria Paulani in Chapter 4, 'The Real Meaning of the Economic Policy of Lula's Government', explains why the hope for a new society and economy that the victory of the PT (Workers' Party) in the presidential elections of 2002 had created did not materialize. The country was on the brink of an economic abyss around the time of the elections of December 2002. Those who took office in January 2003 were given the perfect excuse to continue and to deepen the orthodox and neo-liberal economic policy, which had been the mark of the previous eight years under Fernando Henrique Cardoso (FHC). At the election of October 2006, President Lula was re-elected for a new period of four years (2007–10) and there is no sign that the situation in Brazil will be different in this second mandate. It is actually the case that what had happened at the beginning of 2003 was a deliberate choice. The purpose of this chapter is to recall in detail the arguments that justified that choice, drawing a balance sheet of its outcomes in the first mandate and speculating about the real nature of the 'model' adopted. The main outcome of the discussion of this contribution is the demonstration that the economic policy of Lula's government encourages the country to play the role of an international platform of financial gain (financial valorization).

The natural development on the latter contribution is to enquire into the question of 'The Twilight of Lula's Government: Another Failed Experiment with Left-Wing Administrations?'. Fernando Cardim de Carvalho and Fernando Ferrari Filho in Chapter 5 begin their contribution by examining why politicians elected on the expectation of swift policy changes so often become icons of political and economic conservatism. This is definitely a difficult and complex question, and in this chapter the authors propose to use

Brazil's example to examine two hypotheses. The first concerns subjective factors such as the *quality* of political leadership, the correlation of forces, the existence of a clearly outlined project for the country and the convictions of the governing cadres. The second concerns objective factors, among them the *institutional arrangements* that may or may not facilitate significant shifts in policy orientation. The weight of institutional arrangements is felt in the degree of vulnerability of political authorities to extra-political forms of pressure that can neutralize political initiatives taken by elected political leaders. After a brief introduction, the chapter then presents a critical description of the policies pursued by Lula da Silva's first administration. This is followed by a discussion of whether the subjective and objective factors that may have conditioned policy decision-making in the period under examination are useful in explaining Lula da Silva's failure to promote any significant change of course in Brazil.

Alcino Ferreira Câmara Neto and Matías Vernengo in Chapter 6 turn their attention to 'Lula's Social Policies: New Wine in Old Bottles?'. They posit that it has become common sense to argue that the reforms of social policies after the 1988 Constitution were somehow instrumental in explaining social progress, and that Lula's policies mark a break with the 1988 Constitution. The authors suggest that both propositions are misleading. They proceed in arguing that the financialization of government expenditures has led to worsening income distribution, and by limiting the ability of the state to increase social spending it has limited the ability of the state to reduce social inequalities. The authors conclude that a recovery of Keynesian ideas about full employment and the euthanasia of the rentier should be central to any attempt to develop a more just and civilized society in Brazil.

The following two chapters should be taken together. In Chapter 7, Alvaro Angeriz, Philip Arestis and Tirthankar Chakravarty, in 'Assessing the Empirical Evidence on Inflation Targeting and Possible Lessons for Brazil', deal with the empirical aspects of the 'new' monetary policy framework, known as Inflation Targeting (IT). This is undertaken with the Brazilian case in mind where the IT strategy was very much pursued over the period of investigation. In this sense this chapter should be viewed as preparing the groundwork for the chapter that follows: the Brazilian experience. The authors review the evidence for both developed and emerging economies. The emphasis, though, is on emerging economies, thus heralding the following chapter, which focuses on the experience with IT in Brazil. The results gathered in this study demonstrate that although IT has gone hand-in hand with low inflation, it is very far from declaring the strategy a resounding success. The evidence produced here suggests that non-IT central banks have also been successful on this score. The conclusions of this chapter are very telling for the latter. If non-IT countries have done as well as the IT countries, can we learn further from the IT experience in Brazil? This is precisely the focus of the next chapter.

Philip Arestis, Luiz Fernando de Paula and Fernando Ferrari-Filho, in Chapter 8, discuss 'Inflation Targeting in Emerging Countries: The Case of Brazil'. While this chapter examines this new monetary policy, the IT policy, in the case of emerging countries, the focus is on Brazil and the application of this monetary policy framework in the case of this country since 1999. The chapter begins by discussing the theoretical foundations of inflation targeting, before it turns to an examination of the experience of inflation targeting in Brazil. The Brazilian experience is compared and contrasted with that of other similar countries. The chapter concludes by suggesting that although inflation targeting may have had the intended impact, the non-IT countries examined for the purpose of this chapter have also had a similar experience. Furthermore, the Brazilian experience with IT has been one of low growth and relatively high inflation. It clearly is the case, then, that the conclusions reached in Chapter 7 are reinforced by the evidence adduced, and reported in this chapter, in the case of the Brazilian economy.

Chapter 9 turns to fiscal matters in Brazil. Frederico Jayme and Marco Crocco in their contribution, 'Fiscal Policy, Credit Availability and Financing of Regional Policies in Brazil', provide the relevant discussion. The main purpose of this chapter is to analyse the conditions within which regional policies are financed in Brazil as well as the inequalities in the Brazilian financial system. It intends to analyse the way the first Lula administration financed regional policies in Brazil. It doing so it takes into account three different dimensions: first, the starting point is the financing sources in a context of tax resources sharing and expanding autonomy of the federal states. The authors concentrate on an investigation of the role of federalism in regional financing in Brazil. Federalism is understood as a system that favours, not only the financing autonomy of the subunits, but also the reduction of regional inequalities through an efficient programme of tax transfers. Second, the Constitutional Funds for regional development are analysed; and thirdly, the regional distribution of credit is examined. The outcome is a mixed picture: although the use of Constitutional Funds improved during the first Lula administration, meaning that the government has been able to transform into credit the majority of the resources available, the distribution of credit by the bank sector continued to concentrate in the most developed regions. These conclusions highlight the importance of the financial sector as one of the influential aspects of regional imbalances in Brazil.

By contrast, Lecio Morais and Alfredo Saad-Filho in Chapter 10 take a non-fiscal stance on the matter. In their contribution entitled 'Policy and Politics: Non-Fiscal Implications of the Calculation of the Public Sector Borrowing Requirement in Brazil', they show that the calculation of public sector financial requirements (PSBR), used in Brazil for the determination of the deficit of the federal government and non-financial state enterprises (central government), is contaminated by several non-fiscal components induced by exogenous shocks and by monetary policy costs or gains. The chapter explains these non-fiscal impacts and, in one case, the cost of the Central Bank's discount policy, their value is calculated and its relationship with the PSBR is established for the years 1997–2002. The chapter concludes that these non-fiscal components can distort the perception of the public deficit and, therefore, bias the fiscal policy stance.

Two chapters on interest rates conclude the volume. In Chapter 11 Carlos Vidotto and João Sicsú examine 'The Interest Rate During the Lula Government: A Research Agenda', take the view that a research agenda that focuses on the central role played by the rate of interest in its evolution is paramount to our understanding of Brazilian economic developments. The evidence available poses some questions that ought to be addressed in further research by means of a statistical investigation. This should aim to identify the determinants of the rate of interest and the consequences of its path on the economy. The chapter is divided into three sections. The first section approaches the interest rate/exchange rate relationship after the adoption of a new set of economic policies after the 1998–99 currency crisis. The link between the rate of interest and the fiscal imbalances forms the subject of the second section. In the third one the effective control exerted by the rate of interest on the rate of inflation and the social costs related to it is brought into focus, covering a more recent sub-period. The development of such an agenda can possibly provide more accurate answers to the questions presented at the end of the chapter. All these aspects are of particular importance to the compilation of what could be labelled as a 'dossier' on the rate of interest.

In Chapter 12, 'Fixed Income Debt Management and Uncertainty in the Lula Administration: A Study of the Period 2002–2005', Rogério Sobreira and Paulo Gaya, begin with the observation that in November 1999 the National Treasury and the Brazilian Central Bank implemented a programme of extending the maturity and changing the profile of the domestic public debt. The aim of that programme was to extend the maturity of the domestic debt and increase the share of fixed income debt (LTN and NTN-F) in the total debt. This chapter analyses the debt management in the first Lula administration in order to evaluate the progress in terms of these objectives. It features specifically the role of the uncertainties, which surrounded the debt management of the period, as represented by the volatility in the LTN and NTN-F auctions, in order to understand how the uncertainty that refers to the behaviour of the rate of interest is perceived by the LTN and NTN-F holders. The chapter also shows that this uncertainty is transmitted through the other interest rates in the markets such as the futures market, the interbank market and the secondary market for LTN and NTN-F. It shows that, in times of intense uncertainty, there is a huge increase in the variance of the auction that sometimes leads the National Treasury to cancel the auctions. The final message of the chapter relates to the difficulty of implementing a radical change in the profile of the domestic public debt through a larger share of fixed income debt with larger maturities.

We would very much like to thank all contributors for being unselfishly prepared to revise their contributions time and time again to satisfy our demands and those of the publishers. We would also wish to thank the Departments of Economics and of Development Studies at the School of Oriental and African Studies (SOAS), for hosting a conference, which provided a few of the chapters included in this volume. Amanda Hamilton and Alec Dubber from Palgrave Macmillan and the rest of the staff there have been extremely supportive throughout the life of this project. We are grateful to all these people and their institutions for making this book possible.

2
Neoliberalism, Democracy and Economic Policy in Brazil

Alfredo Saad-Filho
Department of Development Studies, SOAS, University of London

1 Introduction

The presidential election of Luiz Inácio Lula da Silva, the leader of the Brazilian Workers' Party (*Partido dos Trabalhadores*, PT) in 2002 was considered by many commentators to have been an important victory for the Brazilian working class.[1] Lula's election was also claimed to have been one of the most important achievements of the international left in this generation, and evidence of the decline of neoliberalism in Latin America. However, Lula's administration has bitterly disappointed many of his supporters in Brazil and abroad, and it has accelerated the fragmentation of the Brazilian left. Several high profile *petistas* subsequently abandoned the party, and scores of members have expressed their dissatisfaction with the alleged ethical and political degeneration of the PT. In their view, the PT has pursued the same neoliberal macroeconomic policies that it previously scorned, and that characterized the administration led by the ex-Marxist sociologist Fernando Henrique Cardoso.

Although Cardoso's and Lula's neoliberalism may have helped to preserve price and exchange rate stability and to reduce Brazil's country risk indices, they have been blamed for the country's disappointing economic performance and for the insufficiently rapid improvement of the social and welfare indicators in Brazil. For example, the real wages of the low-paid workers have either declined or grown only modestly during the last decade, unemployment and underemployment have remained stubbornly high, the government's attempts to redistribute land have failed, manufacturing output growth has been disappointing for many years, and Lula's electoral promise of 'ten million new jobs' disappeared rapidly from his presidential discourse.

This chapter reviews the transformation of the most important political party of the Brazilian left, and one of the largest left-wing parties in the world, into the new darling of the IMF.[2] The chapter is divided into five sections. This introduction is the first. The second reviews the reasons for the rapid rise of the Brazilian Workers' Party, and the third examines why the PT gradually shifted towards the mainstream. The fourth describes the election of Lula, in 2002, the 'losers' alliance' supporting his successful presidential bid, and it explains the continuity of neoliberalism under his administration.[3] The last section summarizes the argument, and concludes that the PT is no longer a credible left-wing political force.

2 The irresistible rise of the PT

In order to explain the rapid growth and the ensuing political changes in the Workers' Party, it is important to contextualize the trajectory of the party through a brief review of the three cycles of the Brazilian left in recent decades.[4]

The first cycle began in the early years of the twentieth century, and lasted until 1935. It was initially led by anarchist workers based in Rio de Janeiro and São Paulo and, later, by the Communist Party of Brazil (PCB), founded in 1922. This period came to an end when the PCB and other left factions were crushed by the dictatorship of Getúlio Vargas (1930–45) following a failed uprising, in 1935. The second cycle started in the early 1940s, as the PCB gradually reconstituted itself. The party's growth during this period was based on the mass movement against nazi-fascism and for Brazilian participation in the Second World War on the side of the Allies. This campaign was eventually successful, in spite of the early sympathy of the Vargas regime towards the Axis. In the early 1940s the PCB had been virtually destroyed, and most of its leaders were languishing in jail. By the end of the war, the party had become a strongly disciplined organization with hundreds of thousands of members, and the PCB polled almost ten per cent of the votes in the 1945 presidential elections. In addition to the strongly pro-Soviet PCB, the political forces of the left also included the populist Brazilian Labour Party (PTB), the independent Brazilian Socialist Party (PSB), sections of the Social Democratic Party (PSD), and several smaller organizations.

The cold war reached Brazil relatively early, and the PCB was proscribed in 1947. Despite this setback, and the inevitable membership decline, the party's influence continued to be felt among many trade unions and student organizations. A few PCB militants were elected to Congress and to city councils through other organizations, and the PCB forged stable alliances with the PTB, the PSB and the PSD. These alliances with 'bourgeois' organizations were highly prized by the PCB for both tactical and strategic reasons. The PCB claimed – alongside its sister organizations in other developing countries – that Brazil was a semi-feudal country dominated by an alliance between agrarian and imperialist interests. In order to challenge this alliance, the working class (led by the PCB) joined a coalition with the peasantry, the urban middle classes and the national bourgeoisie. This coalition would eventually lead the Brazilian popular-democratic revolution. In the meantime, the PCB demanded a national development strategy based on the expansion of manufacturing capacity through import-substituting industrialization and extensive public sector intervention in the economy. Industrial development would not only support the growth of the local productive forces but also help to emancipate Brazil from the clutches of Western imperialism.[5]

In spite of the growth of the party, the PCB's national democratic strategy was comprehensively defeated in 1964. The domestic bourgeoisie and the majority of the middle classes shunned the reformist administration of President João Goulart, which was strongly supported by the PCB. Goulart was overthrown in April by a military coup promoted by landed and financial interests, and supported by the US government and by many social groups that the PCB was hoping to lead, especially the industrial bourgeoisie. The radicalized workers, peasants and students were left isolated. Although the military coup did not immediately eliminate the scope for all forms of left political activity, most left organizations, trade unions and student associations were destroyed, and the radical factions were firmly throttled. The coup brought to an end this cycle of the Brazilian left. The strategic failure of the PCB and the long-term reflux of the left led to the fragmentation of the Communist Party. Several radical organizations emerged in the mid-1960s, mostly inspired by Trotskyism, Maoism, *foquismo*, and other fashionable left-wing ideologies. Some of these organizations sponsored armed struggles against the dictatorship, especially after the regime adopted a state terrorist strategy in December 1968. The military regime eliminated these movements relatively rapidly, and the left's improvised guerrilla operations were mostly dismantled without great difficulty.[6]

Mass resistance against the dictatorship re-emerged only gradually, in the mid-1970s. The defeat of the organized working class and the guerrilla movements had removed the rationale for state terrorism, and the legitimacy of the regime was badly shaken by its inability to address the economic impact of the first oil shock, in 1973–74. The rate of inflation – an important symbol of the regime's economic 'competence' – rose for the first time since 1964, as it doubled to 40 per cent after the oil shock. Brazil's foreign debt increased rapidly, while the country's GDP growth rate fell. Finally, to the regime's embarrassment, census data showed that the concentration of income and wealth was increasing, and that the benefits of growth were systematically bypassing the majority of the population. It had become difficult to justify the denial of civil liberties in the name of 'public safety' or 'rapid economic growth'. In 1974, industrial capitalists expressed their dissatisfaction with the alleged heavy-handedness of the state's intervention in the economy. Later that year, the regime's political party, ARENA (National Renewal Alliance) was trounced in the Congressional elections. The regime could not ignore these alarming developments. The ruling military circles decided to embark on a slow, limited and tightly controlled process of political liberalization, leading to the transfer of power to reliable civilians in the distant future. This would be the keystone of a constitutional settlement securing the political 'achievements' of the Armed Forces and their role preserving 'national security'.

This strategy was largely successful. The military held on to power for another decade, protected themselves effectively against legal challenges due to the regime's human rights abuses, transferred power to moderate civilians, and maintained a significant influence on constitutional affairs. In spite of these achievements, the military were unable to control the process of liberalization completely for two reasons. First, the Brazilian macroeconomic indicators continued to deteriorate steadily until the mid-1980s. The economy was gripped by a severe crisis after the second oil shock, in 1979–80, and the crisis worsened after the international debt crisis, in 1982–83. These difficulties reduced significantly the regime's ability to deliver welfare improvements to its core constituency, the urban upper and middle classes and the large and medium landowners. The regime eventually alienated most of its supporters through a combination of erratic policymaking, managerial incompetence and corruption. Second, and most importantly for the purposes of this chapter, the dictatorship was challenged by the emergence of a new generation of left-wing mass movements which bypassed the only legal opposition party, MDB (Brazilian Democratic Movement).

In the mid-1970s, the remnants of several left-wing organizations banded together with progressive Catholic groups, leftist intellectuals and young activists to demand the restoration of democracy, respect for human rights and political amnesty, as well as democratic economic policy changes.[7] Petitions were followed by small demonstrations, which were sometimes ignored and often repressed. These protests grew slowly but steadily, especially after the gradual removal of press censorship in the mid- to late 1970s. In 1977, the university students burst back onto the political scene with a wave of strikes and demonstrations demanding resources for higher education and, principally, political freedom. Their offensive was crushed and, in this narrow sense, the students were defeated. However, the harshness of the repression against middle-class youngsters demanding democracy and better education increased the regime's isolation and fuelled the growth of the left among the urban middle and working classes. The military could no longer present themselves as the paternalistic rulers of an immature nation. It was obvious that they ruled by force alone, and did so incompetently. These political developments were followed by the explosive rise of a new trade union movement, born in the key industries nurtured by the military regime's strategy of import-substituting industrialization – the metal, mechanical, auto and household goods industries in the São Paulo industrial belt.

In May 1978, 300 000 workers unexpectedly went on strike in 300 factories, demanding a substantial pay increase. Although the strike was declared illegal and repression was both prompt and violent, the military were unable to bend the workers. Eventually, the regime sponsored negotiations between the workers and their employers. To the surprise of most observers, the strike brought significant economic gains for the workers. It also signalled to the country that resistance was both possible and potentially rewarding, and that the regime was vulnerable to mass action led by the working class. The success of the strike pushed the São Paulo metalworkers to the forefront of the Brazilian working class, and their charismatic trade union leader, Lula, became a political leader to be reckoned with.

The third cycle of the Brazilian left emerged gradually during this period (its origins can be backdated to the MDB victory in the 1974 elections). This cycle was based on the alliance between two wings of the left movement: the 'political' (mostly middle-class) and the 'trade-unionist' (working class) wings. This coalition included Lula's metalworkers' union and, soon, other influential trade unions in the manufacturing and service sectors. It also included the liberation theology sector of the Catholic Church, many student organizations, a large assortment of urban and rural social movements and NGOs, prestigious intellectuals, clandestine left parties, and a wide range of progressive organizations, from small newspapers to theatre groups. The idea of founding a new political party coalesced rapidly around this group. In late 1978 discussions had already started concerning the foundation of a Workers' Party untainted by the traditional features of the Brazilian left: populism, corruption, clientelism and Stalinism. The PT was eventually launched in 1980, under the leadership of Lula. The party included several groups, from Trotskyite political parties to loosely organized tendencies, as well as intellectuals and Catholic activists.

The PT had four distinguishing features in its early stages. First, it was a mass democratic party, where tendencies and groups were not only permitted, but even encouraged to thrive. Second, it was an independent party of the working class, that was controlled and staffed by workers and a few trusted intellectuals, and that tried to maximize the autonomy of the workers' movement vis-à-vis traditional political processes and organizations. The PT shunned alliances with 'bourgeois' parties and even other left-wing organizations. In order to increase its visibility, the PT fielded candidates wherever possible, even if this led to the fragmentation of the democratic opposition. Third, the PT was a centralized party, with a strong (but not overpowering) national executive deciding the political line and demanding adherence to its decisions. Finally, the PT became the hub of an alliance of social movements including, among others, the largest trade union confederation in Brazil (*Central Única dos Trabalhadores*, CUT, founded in 1983) and the landless peasants' movement (*Movimento dos Trabalhadores Rurais Sem Terra*, MST, founded in 1984).

The strategy and the mode of organization of the PT corresponded to the opportunities offered by the crumbling military dictatorship, and the needs and the composition of the Brazilian working class. The party grew extraordinarily rapidly, reaching 800 000 members in less than ten years. CUT represented up to 20 million workers, and the PT made significant inroads into the student movement (although the latter was dominated by the PCdoB[8]). In 1985, the military regime yielded power to a broad centrist coalition, which the PT refused to join. At that point, the PT had already become the most important left party in the country. The PT would grow further in the next few years, when it would consolidate its hegemony in the Brazilian left. Since the early nineties, most left organizations in Brazil have been either affiliated to the PT or controlled by PT militants, and most left parties are either satellites of the PT, and can no longer carry out independent political activity to any significant extent or, alternatively, they have been expelled from the PT and define themselves in opposition to the Workers' Party (especially two Trotskyite organizations, the Unified Socialist Workers Party, PSTU, and the Workers' Platform Party, PCO).

These successes of the PT were reflected in the party's outstanding performance at the ballot box (see Tables 2.1 and 2.2), culminating with Lula's presidential election in 2002, and re-election in 2006. However, these achievements were not unproblematic, and the PT's accomplishments are closely linked to its political degeneration. Taken together, these processes help to explain Lula's election and the character and performance of his administration.

3   The undoing of the PT

The rapid growth of the PT was based on two supporting platforms. First, the party's increasingly popular demand for a socialist democracy – a democratic regime incorporating but not limited to the procedural (formal) democracy associated with Schumpeter and Dahl. Procedural democracy typically includes the protection of minimum civil and political rights, clean competitive elections

Table 2.1   PT election results, 1982–2006 (number of elected candidates)

Year	State Governors	State Deputies	Senators	Federal Deputies	Mayors	Municipal Councillors
1982	0	12	0	8	2	127
1986	0	40	0	16	–	–
1988	–	–	–	–	37	1006
1990	0	81	1	37	–	–
1992	–	–	–	–	54	1100
1994	2	92	5	50	–	–
1996	–	–	–	–	115	1895
1998	3	90	8	60	–	–
2000	–	–	–	–	174	2475
2002	3	147	14	91	–	–
2004	–	–	–	–	411	3679
2006	5	126	11	83	–	–

Sources: Branford and Kucinski (2003, pp.31, 36), www.pt.org.br and PT national committee (personal communication, 5 January 2007).

Table 2.2 Brazilian presidential elections, number of votes and percentage of votes received, 1989–2006

Year	Winner (votes, %)	Runner-up (votes, %)
1989 (1st round)	Fernando Collor (20.6 m, 30.5)	Lula (11.6 m, 17.2)
1989 (2nd round)	Fernando Collor (35.0 m, 53.0)	Lula (31.0 m, 47.0)
1994	Fernando Henrique Cardoso (34.4 m, 54.3)	Lula (17.1 m, 27.0)
1998	Fernando Henrique Cardoso (35.9 m, 53.0)	Lula (21.5 m, 31.7)
2002 (1st round)	Lula (39.4 m, 46.4)	José Serra (19.7 m, 23.2)
2002 (2nd round)	Lula (52.8 m, 61.3)	José Serra (33.4 m, 38.7)
2006 (1st round)	Lula (46.7 m, 48.6)	Geraldo Alckmin (40.0 m, 41.6)
2006 (2nd round)	Lula (58.3 m, 60.8)	Geraldo Alckmin (37.5 m, 39.2)

Source: Saad-Filho (2003, p.10) and www.tse.gov.br.

for the legislature and the executive, civilian government and civilian control of the armed forces. The PT wanted this, but it demanded more: it wanted to transcend the limitations of 'bourgeois' democracy and deliver effective power and immediate economic improvements to the vast majority of the population. Second, the PT promoted the specific interests of the social groups closely associated with the party: the metal and bank workers, low-ranking civil servants, teachers and other members of the organized working class employed in the formal sector of the economy.

Unfortunately for the PT, both platforms collapsed between the mid-1980s and the mid-1990s. The response of the PT to their collapse helps to explain its continuing electoral successes, and the limitations of the Lula government.

The achievement of political democracy, in 1985, radically transformed the terrain in which the PT had initially developed. It was relatively easy for the PT to offer a progressive alternative to a decrepit dictatorship that was increasingly powerless to discipline the populace, but that remained wedded to an anachronistic right-wing rhetoric that sounded pathetic to a growing parcel of the population. The continuing concentration of income and wealth, the evidence of corruption, the military's attachment to the legal apparatus of repression, and the regime's economic ineptitude and abysmal track record providing social and welfare services offered easy targets for the opposition.

The restoration of democracy changed everything. Pluralism diluted political power and removed many of the visible targets that were previously available to the PT and the left. In a democratic state, the locus of political debates shifted to the rarefied domain of parliamentary politics. Mass demonstrations became less effective, partly because they were no longer illegal, and partly because the ballot box presumably offered a constitutional avenue for policy debate. In a democracy undergoing a period of economic crisis, many state officials could plausibly claim that, although they shared the concerns of the majority, they were unable to help because of financial constraints.

The democratic transition satisfied most of the 'political' demands of the left, but only by disconnecting them from the 'economic' demands of the majority. Civil rights, free elections and political pluralism were achieved, but economic redistribution, the nationalization of strategically important firms and the non-payment of the foreign debt, for example, that were inseparable parts of the left's programme, were never seriously considered by the centrist coalition in power. Matters would become even worse in the late 1980s, as the Brazilian elite gradually convinced itself that only a neoliberal economic strategy would permit the resumption of growth, the reproduction of the existing patterns of inequality and the preservation of democracy.[9]

The PT and the left were badly wrong-footed by the democratic transition. Rather than leading legal (and, presumably, more successful) mass campaigns for the radical transformation of the economy and the society, the PT was compelled to submit to the electoral calendar and to operate ever more strictly within the 'bourgeois' framework that it had previously denounced. Since the state institutions had been validated by their democratic veneer, the implementation of PT policies now required a democratic mandate that, although feasible, could be obtained only if the party submitted to the conventional logic of campaign finance, coalition-building, piecemeal reforms, endless negotiations with a myriad of interest groups and the imperatives of 'efficiency' and 'delivery' in local government. These limitations tempered the PT's enthusiasm for direct action and for confrontations against the state. They also increased the weight of the bureaucracy and the parliamentary party within the PT. The party showed growing signs of a split between 'moderates', attempting to implement a social democratic programme by parliamentary means, and 'radicals', seeking to transcend the conventional parameters of political activity in order to build socialism. While the former found it difficult to garner mass enthusiasm for their preferred strategy, the latter could not lead an electorally successful alliance at national level.

The PT radicals were increasingly marginalized, especially after Lula's narrow defeat in the 1989 presidential elections. After that traumatic episode, Lula and the party leadership accepted that, in order to win elections and govern effectively, the PT would need allies in the political centre, even if this required the dilution of the party's principles, political horse-trading, and accommodation with the corrupt practices that dominate Brazilian politics.

This was a very slippery slope. In order to win elections and lead viable administrations, the PT had to accommodate lobbyists and venal politicians, condone the robbery of public assets, and engage in political practices that the party would have found repulsive only a few years before. It will be shown below that, today, there is little to distinguish the PT from the other mainstream political parties.

The PT was hit hard not only by the dismantling of its political platform and identity, but also by the decomposition of its sources of class support. The neoliberal policies imposed by successive Brazilian administrations since the late 1980s hit particularly hard the sectors that were the backbone of the PT, that provided the bulk of its votes, and that were affiliated to the most active trade unions:[10] the industrial working class, the middle and lower-ranking civil servants, and other formal sector workers. One-third of all manufacturing jobs in Brazil were lost during the 1990s. Unemployment and informal employment doubled, and manufacturing industry was radically restructured.[11] The state withdrew partially or completely from several strategic sectors, especially steel, telecommunications, electricity generation, transport and finance. The private manufacturing and financial sectors were restructured and largely denationalized. The trade union laws were tightened up, and the civil service was mutilated by a succession of 'reforms' that reduced the government's capacity to regulate the market and implement targeted industrial policies. They also challenged civil servants' ability to demand economic improvements from the government. CUT lost ground to 'pragmatic' unions wedded to neoliberalism, and the trade union leaders linked to the PT split between a majority seeking short-term economic gains for their members through an accommodation with neoliberalism, and a dwindling minority that continues to demand strategic economic policy changes. Students' organizations have become irrelevant under the combined weight of the rapid expansion of the private university sector, where mobilization is more difficult, and the adverse economic circumstances affecting students and new graduates.

The PT was forced to reconstitute its sources of support under these unfavourable circumstances. In line with its mainstream political strategy, described above, the party leadership decided in the 1990s to appeal to a broader and more centrist constituency, even at the expense of its commitment to achieve immediate social transformations. The PT increasingly presented itself as an 'ethical', 'innovative' and 'responsible' party, rather than as a party of the radical non-communist left, as was the case previously. This shift built upon, and supported, the PT's experiences of municipal administration. In spite of significant failures in the 1980s, especially in Fortaleza and São Paulo, a new generation of PT mayors achieved important successes in such middle-sized cities as Santos, Ribeirão Preto and Santo André (in São Paulo state), Governador Valadares (Minas Gerais) and Vitória da Conquista (Bahia) and, most famously, in the largest city of Southern Brazil, Porto Alegre (the state capital of Rio Grande do Sul). In these cities, PT mayors successfully introduced new priorities for their city administrations, as well as more democratic and accountable political practices. The best-known and most significant example of these practices is the participatory budget.[12]

The participatory budget was originally developed in Porto Alegre, and it later spread to other cities and – less successfully – to states governed by the PT. This is a robustly democratic budgetary process, that is highly resistant against traditional forms of corruption. In the participatory budgets sponsored by the PT part of the available investment funds were allocated through a system of public meetings starting at the neighbourhood level and completed, in stages, at the level of the municipality or state. Although the outcome must be incorporated into the budget law and approved by the local council or state assembly, the political weight of the participatory process renders this share of the budget virtually immune to traditional political bargaining.

In spite of their virtues, participatory budget processes have achieved mixed results. Differences in population size, resource availability, political culture, tradition of independent mass organization and the local correlation of forces have played important roles in the outcome of these experiences. Moreover, there seem to be limits to the type of project that can be successfully funded by participatory budgets. Experience shows that it is difficult to discuss large infrastructure projects at the local level, while smaller initiatives (the expansion of the water or sewerage networks, street paving priorities, and so on) can be addressed efficiently. Finally, the relationship between the PT and the local mass organizations is also important. When they are close the participatory budget process tends to be more successful than when there is political friction and point-scoring between opposing parties at the local level. These limitations have played an important role in the failure of the experiences of participatory budgeting at state level, where the competing projects tend to be larger and political divisions are more significant.

The success of several local and state administrations led by the PT and the party's 'incorruptible' image gradually moved to the forefront, at the expense of the PT's demands for social change. In the 1990s, the PT increasingly presented itself as the only party untainted by corruption, and the PT was widely admired for its managerial capacity at local level. This political shift paid enormous dividends in the short run, and it helped to enhance the party's electoral appeal to an entirely new constituency: the moderate middle class, the informal sector workers, and many industrial capitalists.

The PT repositioned itself incrementally. In the early 1990s, Lula and party president (and, later, cabinet office minister) José Dirceu drew up a two-pronged strategy to isolate the party's left wing. On the one hand, leftists were gradually removed from positions of influence in the party, PT candidates refusing to establish local alliances with mainstream political forces were sidelined, and increasingly moderate resolutions were passed by the party conferences. For example, in 1999, the PT congress approved a 'Programme for the Brazilian

Democratic Revolution', stating that social and democratic reforms could be achieved in Brazil only by a broad coalition. The party congress also gave Lula *carte blanche* to establish any political alliances that may be needed to support his presidential election in 2002.[13] On the other hand, Lula set up the Instituto Cidadania (Citizenship Institute) in the early 1990s, and staffed it with hand-picked loyalists in order to develop public policies outside the gaze of the PT. At the turn of the millennium, the PT leadership felt that the party was finally ready to govern the country.

4   The 2002 elections and the reproduction of neoliberalism in Brazil

The exhaustion of the majority (including a significant part of the Brazilian elite) with president Cardoso's neoliberal policies was evident long before the 2002 elections.[14] It was widely believed that the government was unable to overcome Brazil's chronic economic stagnation, the administration was highly unpopular, and many journalists and commentators claimed that the social tensions in the country were becoming unbearable. The neoliberal camp fractured. No candidate was willing to defend the government's record, and many of Cardoso's supporters deserted his party's candidate, José Serra.

Lula rapidly acquired a commanding lead in the opinion polls. However, his leftist roots, the traditional association of the PT with radical political and economic demands and the party's strong links with large mass organizations, especially CUT and the MST, indicated that his administration might reject neoliberalism and seek a left-social democratic alternative. For example, many *petistas* argued that, in order to reduce the leverage of financial capital over economic policy-making in Brazil, it was necessary to default or, at least, reschedule the payment of the domestic public debt and the country's external debt.

Early in 2002, several financial institutions expressed their concerns by refusing to purchase federal securities maturing after 31 December (the last day of Cardoso's presidency). The timing was especially sensitive because the domestic public debt was equivalent to 44 per cent of GDP, and most of the outstanding bills would mature in less than 240 days. The weekly open market auctions became largely fruitless, as the brokers demanded increasing interest rates to roll over the government debt. If these rates were not forthcoming, the brokers liquidated their positions and shifted funds to the dollar market, devaluing the Real. At the same time, their international partners downgraded Brazilian bonds and foreign debt certificates, allegedly because of 'lack of policy credibility'. This pretext led the foreign banks to start recalling their short-term loans and commercial credit lines, half of which were lost in a matter of weeks. The dollar climbed steadily from R$1.95 in January to R$2.75 in October (domestic inflation was only 4 per cent during that period).

The unfolding crisis had immediate political repercussions. The media stridently demanded that 'all' presidential candidates (i.e., Lula, the only candidate that mattered) must vouch for the continuity of Cardoso's neoliberal policies in order to 'calm the markets'. The Finance Minister and the President of the Central Bank later demanded on television that the presidential candidates must explain their economic programmes to 'the markets'. Lula's poll leadership was shrinking rapidly, and he decided to counter-attack in order to secure the support of the centre. Lula issued a *Letter to the People of Brazil* (22 June, 2002), stating that his government would respect contracts (i.e., service the domestic and foreign debts on schedule), and implicitly agreeing to enforce the IMF programme negotiated by the Cardoso administration.[15] This letter was sufficient to secure Lula's leadership in the polls and, later, to open to the PT the doors of financial institutions and conservative governments around the world. It also offered the opportunity to broaden Lula's coalition further towards the centre-right. Assisted by one of Brazil's best-known advertising agencies, Lula sailed to a tranquil victory.

This episode shows that capital movements can cause significant economic instability and inflict lasting damage to important segments of the Brazilian economy. The ever-present possibility of similar events taking place in the future (in the absence of controls on international capital flows) induced the PT to accept the temporary economic tutelage of the IMF, and to abdicate from considering significant economic policy changes during Lula's administration. After the *Letter*, Lula's platform openly contradicted the historical demands of the PT.

Lula's surrender to neoliberalism was motivated not only by the policy preferences of the PT leadership; it also responded to the demands of his coalition. Lula's presidential bid in 2002 was supported by an *alliance of losers*: a coalition of groups having in common only the experience of losses under neoliberalism. This alliance was structured around four such groups. First, the unionized urban and rural working class, including skilled and semi-skilled manual and office workers, the lower ranks of the civil service, and sections of the professional middle class. It was shown above that these groups are the backbone of the Brazilian left, and that they have lost out heavily under neoliberalism.

Second, Lula was supported by large segments of the unorganized and unskilled working class, especially the informal and unemployed workers of the metropolitan peripheries. Some of these groups had been reluctant to engage with the PT previously, partly for ideological reasons (especially their attachment to clientelist and populist political practices) and partly because of the scarcity of channels connecting them to the party (in contrast, multiple and overlapping channels linked the PT to the formal sector workers, including the trade unions, social movements and the Catholic church). In 2002, these numerically large but relatively unorganized groups were attracted to Lula by their rejection of neoliberalism and by Lula's alliance with several evangelical churches, in whose flocks these workers are disproportionately represented.

Third, several prominent capitalists also supported Lula, especially among the traditional manufacturing elite of the Southeast. They were disappointed by the failure of the neoliberal growth strategy associated with president Cardoso. Many were also exhausted by the prolonged stagnation of the Brazilian economy, the onslaught of transnational firms and the pressure of competing imports, especially after the hasty liberalization of imports in the early 1990s. Finally, some magnates were concerned with the destructive social implications of neoliberalism, especially the perceived deterioration of the distribution of income and wealth and its presumed security implications: violent crime, random shootings, kidnappings, the growing power of drug-trafficking gangs, and so on. These capitalists hoped that Lula would combine economic 'responsibility' with an aggressive strategy to tackle Brazil's ingrained social problems. Their preferred economic strategy was both nationalist and expansionary. It was based on the reduction of the debt burden of productive capital, the minimization of exchange rate volatility, the rationalization of the tax system, the expansion of state procurement and marginal income distribution. Typically, Globo, a historically right-wing and heavily indebted media empire, ditched the official presidential candidate relatively early, and supported Lula hoping that his 'nationalist' administration would help the corporation to avoid bankruptcy.

Fourth, several right-wing oligarchs, landowners and influential politicians from the poorest regions of Brazil also supported Lula. This unexpected development was not due to pressure from below; rather, it was the outcome of a shrewd political calculation. Since the early 1990s, these oligarchs and their *protégés* had been squeezed out of their influential positions in Brasília by the encroachment of a new cohort of upper- and middle-managers of state institutions appointed by the financial interests associated with neoliberalism. In contrast with the previous generation of lawyers, engineers and talentless political appointees coming from the poorest regions, these new managers were economists, financiers and professional managers carefully trained in the neoliberal arts at the best Brazilian and international universities. The traditional oligarchy had also been starved of development funds by the fiscal austerity measures imposed since 1990, which had eroded their political clout. Finally, they felt betrayed by a 'dirty tricks' campaign allegedly inspired by president Cardoso and his party's candidate, José Serra. By switching their support to the PT, the oligarchs aimed to defeat the neoliberal interests associated with Cardoso. They also anticipated that Lula would depend heavily on their support in Congress and in the State Assemblies, and that the PT would be sensitive to the plight of the poor regions – both of which would maximize the oligarchs' political power and influence.

Two important groups resisted Lula's advances, in spite of the PT's effort to broaden the coalition as much as possible. Unsurprisingly, most of the elite refused to support Lula, although their resistance was much less vociferous in 2002 (and, to a lesser extent, in 2006) than in previous elections. The other reluctant group was the urban middle class. This group is relatively small, internally divided and ideologically unstable, but it is also highly influential politically because of its privileged access to the media and the organized social movements, and its ideological influence over the working class. Although the middle class includes a significant left-wing constituency, important segments remain attached to clientelistic politics, landowner interests and right-wing ideology. This group suffered badly under neoliberalism. 'Good jobs' in the private and public sectors have contracted drastically, higher education no longer guarantees sufficient income to satisfy their aspirations, and young adults are frequently unable to emulate the social and economic achievements of their parents. This group as a whole strongly desired expansionary economic policies; however, many were reluctant to abandon the neoliberal-globalist ideology that they had assimilated only recently, and they were also frightened by the 'radical' image of the PT. Under intense pressure from all sides, the urban middle class splintered across the political spectrum.

The analysis in this section indicates that the *Lula administration is structurally limited* in three important ways. First, Lula was originally elected by an unstable coalition of incompatible social forces supporting an expansionary economic programme. Beyond this, the 'losers' had only a very limited range of short-term objectives in common, and their alliance could not offer consistent support to the government. Second, the PT leadership felt that the party had to submit to the power of domestic and international finance because of the threat of a financial balance of payments and exchange rate crisis in Brazil. In doing this, the PT surrendered to the interests that it had attempted to defeat for more than two decades. Finally, the losers' alliance and the forces supporting the Lula administration in Congress and at local level *never* supported a decisive policy shift away from neoliberalism. The disparity between Lula's impressive victories, the distribution of seats in Congress in 2002 and 2006, and the left's lack of influence upon the judiciary shows that radical changes are not unambiguously popular, and they may be unenforceable. In sum, although Lula's two presidential elections created the *expectation* of change, especially among his leftist supporters, the president never had a *mandate* for radical change, and he was never even committed to specific outcomes or processes of change.

The first Lula administration showed that the PT can impose neoliberal policies more consistently and successfully than any other government, however right-wing or ideologically committed to the neoliberal interests. This helps to explain the re-election of Lula in 2006, and the ambiguities surrounding his second mandate. It seems that neoliberalism has achieved the perfect coup: after the corrupt maverick (Fernando Collor) and the aristocratic ex-Marxist sociologist (F.H. Cardoso), it is now the turn of the former trade union leader to impose the policies favoured by the financial interests and the neoliberal elite in Brazil.

5 Conclusion: the end of the PT

The policies implemented by the Lula administration have closed the third cycle of the Brazilian left since the early twentieth century. In power at the federal level, the PT has completed its transformation into a conventional political party: it has become indistinguishable from the parties that it previously opposed. The PT has ditched its commitment to radical social and economic reforms; it has condoned the compression of real wages, deindustrialization and denationalization; it has abdicated from the responsibility to promote rapid economic growth based on the domestic market, and it has sponsored corrupt political practices. The trajectory of the PT as a left-wing organization has been completed. The party has become a mainstream political organization, narrowly pursuing conventional economic policies and promoting the short-term interests of its managers, their wealthy supporters and the financial markets.

At this stage, the role of the PT has become destructive of what remains of the left in Brazil – the PT government promotes neoliberalism, undermines the resistance against it, drags its supporting organizations and political parties down the neoliberal road, and fosters the division of the Brazilian working class. The PT is no longer a party of the left but, essentially, an instrument of the Brazilian right, regardless of the best intentions of the vast majority of its militants, that remain committed to left-wing ideals. In spite of this internal tension, it is impossible to reform the PT. It has been shown recently, in the wake of the corruption scandals that tainted the first Lula administration, that the institutional structure of the party does not permit the defeat of its ruling group and, more to the point, the shift of government policy. This group has become hegemonic through ideological indoctrination, organizational control, state power, and the promotion of the economic interests of their supporters. The most likely outcome is that the members dissatisfied with the transformation of the PT will gradually leave the party or abandon any attempt to participate in political life. Like the PCB at the end of the previous cycle of the Brazilian left, the PT is likely to survive for many years. It may dwindle as its disillusioned militants abandon ship, but it may also grow substantially, from time to time, through serendipitous electoral successes.

The current state of fragmentation of the left and the working class in Brazil indicates that the present crisis of the Brazilian left defies rapid resolution. It is likely to last many years, and it cannot be resolved simply through the creation of another political party (as was attempted recently by the founders of the Party of Socialism and Freedom, PSOL). Attempts to address this crisis will need to address two questions consistently: what is the nature of the Brazilian working class under neoliberalism, and what forms of organization and political activity can promote its interests? These questions cannot be answered purely academically. Responses can be found only in practice, as the Brazilian workers struggle to discover new forms of political activity in order express their interests in the face of a bitterly hostile political environment.

Notes

1   Myself included; see, for example, Saad-Filho (2003).
2   In April 2003, IMF managing director Horst Köhler stated: 'I am enthusiastic [about the new Brazilian administration]; but it is better to say [that] I am deeply impressed by President Lula ... because I do think [that] he has the credibility which often other leaders lack a bit, and the credibility is that he is serious to work hard to combine growth-oriented policy with social equity [*sic*]. This is the right agenda, the right direction, the right objective for Brazil ... I [also] think [that] what the government, under the leadership of President Lula, has demonstrated in its first 100 days of government is also impressive and not just airing intention' (http://www.imf.org/external/np/tr/2003/tr030410.htm). Later, Anne Krueger, IMF first deputy managing director and acting chair, declared that 'The [Brazilian] government's sound policies have contributed to increase international reserves, helped improve the composition of public debt, and fostered a swing in the external current account ... The conduct of fiscal and monetary policy remains commendable ... Within this fiscal framework, the government's focus on modernizing Brazil's infrastructure and implementing a prudent mechanism for private–public partnerships ... should help increase growth ... The conduct of monetary policy has been appropriately cautious in light of recent uncertainties, solidifying the credibility of the monetary authorities and maintaining inflation on a path toward the government's goals' (http://www.imf.org/external/np/sec/pr/2004/pr04118.htm).
3   This section does not assess in detail the performance of the Brazilian economy under the Lula administration; see, however, the other chapters in this book.
4   These cycles were initially suggested by Cesar Benjamin (personal communication, June 2004), but they have been adapted and modified in this chapter. For a similar interpretation, see Bianchi and Braga (2003) and Boito (2003). The review of the history of the PT in this chapter draws primarily on Branford and Kucinski (2003).
5   See Goldenstein (1994), Löwy (2003, part 2, V–VI) and Mantega (1984).
6   For a review of the Brazilian left during this period, see Mir (1994). The only minimally successful guerrilla operation in the country was sponsored by the Maoist Communist Party of Brazil (PCdoB) in the southeastern fringe of the Amazon rainforest. A few dozen guerrillas based in the region since 1966 managed to resist three Army incursions in 1972–74, but they were eventually defeated (see Morais and Silva 2006).
7   Two especially important organisations were the Brazilian Movement for Amnesty (MBA), a broad front campaigning for amnesty to all political prisoners and the right of return of Brazilians exiled or banished for political reasons, and the Movement Cost of Living (MCV), that collected millions of signatures in petitions demanding inflation control and real wage increases for the low paid.
8   The PCB changed its name to Brazilian Communist Party in 1958, in order to apply (unsuccessfully) for its legalization. A Maoist splinter group recovered the name

Communist Party of Brazil in 1962, and adopted the acronym PCdoB. In the late 1960s this party shifted towards Enver Hoxha's Albania. The PCdoB has been a satellite of the PT since the late 1980s.

9 See Saad-Filho and Morais (2002).
10 See Saad-Filho and Mollo (2002, 2006).
11 For an assessment of the transformations in the Brazilian working class under neoliberalism, see Pochmann (1999).
12 See Branford and Kucinski (2003, ch.4).
13 See Branford and Kucinski (2003, pp.45–52).
14 See Morais and Saad-Filho (2003, 2005), Saad-Filho (2003).
15 This letter is available in English and Portuguese at www.pt.org.br.

References

Bianchi, A. and Braga, R. (2003) Le PT au Pouvoir: La Gauche Brésilienne et le Social-Liberalisme. *Carré Rouge* 26, pp.49–60.

Boito, A. (2003) A Hegemonia Neoliberal no Governo Lula. *Crítica Marxista* 17, pp.10–36.

Branford, S. and Kucinski, B. (2003) *Politics Transformed – Lula and the Workers' Party in Brazil*. London: Latin American Bureau.

Goldenstein, L. (1994) *Repensando a Dependência*. Rio de Janeiro: Paz e Terra.

Löwy, M. (2003) *O Marxismo na América Latina*. São Paulo: Fundação Perseu Abramo.

Mantega, G. (1984) *A Economia Política Brasileira*. São Paulo and Petrópolis: Polis/Vozes.

Mir, L. (1994) *A Revolução Impossível: A Esquerda e a Luta Armada no Brasil*. São Paulo: Editora Best Seller.

Morais, L. and Saad-Filho, A. (2003) 'Snatching Defeat from the Jaws of Victory? Lula, the Workers' Party and the Prospects for Change in Brazil', *Capital & Class* 81, pp.17–23.

Morais, L. and Saad-Filho, A. (2005) 'Lula and the Continuity of Neoliberalism in Brazil: Strategic Choice, Economic Imperative or Political Schizophrenia', *Historical Materialism* 13 (1), pp.3–32.

Morais, T. and Silva, E. (2006). *Operação Araguaia*. Brasília: Geração Editorial.

Oliveira, F. (2003) 'The Duckbilled Platypus', *New Left Review* 24, pp.40–57.

Pochmann, M. (1999) *O Trabalho sob Fogo Cruzado: Exclusão, Desemprego e Precarização no Final do Século*. São Paulo: Contexto.

Saad-Filho, A. (2003) New Dawn or False Start in Brazil? The Political Economy of Lula's Election, *Historical Materialism* 11 (1), pp.3–21.

Saad-Filho, A. and Mollo, M.L.R. (2002) 'Inflation and Stabilization in Brazil: A Political Economy Analysis', *Review of Radical Political Economics* 34 (2), pp.109–35.

Saad-Filho, A. and Mollo, M.L.R. (2006) 'Neoliberal Economic Policies in Brazil (1994–2005): Cardoso, Lula, and the Need for a Democratic Alternative', *New Political Economy* 11(1), pp. 99–123.

Saad-Filho, A. and Morais, L. (2002) 'Neomonetarist Dreams and Realities: A Review of the Brazilian Experience', in P. Davidson (ed.) *A Post Keynesian Perspective on 21st Century Economic Problems*, Cheltenham: Edward Elgar.

Tavares, L. (2003) *O Debate sobre o Gasto Social do Governo Federal, ou 'Os Economistas da Fazenda Atacam Outra Vez'*, www.lpp-uerj.net/outrobrasil/Link_OutroBrasil/ANALISES/Laura.11.2003.pdf

Watson, M. (2002) 'The Institutional Paradoxes of Monetary Orthodoxy: Reflections on the Political Economy of Central Bank Independence', *Review of International Political Economy* 9 (1), pp.183–96.

3

Lula's Government in Brazil: A New Left or the Old Populism?

Fernando J. Cardim de Carvalho[*]

Professor of Economics, Institute of Economics, Federal University of Rio de Janeiro

1   Introduction

The election of Brazilian President Luiz Inácio Lula da Silva in 2002 was surrounded by a diffuse but very strong expectation of change. In fact, the new president himself, in his inaugural address, opened his speech stressing the word *change*. Lula's voters expected him to take the necessary steps to resume economic growth, after almost 25 years of semi-stagnation, and to achieve some measure of income and wealth redistribution. A few segments of his electorate seemed to expect him to move even beyond these goals, to promote some form of radical structural change in the Brazilian society, although different groups could entertain different ideas as to which structural reforms should be given priority. At a minimum, both Lula's voters and opponents seemed to expect (or to fear) a change in the macroeconomic policy mix implemented by President Cardoso in his second term, particularly in relation to the maintenance of high interest rates and of a fiscal policy that privileged financial transfers over public investment.

Lula's administration, however, was characterized, in his first year, by an over-cautious behaviour, maintaining and in fact intensifying Cardoso's monetary and fiscal policies. To signal that his choice to persist with Cardoso's policies was not temporary, Lula placed conservative economists in posts of the highest authority in the economic ministries, in complete disregard of the economists historically associated with the Workers' Party (PT, in Portuguese). Still, the president's rhetoric was ambiguous in this period: in his first year as president, Lula frequently explained the maintenance of Cardoso's policies as a result of the latter's *damned legacy*, the 2002 balance of payments crisis, which forced him to adopt policies destined to calm down financial markets rather than to satisfy his supporters. This ambiguity allowed a large number of his followers to keep faith, expecting that, once the crisis was over and financial markets had at last calmed down, the 'PT style of government' would then prevail.

Lula's first term in government drew to a close in 2006.[1] The rhetoric of the damned legacy is long gone, replaced by the idea that Lula in fact represents a new, modernized left. This characterization, often proposed by conservative analysts, opposes something like Tony Blair's combination of fiscal austerity with sensible social policies (providing public support to targeted vulnerable social groups), to Berlin Wall-types of leftist thought which would bring back the nationalization of firms, fiscal irresponsibility (and, in South America, complacency with inflation), disrespect for the law (as in the cases of invasion of private property), and so on. Lula is praised by local conservatives as well as by foreign entities and politicians for his *social sensibility*, which, allied to his *fiscal responsibility*, would define him as a man of the 'modern left'.[2,3]

This characterization has suited Lula very well. Beginning in 2005, a succession of corruption scandals has plagued his administration. PT's first, and so far the most important, line of defence has been to acknowledge some guilt but to argue that Cardoso's politics, during the latter's presidency, were no better. Thus, the focus of the political debate was displaced. A very dear argument to PT in the past, that it was a *different* political organization, compared with the other parties (and the derived argument that PT administrations were different from the others), had to be abandoned. Most of the debate now in Brazil is reduced to wholesale comparisons between the quantitative results achieved by Lula's and Cardoso's respective administrations. Thus, consciously or not, Lula and his supporters came to accept implicitly the thesis that his policies are the same as Cardoso's. The question that has to be settled is which one has been more successful (and which one has been less corrupt or less complacent with corruption).[4]

The impossibility of essentially distinguishing both leaders' policies was in fact reaffirmed during the 2006 electoral process. Lula's opponent ran under the slogan 'the same policies, but better managed', which is essentially Lula's own point when he compares his own performance with that of Cardoso. The campaign rhetoric changed somewhat between the two ballots of the 2006 election. Feeling the pressure to be more affirmative in his attempts to differentiate himself from the candidate running for Cardoso's party, Lula radicalized his discourse, focusing, however, on one point: his opposition to any new privatization initiative. But even here, one can doubt the relevance of the apparent shift: his opponent had not, in fact, defended new privatizations. He was forced by Lula, however, to defend Cardoso's privatizations that are, in fact, quite unpopular. Be this as it may, the important point was that by focusing on something that was not in fact under discussion, Lula could exhibit a radical campaign rhetoric without actually committing himself to any change of ways with respect to the conservative policies he adopted in his first term.

One should not underestimate, though, the importance of being able to present oneself as representing the 'left' in Brazilian politics. No political group in Brazil dares to present itself as right wing, because the right is still heavily identified by voters as those nostalgic of the military regime. Cardoso, before Lula, had already tried to advance the concept of a *modern left*. In fact, he had invested heavily in the construction of this notion through his participation in the Clinton/Blair 'Third Way' meetings, which had also involved politicians like Lionel Jospin and Massimo D'Alema. The 'third way' seems to have been forgotten once most of its sponsors lost power. Lula now claims to be the true heir to the notion of a modern (more responsible, perhaps?) left.

Whether Lula's recent adhesion to a policy strategy characterized by the combination of fiscal austerity with targeted social spending is sincere or not, his administration has deeply disappointed many (if not necessarily most) of his voters. This chapter tries to evaluate his government's policies. To that aim, in section 2 we present the most important achievements of Lula's administration so far, trying to identify his successes and failures in a rather matter-of-fact, descriptive way. Section 3 presents an assessment of these results, having in mind the expectations created by Lula's election. Section 4 discusses whether Lula could have made different choices. Section 5 concludes. It is important to bear in mind that the discussion in this chapter is mostly confined to economic problems. The political dimension is taken mostly as an element of the context within which policies were selected and, as such, it is sometimes, but not always, explored in more detail.

2   Achievements and shortcomings

In one of the first speeches delivered after his inauguration, already under criticism for nominating conservative economists for all key posts in the Finance Ministry and in the Central Bank, for raising the primary surplus target to 4.25 per cent of GDP (from 3.75 per cent maintained by the Cardoso administration), and for the steep increase in interest rates decided by the Central Bank, which would certainly choke whatever impulse to growth could have survived the turbulences of 2002, Lula replied to his critics that his past rhetoric should be disregarded as 'bragging' (*bravatas* in Portuguese), which one is free to do when in the opposition, but which is inadequate in a responsible politician as he had now become by getting elected president.

In terms of macroeconomic policy, Lula maintained Cardoso's second-term mix of inflation targeting (monetary policy), primary surplus targeting (fiscal policy) and floating exchange rates (exchange rate policy). He resurrected other policies, such as industrial policies, but they were implemented in a way that has been usually described as *erratic*, in which some good ideas are advanced but are seldom consistently implemented. The general results achieved are presented in Table 3.1. Data for Cardoso's second term are added for comparison.

Overall macroeconomic performance, measured by the growth rate of GDP has not changed. Under Lula, the economy exhibited the same stop-and-go pattern it showed during Cardoso's term. The stop-and-go cycle has been explainable since the 1990s by the behaviour of the interest rate. In fact, after initiating a protracted process of reduction of the basic interest rate in the second semester of 2003, the Central Bank reversed course, choking the

Table 3.1   Short-term macroeconomic indicators

	1999	2000	2001	2002	2003	2004	2005
GDP Growth (%)	0.8	4.4	1.3	1.9	0.5	4.9	2.5
Per capita GDP	93.9	96.5	96.3	96.8	95.9	99.2	100
Price Changes (%)	8.9	6	7.7	12.5	9.3	7.6	5.7
Interest Rate (%)	25.5	17.4	17.3	19.2	23	16.4	19.2
Primary Surplus/ GDP (%)	3.2	3.5	3.6	3.9	4.3	4.6	4.8
Trade Balance (US$ billion)	−1.2	−0.7	2.6	13.1	24.8	33.5	44.8

Notes: Per capita GDP index: 2005 = 100; the interest rate is SELIC, annual average.
Sources: IPEADATA and Central Bank of Brazil, in Carvalho and Ferrari Filho (2005).

recovery that began in 2004. Having its monetary policy oriented exclusively by an inflation target, the Central Bank did not seem to care for the negative impact its policies would have on the rate of growth of GDP, pulling it down in 2005.[5] Inflation, however, did respond to the slower economy, falling continuously since its upsurge in 2002.

Turning to fiscal policy, Lula's government overshot the primary surplus target (4.25 per cent of GDP) in the first three years of his term. For 2006, the last of his first term, all indications are that the target will be reached but without any overshooting, given the increase in government expenditures resulting from electoral pressures. Nevertheless, public debt reduction targets were missed because the Central Bank kept interest rates too high, to the point of generating deficits in the overall budget. Be that as it may, management of the federal public debt can be counted among the successes of Lula's administration, given the adverse context in which the Treasury operated, including the policies of the Central Bank.

Also among the successes one should count the very impressive turnaround in the evolution of trade balances. In fact, Brazil began showing surpluses in its trade balance under Cardoso, when, at last, the change in the exchange rate regime implemented in 1999 began showing its effects more clearly. The rapid increase in the trade balance made it possible to reach significant surpluses also in the current account, reducing one important (although not the only) source of external vulnerability. Of course, one cannot forget that this performance was favoured by the intense growth of international trade and by the significant rise in the prices of commodities, including those exported by Brazil.[6]

The publication of the results of the 2004 Household Survey by the Central Statistical Office of Brazil (IBGE) brought some good news too with respect to social indicators. Table 3.2 shows that the proportion of the population living under poverty had fallen from 35.26 per cent in 1999 to 33.57 per cent in 2004. The numbers of those living in extreme poverty were 13.13 per cent in 2004, down from 15.03 per cent in 1999. In the case of people living in poverty,

Table 3.2   Social indicators

	Share of population below poverty line (%)	Share of population below extreme poverty line (%)	Gini Coefficient
1999	35.26	15.03	0.594
2000			
2001	35.11	15.24	0.596
2002	34.34	13.95	0.589
2003	39.16	16.7	0.581
2004	33.57	13.13	0.572

Source: IPEADATA.

absolute numbers actually went up, because of growth of population, while those living in extreme poverty remained roughly the same absolute number. The Gini index of inequality fell from 0.594 in 1999 to 0.572 in 2004.[7]

These good results should be approached with some care, first, because the survey was from 2004, a year in which the highest growth rate of GDP since 1999 was reached. What happened to these indices in 2005, with the slowing down of the economy is not yet known. Secondly, the Household Survey is a reasonably accurate source of data about labour income distribution, but it is much less reliable with respect to other sources of income such as profits and interest. Therefore, one can be sure that intra-labour sources of inequality may have been attenuated but very little can be said with certainty about the functional income distribution profile. In fact, available indications are that profits have increased considerably in the period (particularly in the financial sector) and interest payments, led by the service of the public debt at those rates appointed in Table 3.1, have also been very high.

Finally, and also somewhat controversially, the government also counts among its successes the behaviour of the labour market. In fact, one can see in Table 3.3 that total formal employment (that is, of people hired under a formal labour contract) has grown monotonically, if not very quickly, since 2000. It has grown even in slow growth years, such as 2001 and 2003. There is some scattered evidence that the *net* expansion of employment has been in fact much lower, with formal employment expanding at the expense of informal jobs, as a result of monitoring crackdowns on employers. The behaviour of the unemployment rate is also ambiguous, with some decrease in unemployment rates during 2005. Unfortunately the data in the table does not allow us to discriminate between reductions of the unemployment rate due to expansion of jobs and those due to discouraged workers abandoning the labour market.

Among the failures of Lula's government the inability to sustain a regular rhythm of growth for the economy stands out. Even the most enthusiastic supporters of his modern left style, such as the IMF staff, stress that this is

Table 3.3 Level of employment – formal labour market

Period: December of	Index	
	Observed	Seasonally adjusted
2000	81.7	81.71
2001	83.89	83.91
2002	86.88	86.91
2003	89.38	89.45
2004	95.2	95.2
2005	100	100

Source: Central Bank of Brazil.

their one big disappointment: the inability to accelerate growth beyond the 2.5 per cent/3.5 per cent range. If one takes into consideration the exceedingly favourable external environment, with expanding trade, rising prices of commodities, and quiet financial markets for the last four to five years, Brazil has actually missed an important opportunity to accelerate its growth rate. In fact, the Brazilian economy has grown at some of the lowest rates of growth in the world in the last three years.[8] In addition, the expansion of private investments, key to sustain long-term growth, has been aborted repeatedly. As to public investments, they have been continuously sacrificed in favour of financial transfers (servicing public debt) and current expenditures. Thus, one can make a favourable evaluation of Lula's option for 'fiscal austerity', repeatedly overshooting the primary surplus targets, but when one checks out how public expenditure is being allocated it is inevitable the conclusion that expenditure cuts are entirely *ad hoc*, actually reducing the growth potential of the economy.

3   An examination of the performance of Lula's government

Even though the performance of Lula's administration has not been brilliant, it may be difficult, at first sight, to understand why some of his critics have been so harsh in their judgements. Even if one disregards the seemingly endless string of scandals that have been uncovered since mid-2005, which has shattered, perhaps fatally, the ethical image PT has cultivated for so long, Lula's policy choices have been the target of continuous and relentless criticism, coming particularly from his left.[9] Of course, one should keep in mind that since Lula is widely judged to have moved significantly to the right, the critics in the 'left' now cover a wide political spectrum, ranging from Keynesian 'social democrats' closer to the political centre to Marxists at the more extreme left, including left-leaning liberals and traditional leftist intellectuals disappointed with the performance of Lula and PT in regard to their 'ethical' conduct.

Of course, with such a diversity of views, one would expect a wide variety of criticisms to be levelled against President Lula, and actually this is precisely the case. If one disregards criticisms coming from more radical quarters, it can be said that even a nominally left-wing government in a developing country should pursue at least four goals: full employment of labour; economic growth; income and wealth redistribution; and the empowerment of dispossessed groups, spreading out citizenship rights. A left-wing administration should not be 'generous'. On the contrary, it should advance a redefinition of duties and rights, redistributing power away from those used to rule towards those in position of subordination. It is structural change that is to be sought, not 'generosity' or even 'social sensibility'.

The first and more widespread criticism directed at Lula relates precisely to the perception that growth opportunities have been lost because of wrong-headed macroeconomic policies. As already observed, the international economy has behaved in an extraordinary benign manner in the last few years. Although the Brazilian economy has grown at positive rates during the whole period, these rates have been consistently lower than those reached by the international economy and by most of the emerging economies. Also, in contrast with economies like Argentina's, most of the problems faced by the Brazilian economy have been self-inflicted.

In fact, the macropolicy mix implemented by Lula's economic authorities exhibits a strong anti-growth bias. The Central Bank sustains exceedingly high interest rates to keep aggregate demand under its control so to allow reaching its inflation target. The monetary authority does not acknowledge any responsibility for the 'real' side of the economy, alleging that the best contribution it can give to ensuring fast growth is to make sure that inflation will be low. Most inflation surges in the last years have been due to supply shocks. Combating inflation as if it was caused by excess demand depresses the level of activity and keeps unemployment high.

In fact, the inflation targeting regime is generally biased against the level of activity and growth; not only because it absolves the Central Bank of any responsibility for the negative impact its policies may have on employment, production and investment. In fact, this regime is asymmetric with respect to real production. If the Central Bank believes that the output gap (the gap between actual and potential output) is closing and the economy may become overheated, it will raise interest rates to cool down economic activity. However, in the opposite situation, if the output gap is opening because actual output is falling further below its potential level, it does not feel obliged to reduce interest rates unless inflation rates may fall below the floor of the acceptable range. In sum, interest rates tend to rise when output growth accelerates, but they do not fall when output falls.

In the Brazilian case, the extreme conservatism of the board of directors Lula appointed to the Central Bank made things even worse. As we just argued, the inflation targeting regime by itself may be biased against growth, but monetary policy action still depends on the evaluation of how far output can grow before the output gap reaches a dangerous value. One has to remember that the monetary authorities do not react to *actual* inflation but to *expected* inflation. To do it, the Central Bank builds a model of inflation to estimate the parameters for action econometrically. Although it may seem that this procedure is more scientific, appropriate for a neutral, technical body as the Central Bank likes to present itself, these models are in fact wildly simplified versions of how an actual economy really works. In other words, in policy-making, one should not attribute to models a degree of precision that is not warranted either by actual knowledge of the real economy, or by the accuracy of the data with which the model is fed.[10] In the case of Brazil, these commonsense concerns are even more serious. Econometric models are built with data obtained from time series. The Brazilian economy has gone through deep changes even if we take only the last ten to 15 years, be they matters of policy regime or of productive characteristics. When decisions are made without taking into appropriate consideration the uncertainty surrounding the adequacy of the models used, or of the data on which they are constructed, among other problems, the policy-decision process is bound to be inefficient. The Brazilian economy has paid a high price for the behaviour of Lula's Central Bank directors in terms of lost output.[11]

The fiscal component of the policy mix also exhibits an anti-growth bias. The biggest debtor in the Brazilian economy is the government itself. When the Central Bank keeps interest rates high, it is contributing directly to fiscal disequilibria. A large share of current expenditures is protected by legal dispositions or by the action of strong lobbies. When the burden of the service of public debt is raised (or kept high) by the monetary authorities, the government can either raise taxes or curtail public investments, most frequently both.

This combination of monetary and fiscal policies exerts a strongly regressive impact on income distribution, redistributing income from workers *and* productive firms towards rentiers. Punishing, as it does, productive activities to favour purely financial investors and other rent-seeking groups that benefit from the inability of the government to change the profile of its expenditures, this policy mix is not only regressive but also anti-growth.

Finally, floating exchange rates is probably the best choice at the disposal of a relatively small economy under current international economic conditions. Fixed exchange rates could be conducive to better coordinated processes of international coordination, but if the conditions for these forms of organization do not exist, smaller economies do not have any choice but to keep their possibilities open and a flexible exchange rate system allows that. However, the Brazilian Central Bank oscillates between a pure floating exchange rate regime and some half-hearted intervention when overvaluation seems to break into particularly dangerous ranges. As a result, exchange rates are unnecessarily unstable, particularly because of the capital account liberalization processes initiated by F.H. Cardoso, and continued under Lula. Furthermore, volatility occurs around a sustained trend toward overvaluation. Although exports are still growing, due to strong world demand particularly for commodities, Brazilian manufacturing exports are losing strength at the same time imports of manufactured goods rise.

In sum, the macropolicy mix implemented by Lula's team allows opportunities to pass by unutilized, keeping growth rates at very low levels, much below the capacity to grow demonstrated in the past. The Keynesian lessons accepted by the democratic left in practically all Western countries in the postwar period, as to how to set macropolicies towards achieving full employment and maximum growth, were simply forgotten both by Cardoso's self-titled social democrats and by Lula's socialists.[12]

Lula's government seems to operate under the assumption that macroeconomic policy is not important to determine growth rates. The concept of macroeconomic stability advanced by its economists is restricted to *price stability*, in the belief that if government is successful in ensuring price stability, the private sector (the 'free' markets) will promote growth spontaneously. This was, in fact, the prevailing view among the liberal economists who populated F.H. Cardoso's government. Although the liberal discourse was rejected by the *political* sectors of Lula's government, his former Finance Minister (who was fired amid a corruption scandal and power abuse early in 2006) brought to the ministry and to the Central Bank economists that shared the same liberal beliefs. In fact, some of Cardoso's economists remained in authority posts under Lula. On the other hand, some of PT's economists were also converted to the liberal position. A few hardliners remained in the belief that the adoption of liberal policies had been forced on Lula by adverse circumstances (the 2002 balance of payments crisis), but that the anti-growth bias of the macropolicy could be countered by pro-growth structural policies, such as industrial policies.

This reasoning is flawed for various reasons. First, in a capitalist economy, investments on capital assets (on which growth depends) depend on favourable expectations of demand for the additional goods to be produced by the capital equipment to be added to existing facilities. If expected demand is choked by contractionary macropolicies, industrial policy incentives are unlikely to be enough to induce investments. Secondly, industrial policies involve the allocation of current fiscal resources (as subsidies or revenue renunciation), which may be prevented by a fiscal policy oriented by short-term goals. Thirdly, it is naive to think that liberal economists (and the interests they represent) will be satisfied with running the short-term macroeconomic show. Liberalism is a long-term political programme. One cannot expect to enlist liberal economists to pursue short-term policies and be free to implement interventionist long-term policies. Liberals have their own ideas as to the reforms an economy needs to operate properly in the long run and will try to implement them through so-called *microeconomic* reforms. PT's economists were deluded in thinking that they would be free to pursue their long-term goals. Were it not for the weakening of the federal government's political weight resulting from the revelation of scandals, Lula's former Finance Minister would likely be successful in pushing the long-term liberal programme of reforms his helpers had already formulated and made public.

Finally, and more importantly, to expect that entrepreneurs' *animal spirits* will be awakened by structural policies alone is only reasonable if the political leadership is able to point clearly the ways of the future, and to strongly commit themselves to their achievement. In the case of Brazil, all indications are that there is a significant leadership deficit with respect to both the ability to formulate clear strategies and, consequently, to commit to them. When the government announced, in very general terms, the principles of the industrial policy it would pursue, it was widely (if not unanimously) praised. In the twilight of Lula's term, many of its previous supporters ask themselves whatever happened to that policy. Lula, as Cardoso before him, does not seem to conduct the country according to some plan, with definite goals and definite instrument choices. In the case of Cardoso, this anomie seemed to be rooted in his theory of dependence, according to which only by associating with developed countries could a developing country experience some 'development situation'.[13] In the case of Lula and the PT the reasons for the absence of strategic thought are unclear. The party had apparently invested for many years in the definition of an appropriate concept of development and of the instruments and ways to reach it. When in power (or in government, as Lula and his followers are fond of saying), these efforts seemed to have been simply forgotten.[14]

In the absence of well-defined strategies, Lula's policies seemed to have consisted mostly of surfing on the favourable winds of the international economy that preserved the Brazilian economy from suffering any significant adverse shock. Some important institutions, such as the National Social and Economic Development Bank (BNDES), were able to focus their policies and actions, exercising their role efficiently. Others, such as the Central Bank, took advantage of the unheard of degree of autonomy that was conceded to them to define their own ways, strengthening the perception of absence of any strategic principle unifying and explaining the government's actions.

The lack of clarity as to what would constitute an effective alternative to the liberal ways of the Cardoso presidency seems to have been perceived by Lula and the political leadership that support him. As already pointed out, in the electoral campaign for the presidential election of October 2006 Lula defended his bid for re-election mostly by proposing a comparison between his results and those exhibited by Cardoso, instead of by pointing out how different objectives could (or should) have been proposed.

It is interesting to notice that criticism of the government's social policies has also been somewhat severe. Lula's leading social programme is the 'Family Grant' (*Bolsa Familia*), through which money transfers are made to families that fulfil a certain number of conditions. The Family Grant programme unified previously existing money payment programmes that applied to different groups according to particular criteria, including perhaps Lula's most famous social programme, the Zero Hunger Initiative (*Fome Zero*).

Criticism levelled at Lula's social policies are often not directed at the policies themselves, but at the lack of complementary policies that would consolidate the gains obtained by the money transfers. The first and most obvious criticism is raised against the inconsistency between economic policies that prevent the economy from growing at its true potential (with damaging effects on welfare such as maintaining high rates of unemployment) and social policies protecting the most vulnerable groups. A second criticism refers to the lack or inadequacy of supporting policies that would not only attenuate vulnerability or poverty but would also strengthen the position of the dispossessed. Public education, particularly primary and secondary schooling is widely considered to be gravely inefficient. Children go to school mostly to get meals instead of an education and to improve their chances of raising their life standards. A similar situation is found in public health services. As meritorious as any programme to feed the malnourished is, the main social policy does not offer the beneficiaries the possibility of rising definitively above poverty levels. Offering subsistence for a large number of people is certainly needed, but as a social policy it does not go far enough.

A particularly problematic aspect of Lula's social policy is its *political* form. For most defenders of money transfer programmes, a minimum income programme should serve to empower citizens, to ensure that the right to live is not a *market* problem, but a *citizenship right*, to be recognized and guaranteed by society itself. Money payments should not be confused with charity. It is a duty of a civilized society to guarantee the survival of its citizens in as dignified conditions as possible.[15] Lula's government, however, and the president himself frequently seem to approach social programmes in a completely paternalistic fashion. The President's language is always full of family metaphors in which Lula is the *pater familias* and society his (not always well behaved or endowed with good sense) children. Criticisms and demands are not taken as the exercise of citizenship rights but the complaints of 'adolescents' unable to see the bigger picture, or to understand that the family head cannot give them everything they want and so on. President Lula may be personally innocent of the authoritarian vice that accompanies this posture, but under these conditions social policies do not serve a liberating function, but its opposite, as it was frequently the case with populist leaders of the past.

Lula's re-election seemed to have re-kindled the expectations of his supporters in the left. Partly because of the already mentioned radical rhetoric used by Lula between the two ballots, many of his supporters tried to spread the notion that a second term would be radically different from the first. Many reasons are adduced to defend this view. They range from subjective factors, such as some supposed concern of Lula to go down to history not only as a continuation of F.H. Cardoso, but as an authentic left-wing leader, from more objective reasons such as the increasingly undeniable inability of his government's policies to promote growth.

In fact, many PT leaders advanced the idea that, after being re-elected, Lula would finally be able to begin governing as a PT leader. One of his ministers has publicly declared that 'the [former Finance Minister] Pallocci era is over', only to be immediately rebuked by the President himself. This group seems to want to revive the 'damned legacy' thesis, now in an extended version. Lula is supposed to be finally free from the need to stabilize the economy, so he could at last dedicate himself to make the economy grow and change so the country could finally resume development. This argument is sometimes strengthened by a supposed realization by Lula that no matter how conservative the policies he implements may be, the ruling 'elite' will never support him.[16] So, he might as well begin governing for his constituency rather than to the benefit of the 'elites'.

It is common knowledge that the President is deeply dissatisfied with his inability to begin what he once called the 'spectacle of growth'. It is also common knowledge that his government does not have any strategy that could lead to the resumption of growth. Most of the liberal economists in his administration are now gone. After about 12 years of hegemony in policy-making, it became clear that the notion of spontaneous growth as it was believed in the Cardoso period is doubtful at the very least. The President still refrains, however, from making any risky decision, insisting that any other policy mix than what he implemented is 'magic'. Lula remains as the prince of Denmark and runs the risk of making decisions when it will be too late anyway, if at all.

4   Could it have been different?

In itself, asking whether it all could have been different takes us from the strict economic field to the political debate, where the notions of limits and of possibilities are usually treated in a more flexible way, since they perforce incorporate the idea of conflict and, with it, the uncertainty of its results. One does not question whether something can or cannot be done as much as what is necessary to make a given alternative viable. Therefore, it may not be worthwhile discussing whether there were alternatives as such (because there always are) but, keeping in mind that alternatives create different configurations of winners and losers, rather how one could make sure that a preferred alternative would be politically feasible.

From this point of view, many analysts debate whether the so-called 'modern left' or the third way represents a true alternative for progressive politics or if it is just a surrender to the current dominance of markets (in particular financial markets). In its 'pure' form, which was actually pursued in Brazil during the Cardoso presidency, the modern left would combine orthodox economic policies giving support to the unfettered operation of free markets with sensible social policies, with the goal of protecting the more vulnerable social groups.[17] Of course, some residual tension remains given the conflict between the attempt to curtail fiscal expenditures and the objective of increasing social protection, making the boundaries between the two objectives somewhat fluid. Lula's policy, for instance, seems to have taken some distance from the pure model adopted by Cardoso, although in an ambiguous way. The orthodox character of his government's macropolicies was in fact strengthened but, at the same time, some interventionist rhetoric was adopted, as in the already mentioned case of industrial policy. In addition, social policies supporting the most vulnerable groups were extended and intensified.

Whether it is the result of the persuasion that past economic policies were wrong or just a simple act of surrender to conservative liberalism and to market pressures, one can raise some hypotheses to explain the sudden and drastic about-face of Lula and the PT and the apparent complete conversion to the Thatcherian motto that 'there is no alternative'.[18] On the one hand, we can point to two possibly relevant subjective factors in operation. The first may relate in fact to an 'optical illusion'. Since its creation, PT has attracted some of the brightest intellectuals in the country, fascinated by an organization formed in the union battles of the late 1970s. Even though the party has lost considerably its past shine, especially after the accumulation of corruption scandals since 2005, there was no doubt that a large number of Brazil's finest thinkers and intellectuals could be counted in its ranks at the moment of Lula's inauguration as President in 2003. Many analysts have been surprised by the inability of Lula's government to propose any strategic goals for the country because PT's intellectuals in the past had been able to produce diagnostics and proposed solutions for virtually all ailments of Brazilian economy and society. The party, however, was not its intellectuals. The party that went to Brasilia in 2003 was the other 'half', that of professional politicians and former unionists, many (or most) of which were now simple bureaucrats. The highest authorities of the Republic under President Lula showed no ability to formulate strategic thinking, and therefore no ability to lead and to mobilize toward any development project. They were consumed by the bureaucratic routine of the federal administration and seemed to be happy with it. As already mentioned, the 'federal' PT is happy to run for re-election on the basis of being just better administrators than Cardoso's team.

Another subjective factor is harder to define. It is only in part related to the preceding argument and refers to the quality of political leadership. F.H. Cardoso was for decades one of Brazil's most important intellectuals, his works being required reading for those wishing to understand how Brazilian society was formed and how it worked. He was also an influential progressive politician after his return to the country in the final years of the military regime. Lula, on the other hand, was perhaps the most influential union leader to emerge in the country, leading workers' movements that helped to change the face of the country while also becoming an important progressive politician after he led the process of creating PT. However, as presidents, both Cardoso and Lula showed themselves to be indecisive, unable to formulate and pursue strategic goals and to transcend everyday petty politics. Both Cardoso and Lula have actively tried to present themselves as heirs to the late President Kubitschek, but these attempts were received derisively because the one quality generally attributed to Kubitschek was precisely his ability to design a future for the country and to forcefully move the country towards that future, 'fifty years in five'.[19]

One can legitimately ask whether, if the two preceding hypotheses are true, the adherence to the modern left, by combining orthodox free-market economic policies with social sensibility, was not just the *default solution* to two governments led by former progressive leaders unable, however, to offer any substantive vision of a different future.

Naturally, subjective factors do not exhaust the possible explanations of the shortcomings of Lula's government (or Cardoso's for that matter). Some objective obstacles to the pursuance of progressive politics are in place. The most important of them is certainly the liberalization of the capital account of the balance of payments promoted in the mid-1990s. The key element of these liberalizing reforms was to allow residents in Brazil to make financial investments abroad. Although Brazilian legislation did not in fact allow it (it still doesn't), the Central Bank broke the limits of its authority in 1996 to remove, for all practical purposes, barriers to outflows of domestic financial capital. As a result, wealth-holders can now supersede domestic political processes, voting, as the Americans say, with their feet. A policy or government decision that does not meet with favour among wealth-holders and their financial agents may lead them to leave the country (or *to threaten* to do so), generating a balance of payments crisis through capital flight. In fact, this was precisely what happened during the electoral campaign of 2002. By mid-2002 it became clear that Lula's lead in the presidential campaign could not be overcome by Cardoso's candidate. Financial markets became agitated by the fear of a default on the public debt and other 'leftist' policies when Lula became president. Some financial agents engineered an episode with the characteristics of a capital flight (even though actual capital outflows remained relatively subdued). The exchange rate rose quickly from around R$ 2.50 to the US dollar to R$ 4.00 to the dollar in two to three months. Private investors refused to accept public securities maturing after inauguration day. The crisis went on until Lula agreed to address directly the financial market's worries issuing a 'Letter to the Brazilian People', which marked his commitment to respect the rules of the game. After his election, Lula nominated, as already noted, a conservative team to run the Finance Ministry and the Central Bank.[20]

The removal of capital controls in the mid-1990s ensured the dominance of financial markets over the formal political process in Brazil. Policies are now explained to the markets rather than to the people. Voters elect the politicians but the markets define what the latter have to do.

In sum, the combination of low-quality political leadership, poor (or non-existent) strategic thinking and weaknesses in the face of financial markets made the adoption of 'a liberal capitalism with a human face' a done deal. It is not a step in any direction, it is the very end result itself.

5 Summary and conclusions

Progressive or left-wing thought in some places, particularly in Latin America, came to equate conservative or right-wing governments with unnecessary meanness or cruelty. It is thought that a conservative government *has* to embody some sort of social Darwinism, where each one has to fight for him(her)self. If one believes that, any demonstration of generosity or solidarity is, by elimination, 'left-wing'. This allows any government with social sensibility to call itself progressive or left-leaning. Although capitalism seems in fact to have adopted of late a mean face in some countries (the US inevitably comes to mind, even if the characterization may not be entirely appropriate), this simplistic dichotomy could not explain the behaviour of Christian Democrats in Germany or even the conservatives in France, among many other cases. Lula's government has been in fact more *generous* than preceding administrations in Brazil, even though the expression of solidarity for the dispossessed has been the mark also of Franco's and Cardoso's presidency before Lula.

What should be, at the end of the day, the mark of a left-wing administration? We would risk suggesting that it would be the empowerment of the classes and groups in subordinate positions in society. This is the true meaning of changing structures. It is not just improving living conditions of the poor (although this is supremely important) but is also, and mainly, to recognize their *citizenship rights* and the *society's duties*, to acknowledge their right to participate and to influence the fundamental choices made by society. Power, however, is largely a zero-sum game. Dominated groups are empowered when the dominant groups are weakened. That is why 'social sensibility' may be a necessary but certainly not a sufficient condition to characterize a progressive government. In what relates to the economy, it is not enough to make money transfers, for instance, it is also necessary to implement progressive taxation, so as to not only make the burden of the provision of the public goods that will empower the dispossessed to fall on those who benefited the most in the past, but also to engrave the principle in society's laws. You cannot change a hierarchical structure just by raising the bottom, it is necessary also to lower the top. The absence of any serious proposal to implement progressive taxation is one of the most eloquent evidences of the essentially conservative character of the Brazilian governments of the 1990s and 2000s.

In an objectively conservative government like Lula's, money transfers are not entitlements explained by the duty of society to guarantee the dignified subsistence of its citizens, but are the result of the sensibility of a particular leader and can disappear when the leader is eventually replaced.

In sum, Lula's first presidency did not represent any substantial change in the conservative ways of Brazilian politics. His personal history is a novelty, but the character of his administration is not. One need not join his detractors (many of them guilty of the very same shortcomings they accuse Lula of) and exaggerate the limitations of his administration. In fact, it is very much likely that, all things considered, his administration has indeed been the most generous to low-income groups in recent Brazilian history (possibly remaining so even if we consider longer periods of Brazilian history). This, however, is not the point. Lula's government, like the nominally social democrat administration of F.H. Cardoso before him, did not promote full employment, did not push for growth, did not push for structural changes that would empower the dispossessed and reduce the power of the ruling groups. It is not by accident that we witnessed the last presidential election having the leading candidates vying for the 'best manager' prize. After all the missed opportunities of the last ten to twelve years, it definitely has an ironical ring to it.

Notes

* The author thanks his colleague Fernando Ferrari Filho, with whom the questions raised in this chapter were discussed many times, and Fernanda Lopes Carvalho for the comments and suggestions made to a previous version of the paper. The author also thanks financial support by the National Research Council of Brazil (CNPq) and from Faperj in the context of a Pronex Project.

1 Brazilian law allows sitting presidents to run for a second term. Lula was re-elected president in a run off ballot after missing a first-ballot victory by less than 2 per cent of the vote.

2 Castañeda (2006), for instance, proposes the existence of two 'lefts' in Latin America. On the one hand, one would find Lula and the Chilean Socialists, professing a modernized left, defined as politically moderate, macroeconomically prudent, aiming to combine the concern with economic efficiency through the adoption of market-friendly policies with 'social' concerns attempting to improve the lot of the poorer segments of society. In contrast, there would be an old left, led by people like Evo Morales, closer to Cuba's Fidel Castro. Castañeda includes in this last group Lopez Obrador, the defeated candidate in the last Mexican presidential election. Castañeda approaches the issue of the nature of the political with the eyes of a Mexican analyst: one of the criteria he proposes to classify the existing left-wing groups as modern or old is the degree of friendliness shown to the Bush administration in the US.

3 It is very interesting that politicians like President Bush, widely associated with extreme conservatism, actually seem to support Lula's policies, even as they call his government leftist. The same comment applies to institutions such as the IMF which seems happy to be able to show support to a supposedly leftist administration.

4 The old ghost of the reformist left, that it aims to manage instead of changing capitalist economies, seems to have staged a comeback, not without some irony, in the debate about who was the best manager, Lula or Cardoso. It is ironic because PT has always expressed publicly its rejection of the reformist left and social democracy!

5 The chairman of the Central Bank of Brazil, Henrique Meirelles, recently stated: 'And I mentioned that this is a successful process. Because the inflation rate, which is the main measure, *practically the only measure in fact to assess the performance of the Central Bank*, has gradually approached the center of the target, which demonstrates that it is a successful monetary policy'. Statement reported by Folha-online, 3 April 2006, emphasis added.

6 One feat widely commemorated by Lula's government was the liquidation of the debt with the IMF, established with the rescue package of late 1998 and renewed many times since. One has to consider it carefully though. On the one hand, the possibility of paying the remaining debt should be welcome, and it was possibly, due to the good results obtained with the current account of the balance of payments. The government's commemoration, however, is overdone. The main gain a country derives from getting rid of an IMF rescue programme is the possibility of choosing autonomous policies, free from the constraints posed by the Fund's conditionalities. Lula's government had no intention of pursuing any other policy different from that prescribed by the Fund. In fact, a large number of the key officers in the Ministry of Finance and the Central Bank were former IMF officials who ensured that the Fund's policies were followed without interruption. Therefore, the liquidation of the debt should be welcomed because it reduced the country's financial obligations. The main benefit, however, the recovery of policy autonomy, was never meant to be enjoyed.

7 Again, one has to be careful praising these results. Critics point out that 2004 results are a continuation of a trend that comes from Cardoso's presidency. The point is also raised that the changes are very small for such a long period of measurement.

8 The IMF forecasts similar results for 2006 and, possibly, 2007. See IMF, World Economic Outlook, April 2006, table 1.1.

9 It is interesting to note, however, how small was the influence of 'ethical' factors in the 2006 election. Not only did Lula maintain quite a comfortable lead over his opponents for the whole campaign (after a very difficult 2005), but PT itself fared very well in the elections for Congress and the Senate. It is still far from becoming a 'majority' party, but with about 16 per cent of the votes for Congress, PT was actually able to elect the largest group of deputies. In fact, among the re-elected Congressmen are included many of those involved in the scandals of Lula's first term, and who are now being criminally prosecuted. One should keep in mind that according to Brazilian law, members of Congress can only be prosecuted by the Supreme Court, no matter what the nature of the crime they are accused of. It has long been a tradition in Brazilian politics that for some politicians the election for Congress is tantamount to obtaining habeas corpus against criminal prosecution.

10 It has already become legend how former Federal Bank Chairman Alan Greenspan used to consult businessmen prior to the meetings of the FOMC so his decisions would not be unduly influenced by models' results.

11 Although the Central Bank refuses to engage in public debate, it is widely known that the bank's model assumes that sustainable yearly rates of growth (potential output growth rate) is only 3.5 per cent. This means that if the Brazilian economy begins to accelerate beyond this threshold, it will be repressed by the interest rate policy of the Central Bank.

12 In fact, as observed by James Tobin, not without sadness, these lessons seem to have been forgotten also in Western Europe, where economies are crawling since the 1990s under the weight of contractionary policies and reactionary ideologies like the ones embedded in the Maastricht Treaty.

13 The consistency between Cardoso's theses on dependence and the general orientation of his policies when president was pointed out by Professor Yoshiaki Nakano in a lecture given at the Institute of Economics, Federal University of Rio de Janeiro. See Cardoso and Faletto (1970).

14 One is not judging here the *quality* of the strategies designed by PT militants and sympathizers. Interestingly enough, most of these studies were developed by the

Citizenship Institute, an NGO created and led by Lula himself, as a supporting element of his persistent attempts to reach the presidency. Nevertheless, these studies were never given any privileged status as government programmes or strategies once Lula was inaugurated.

15 See Davidson and Davidson (1996).
16 The evidence for this would be the voting maps that show that Lula lost in all southeastern and southern states, where per capita income is higher.
17 One should notice that institutions like the IMF and the World Bank are very supportive of this kind of 'leftist' programme. The Fund was candid enough, however, to admit that the protection of vulnerable groups was necessary to maintain the political viability of liberalizing reforms. Cf. Carvalho (2003).
18 Prime Minister Thatcher's motto is translated to Lula's language as 'we can do no magic'.
19 The argument about the quality of leadership is explored in more detail in Carvalho and Ferrari Filho (2005).
20 See Carvalho and Ferrari Filho (2005).

References

Carvalho, F., 'On the ownership of reform proposals. How social policies found their way into IMF's adjustment programs', *Econômica* (UFF), 3 (1), June, pp. 67/94, 2003.

Carvalho, F., and Ferrari Filho, F., The twilight of Lula's Government. Another Failed Experiment with Left Wing Administrations?, manuscript, 2005.

Cardoso, F.H., and Faletto, E., Dependência e Desenvolvimento na América Latina, Rio de Janeiro, Zahar Editores, 1970.

Castañeda, J., 'Latin America's Left Turn', *Foreign Affairs*, May/June 2006.

Davidson, G., and Davidson, P., *Economics for a Civilized Society*, Armonk: M.E. Sharpe, 1996.

4

The Real Meaning of the Economic Policy of Lula's Government

Leda Maria Paulani
Economics Department, University of São Paulo, Brazil

1 Introduction

The victory of the PT in the 2002 presidential elections gave rise to different expectations: gloomy for some, bright for the great majority. The expectation that the people would start to transform Brazil into a nation became stronger. Forged from the bottom up in the difficult times of struggle against military dictatorship, starting with the movements of the workers in the ABC region in the state of São Paulo (the most important industrial area in the country), and under the leadership of Luiz Inácio Lula da Silva, the Workers' Party seemed well-suited to accomplish the task of pulling Brazil out of its centuries-long lethargy and freeing it from the unparalleled inequalities which that lethargy sustains. It was not going to be this time, however. The hope for the refoundation of society was postponed. On the basis of a catastrophist diagnosis, according to which the country would be on the brink of an economic abyss after the 2002 elections, the incoming administration decided to continue the orthodox economic policies that were typical of the previous eight years under President Fernando Henrique Cardoso (FHC).

At the time of writing (winter 2006–07) and after Lula's re-election for another term in office (2007–10), and with no signs of significant change in economic policy, it has become clear that the path taken was not at all, as it was claimed, a 'tactic' of clenching one's teeth and accepting a policy which was bitter, odious, but necessary in order to 'save the country'. Quite the contrary, it was a deliberate choice of maintaining Brazil locked in the same trap, under the condition that it would not jeopardize the PT power project. In what follows, I review in detail the arguments that justified that choice, drawing a balance sheet of its results after four years, and speculate about the nature of the 'model' adopted.

2 The fallacy of the Brazilian economy on the brink of an abyss in December 2002[1]

Faced with the surprise of those who had hoped not for an adventurous economic policy, but for a clear signal showing the intention of the new government to free the Brazilian economy gradually from the trap in which it was caught, the new authorities had a ready explanation for their unexpected behaviour: it was necessary, before anything else, to get the country away from the verge of the abyss. This was the main argument that justified the rise in the basic rate of interest rate (Selic) to 26.5 per cent, the reduction in liquidity via the rise in the reserve requirements of the banks, and the increase in the primary surplus beyond that required by IMF (4.25 per cent of GDP, against 3.75 per cent).

What was the basis for the government's pessimistic assessment of the situation? It was due to the behaviour of three variables which were, from then on, elevated to the status of absolute indicators of the country's economic health: the price of the US dollar (the exchange rate), the value of the C-Bond (the main public debt bond negotiated in international markets), and the country risk indicator. These variables were at undesirable levels at the end of 2002. The dollar had reached R$4.00, indicating a depreciation of the domestic currency of approximately 47 per cent since June, the C-Bond was below 50 per cent of its face value, and the country risk was close to 2000 points. But what was the reason for those adverse indicators? Basically, the speculation generated by what became called 'electoral terrorism', orchestrated by the elites and by national and international interests in view of the possibility of Lula's victory. Without the elections, those indicators would not have behaved in that way.

The most important risk influencing the behaviour of these variables was the prospect of an external default, that is, the risk that Brazil would not have enough hard currency to honour its external obligations. What was the situation at that point? First, the behaviour of the trade balance took the FHC administration by surprise, since it overshot the target by more than 50 per cent. Moreover, the prospects were even better for the future, since the exchange rate adjustment of January 1999 seemed, since early 2000, to be finally pushing the trade balance in the right direction.[2] In addition to this, the change of the foreign exchange reserves, the relevant variable for the assessment of external solvency, shows a surprising outcome: in contrast with the period between September 1998 and January 1999, when more than US$ 40 billion were drained from the country, the quantity of dollars held by the central bank was stable during 2002. The level of reserves starts the year at US$ 36 billion (the average for 2001 was US$ 36.3 billion), declines to US$ 33 billion in April–May, reaches US$ 40 billion in June–July, stays at US$ 38 billion in August–September, and 36 billion in the following two months, closing the year at US$ 37.8 billion. The numbers speak for themselves: there had been no uncontrollable bleeding, and there was certainly nothing that could be compared to the speculative attack against the real between September 1998 and January 1999.

Of course there were problems concerning the external accounts. They existed then and continue to exist now. But they have a *structural* nature: the rise in the import dependence due to the abrupt opening of the Brazilian economy promoted by the FHC administration, the rise in the liquid external liabilities due to the internationalization of the productive capital promoted by the FHC privatization programme, and the rise in expenditures linked to the enormous increase in portfolio investment due to the financial opening of the Brazilian economy. The outcome was a permanent increase in the expenditures in dollars. This kind of problem is quite far from the worsening economic *conjuncture* which was the argument used by the new government. And even if a significant crisis were to take place, the agreement with the IMF had already been signed in August, and it would allow the government to address any unexpected difficulties.

The other reason often raised by the authorities in the Lula administration to justify the direction they gave to economic policy was the presumably imminent risk of monetary disorder. In those circumstances, it was claimed, the government had to take the 'necessary measures' (whatever they may be) to curb the momentum of that process. To act in any other way would be tantamount to signing straightaway a certificate of economic incompetence, which would put into jeopardy the viability of the new administration. It was this kind of consideration that justified the high interest rates and the increase in the bank reserve requirements in February, which withdrew quite suddenly, around 10 per cent of the supply of money in the economy. Still, an interesting question relates to the main reason for the unfavourable behaviour of the price indices. The main problem was the depreciation of the Real starting in June 2002, which had been due to the electoral turmoil. With the inevitable time lag, the price indices started to show the impact of that shock by October–November. But the asynchrony that exists in the process of realignment of prices, and the weight that the public tariffs and the so-called administered prices (fuel, gas, etc.) have in them, made it impossible for the price impact to be absorbed in one go. Thus, with or without a tighter monetary policy, the price indices would continue to rise until all the impact had been incorporated. They would then start to decline, pushed also by the fall of the exchange rate (which is exactly what happened). Thus, there was no significant risk of inflation running out of control. And how could there be one, if the economy had been moving sideways, and had been almost stagnant for a long term? The mechanisms to switch on inertial inflation, which were inadvertently suggested by the president of the Central Bank, Henrique Meirelles, in August 2003, did not exist then, nor do they exist now.

Thus, the hypothesis of the 'abyss' has not been substantiated. The existing data about reserves and a minimum of knowledge about the formation and the behaviour of the price indices do not confirm its validity. The government also claimed that the country's external credit lines had been cut, and that it was necessary to re-establish them rapidly. But it was never revealed which were those lines, and by how much they had been cut.

3 The fallacy of the 'short-term' in the orthodoxy

The government's justification for orthodox economic policy and management always included the need to recover credibility. It would be necessary to recuperate to avoid compromising the country's external accounts, since the adjustment of Brazil's balance of payments was still in process. The sign of the recovery of that credibility was precisely the fall in the country risk, the rise in the price of the C-Bonds and the increase in the value of the domestic currency. To achieve these results it was necessary to reduce drastically the rate of inflation and to declare faith in the therapy of liquidity contraction and monetary and fiscal restrictions. In sum, it was necessary 'to kiss the cross' of economic orthodoxy,[3] and it was kissed with devotion.

That discourse had ambiguous implications, since it suggested that, once the 'credibility' had been recovered, it would be possible finally to make development the main priority of the government's economic policy. It suggested that the orthodox stage was only short-term, and it was necessary to make possible a non-traumatic transition to another policy regime. Those who knew the dynamics of the economic model embraced by the PT government were aware that such an assumption was fallacious. The 'logic of credibility' simply does not allow sharp changes of trajectory. 'Credibility' can be maintained only if implacable fiscal adjustment, high interest rates, contractionary monetary policy, and so on, are maintained permanently. Once one has joined this game, any attempt to move in the opposite direction spoils the country's hard-won 'achievements' and, with them, the supposedly necessary conditions for stable development. One could imagine that the new government core team had failed to realise these limitations and genuinely believed that they could, initially, 'play the game' in order to to obtain, later on, the necessary conditions to implement its own economic policy. Presumably, these policies would finally promote economic growth and the ten million new jobs promised by Lula during his campaign.

Even that hypothesis seems difficult to sustain today. After hearing, first, the secretary for economic policy of the Finance Ministry declaring that Pedro Malan (minister during the eight years of the FHC administration) deserved a statue in his honour and, later, Lula's first finance minister Antonio Palocci (who resigned because of a corruption scandal in March 2006) stating, in the presence of FHC, that he would 'maintain the same economic policies for another ten years', it is difficult to imagine that policy continuity was merely a tactical move. The only alternative hypothesis is that a deliberate and fully conscious choice has been made. Even with the support of 55 million votes and in possession of unprecedented political capital, the new power holders did not want to risk anything, and opted for the line of least resistance. They decided to avoid confrontation against internal and external interests, which reserved for the government the paternalistic and 'focused' role of looking after the poor. The latter did not question the regional and personal disparities in income and wealth, which did not even threaten to scratch the country's iniquitous patrimonial structure. In sum, the policy reproduced the submission to the imperatives of financial accumulation that had dominated capitalism internationally since the mid-1970s.

4   The economic achievements of the first Lula administration

At the beginning of 2004, at the end of the first year of the new administration, newspapers started printing damaging headlines:[4] 'Brazilians buy less food in 2003'; 'Domestic consumption, which grew for ten years, remains stagnant in 2003'; 'With Lula, income falls and unemployment rises'; 'Industry has its worst performance since 1999'; 'The number of underemployed workers grows 42.5 per cent'; 'Economy shrinks in Lula's first year'; 'GDP has its first fall since 1992';[5] 'Household consumption has record fall'; 'Slow growth of investment'; 'Social spending does not grow with Lula'; 'Unemployment in São Paulo goes back to record levels', and 'São Paulo metropolitan region has 2 million unemployed'. On the other hand, 'Fiscal tightening exceeds IMF target'; 'Interest spending at record levels'; 'Brazil has highest interest rates among emergent countries'; 'Lula promotes the biggest fiscal tightening in history'; 'Country invests little and has record fiscal squeeze'. Even with all this belt-tightening, 'Fiscal surplus does not pay half of the government's debt service'; 'Country risk exceeds 500 points again'; 'Standard & Poor sees vulnerability in Brazil'; 'JP Morgan downgrades Brazil and country risk rises', and 'Brazilian economy remains fragile'.

It is true that on the basis of newspaper headlines, the argument that we are developing here cannot be sustained. But these headlines were chosen by the newspapers on the basis of official data. Thus, even taking into account the adversarial relationship between the press and Lula's government, it would have been impossible to create more positive headlines. In fact, from the economic point of view the Brazilian economy practically stagnated in the first year of the PT administration. GDP increased only 0.5 per cent, and unemployment increased. In May 2004 the output and employment indicators pointed to a minor recovery.[6] The authorities celebrated, and claimed that those improved indicators showed that their chosen economic policies were 'correct'. In mid-July, speaking to the Federation of Industries of Rio de Janeiro, finance minister Antonio Palocci declared, in a fit of optimism, that 'Brazil has set right the economic fundamentals to grow steadily for at least fifteen years. Our country certainly does not have the vocation to grow slowly. Our vocation is to grow 5 per cent per year, or more. We are going to reap these amazing results'.

Palocci was correct when he said that the vocation of Brazil was not to grow slowly. In fact, for 50 years – from the mid-1930s to the mid-1980s – Brazil was one of the fastest-growing countries in the world, with average GDP growth in the region of 6.5 per cent annually. However, he was wrong to expect that the Lula administration would restore this pattern of growth. If we consider that GDP growth in 2006 did not exceed 3 per cent, the average growth of the Brazilian economy during Lula's first government was only 2.5 per cent. This is only marginally higher than the 2.3 per cent average annual growth in the two FHC administrations (1995–98 and 1999–2002) – which was battered by several international financial and balance of payments crises. In contrast, 2003–06 was a period of rapid international growth and relative calm international financial markets. That is why several economists have argued that Lula's first administration benefited from a positive external shock.

Considering the last point, it has often been argued that the recent growth of exports and the substantial improvement of the Brazilian current account has contributed to the reduction of the country's external vulnerability and, in this manner, it has strengthened the basis for the sustainable growth predicted by the government. In fact, in 2002–06, exports rose significantly from US\$ 60 billion to US\$ 135 billion. However, it is important to examine this growth process in more detail.

This significant improvement was due more to the favourable conditions in the global market than to any structural improvement of Brazilian exports in terms of competitiveness, quality or value added. In fact, Brazil has not only been falling behind in the ranking of multilateral agencies, but its participation in global manufactured value added has declined.[7]

The Brazilian export boom is fundamentally based on primary products and low value added manufactures (high volume, low price and standard technology). In contrast with the 1980s, Brazilian insertion into global trade has taken a large step backwards. With few exceptions (for example, Embraer), it is as if Brazil had returned to the 1930s, when the economy was an appendix to the developed world. This type of assertion reduces the country's sovereignty and autonomy, and reinforces the tendency to the extraction of absolute surplus value, which is a step backwards for the country to achieve the goal of building the nation and offering the majority of its people the conditions to lead a dignified life. For this reason, Brazil was included in the bottom category of the 2004 UNCTAD Report ranking of developing countries, among those countries about to become de-industrialized.[8] Clearly, then, the Lula administration has maintained the economic model that created that situation.

5   The chosen model

In mid-1996, Gustavo Franco, then director of external affairs of the Central Bank, wrote a widely-read article entitled 'External insertion and development'. This paper was praised by FHC as a 'Copernican revolution in economics'. Wrapped in the idolized garb of mathematics, the article was nothing more than an apology for Washington Consensus policies, which the FHC administration was already implementing in Brazil. These policies included the reduction in the size of the state (privatization), trade liberalization and restrictive monetary and fiscal policies. Gustavo Franco claimed that, in correct combination, the country would eventually be ready to 'catch the train of history'. The shock of competition imposed by the liberalization of trade would induce a process of productive restructuring that would get Brazil a place in the brave new globalized world, and secure the necessary conditions for growth and stability. The minimalist state and the rigid fiscal and monetary policies would prevent inflation and reassure the external investors, resolving the problems of the balance of payments. To complete the recipe, productive restructuring would raise productivity, raise salaries and reduce inequality.

A decade after the imposition of these policies, the outcome has been economic stagnation, record levels of unemployment, a large increase in external vulnerability, the return of the economy to a position of dependence on primary exports, and the reproduction of the same distributive pattern, with higher levels of absolute poverty, violence and barbarism in the country's urban centres. Just before the publication of Gustavo Franco's article, his Central Bank directorship was taking measures to secure the country's insertion in the international circuit of financial valorization. The renegotiation and securitization of the external debt and the creation of C-Bonds, quoted in international markets, had already done part of the job. At the same time, the Central Bank board of directors quietly took charge of another, equally fundamental, task: the deregulation of the Brazilian financial system.

Making use of an instrument created in 1962 – the so-called CC-5 accounts, exclusive to non-residents, which permitted the free transfer of funds in foreign currency – the Central Bank promoted the financial liberalization of the country. Two important changes were made. First, the concept of 'non-resident' was widened to include corporations 'in transit' in the country and financial institutions not authorized to operate in Brazil (originally only individuals were allowed CC-5 accounts).[9] Second, CC-5 account holders were permitted to export not only the domestic currency surplus due to the conversion of foreign currency, which non-residents had brought into the country, but *any* surpluses. Through a simple administrative measure it became possible for any agent, resident or not, to send funds abroad by depositing domestic currency in the account of foreign financial institutions.[10] In July 2006, the last year of the first Lula administration, the transfer rules were relaxed even further.

These legal and regulatory changes have helped Brazil's pathway into the international financial markets a great deal. The Brazilian debt certificates quoted abroad have confirmed the country's role as creator of fictitious capital (in the Marxian sense). Financial liberalization guarantees the free flow of international capital, which can maximize the advantages offered by the restrictive monetary policies imposed by the government. Without that new freedom, the US$ 40 billion, which left the country between September 1998 and January 1999 before the devaluation of the Real, would not have been able to do so, and would have sustained heavy losses. In spite of this, the transformation of the country was not yet complete. Despite serious attempts to reform social security, the FHC administration failed to implement all the changes that would be required to adapt the Brazilian system to the requirements of the new model.

The pensions reform was the first substantial project of the Lula administration. In the first weeks after taking office, the new government sent to Congress a bill proposing several changes in civil service pensions (private sector pensions had been reformed by the previous administration). In essence, the Lula reform changed the retirement system for public sector workers. Armed with the justification that the social security deficits were unsustainable and would rise over time, the government changed the pensions system from pay as you go (PAYGO) sector workers, the main tool used to impose the change in the public sector, to the imposition of a benefit ceiling, which would force the workers to join a funded regime; just as FHC had done with the pensions system of the private sector thus, ostensibly having the '*Fome Zero*' [Zero Hunger] programme as its main marketing strategy, but without assigning great importance to this goal and pension funds.[11] Without channelling substantial resources to it,[12] the government in fact tried from the start to complete the social security reforms started by FHC. That the government started in this particular way, and that it mobilized all its political weight and its main appointments in order to get this reform approved, is anything but casual. This was an unequivocal sign of the path chosen by the new government, and the economic policies it has embraced. This makes it more plausible that there has been a conscious choice, rather than an inescapable situation that had forced the government to deepen the model that the PT had so firmly rejected during the 2002 presidential campaign.

In completing the FHC pensions reform, the PT administration killed several birds with the same stone. First, it created a large market for complementary pension plans, which had excited the imagination of domestic and international financial institutions for more than two decades. In this sense, the public sector pensions reform has opened new perspectives for accumulation, which were not possible only through the private section pensions. Although the Brazilian private sector is a much larger employer than the public sector, private sector average incomes are much lower, and these workers face a much greater threat of unemployment. The opening of this new market was the first achievement of the new government. Second, the requirements for higher contributions, higher retirement age and longer service supported the government's aim of fiscal adjustment. Third, a well-designed propaganda campaign successfully presented the civil servants as the 'great villains' of the country's social disaster scenario, and claimed that the reform would foster social justice. Last but not least, a social security system predominantly under the PAYGO regime and under state control did not fit well with the policies implemented in the early 1990s to establish Brazil as an important platform of financial valorization. The reform championed by the PT helped to achieve that goal.

The funded regime has, by definition, a *rentier* nature, favouring high real interest rates and investment in guaranteed assets, especially government securities, since the fund managers have to make sure, in the long run, that sufficient resources will be available to honour the contracts. In contrast, the PAYGO regime is closer to productive capital, because those who work pay those who have already retired. Thus, the pensions reform not only infringed rights, but it also induced macroeconomic instability.[13] This outcome was probably considered a matter of detail in high government circles, given the need for the institutional modernization of Brazilian capitalism and the potential credibility gains that the reforms would entail.[14] In this context, it comes as no surprise that the World Bank 'suggested' to the new government, even before it took office, that it should complete the social security reform as well as implement the fiscal and university sector reforms (this was essentially the same advice that the Bank gave to the Argentine government).

Once that stage was completed, Brazil was nearly ready to be incorporated into the international circuit of financial valorization. With the addition of some minor elements, which are perceived to be necessary to secure this sort of 'minimum income guarantee for capital',[15] nothing else would be lacking. These measures include the approval of the new bankruptcy law (achieved in February 2005) and the formal autonomy of the Central Bank (which has not been sent to Congress because of the higher political temperature caused by the corruption scandals of the Lula administration since May 2005). That moment will not take long to arrive, since the government has taken all necessary steps to implement these modernizing reforms as soon as possible. The dressing up will then be complete. The autonomy of the Central Bank will make the 'markets' see, once and for all, that the Brazilian state will not relinquish its role of subtracting part of society's income to transfer it to the financial sphere,[16] thus securing the revenue of the fictitious capital which it issues.[17] At the same time, the state transforms the country's currency into an object of speculation, subjecting it to arbitrage operations that make its value fluctuate according to transitory imperatives. As an object of speculation, the Real is always available as a vehicle for exceptional gains in hard currency. The pension funds (which will become larger and more numerous) operate in the same way as the public sector debt, subtracting from the sphere of productive accumulation substantial portions of the real income which could otherwise be transformed into productive capital. The pensions funds will indirectly do, through voluntary contributions, what the state does directly through compulsory taxation.

The government of the largest purportedly left-wing party in the world, in the largest country in Latin America, will have provided an invaluable service to financial capital and its ideology. It will have demonstrated that there is no alternative. This is the model adopted by Lula and by the PT to promote the development of Brazil. Mainstream rhetoric assures us that fiscal austerity and monetary contraction are the only certain and 'scientific' ways to achieve development with stability. Given the size of its domestic public debt, it is claimed that the country needs to achieve fiscal surpluses in order to reduce the weight of the debt and create space for the economy to grow again. It never occurs to them that the growth of the debt was not due to 'irresponsible' government spending, but to the orthodox recipe which prescribed high interest rates to sustain the appreciation of the exchange rate between 1995 and 1999. It also never occurs to them to say that the high interest payments are the main reason for the nominal public deficits, which not only make the public debt grow further, but also lead to the deterioration of public services and to higher unemployment.

Finally, it also never occurs to them to admit that the public sector debt is not supposed to disappear; it is not an anomaly or a sin to be purged. Quite the contrary, it is a necessary aspect of capitalist development. It derives from the relationship between the state and private accumulation, between power and money, and it helps to secure the social wage.[18] Today, the debt supports the space of value and capital, prevents the destruction of excess capital, and guarantees its minimum income.

The last point makes the responsibility of the Lula government in promoting the continuation of the Brazilian disaster (which has already lasted more than two decades) even more significant. The purported 'conflict' between productive and finance capital only appears clearly at the aggregate level, where the irrationality of grounding economic growth in the transfer of income, rather than its generation, becomes evident. At the level of individual capital, particularly the large internationalized capital, which operates internationally, the combination between *rentier* gains and productive gains is part of normal operations. If there are high interest rates in the capitalist periphery, production adjusts to that circumstance in order to maximize the combination of productive and financial gains. Thus, instead of reflecting a problem faced by big business, the criticisms that capitalists raise against high interest rates are merely a pretence. The relationships that connect finance and productive capital and the state (as creator of fictitious capital) show that these differences only exist for small businesses that are condemned to generate real income.[19] In other words, it is the productive and fictitious-financial logics of capital that are in conflict, not the individual capitals, which benefit from both.

This indicates that the direction to be followed by the type of association between the state and capital remains a choice of the state. It can play in favour of the *rentiers*, which is perverse from the social point of view, or the state may confront that logic and use its power not to extract real income from society and fatten capital financially, but to force it into the area of productive accumulation and the expansion of real income. The insistence of the government's economic establishment in the path of austerity, hailed as a safe and sure recipe for 'growth' – that is, the growth of production and, therefore, of employment and real income – expresses the need for the state to assure capital, through interest payments, that the state's fictitious assets are sufficiently safe.[20] The PT government, lacking the courage to confront these vested interests, and with no wish to risk a change in the policies of the state that would make it capable of dealing with the real problems faced by the country, decided to confirm the perverse logic which was already at work.

6   Final remarks

How could this be possible? How could a leftist government or, at least, the government of a party that used to be known as leftist, be so petty, so unconcerned with national construction, sovereignty, and the prospect of real development in Brazil? How could they be so subservient to financial interests and large capital? We do not have definitive answers to these questions. But one thing is clear: Lula and the PT government have made an important contribution to Brazil's attempt to find a niche in which, as the discourse of globalization proceeds, the country could find its place in the brave new 'globalized' world. Its specialization is in the generation of financial gains (financial valorization). Today, for investors – whether or not they are residents, businesses transacting in Brazilian currency, public securities or Brazilian bonds – Brazil offers the fastest way in the world to increase values in hard currency. This is the only comparative advantage that Brazil has managed to achieve after 15 years of the model that was firmly criticized by Lula and the PT during the time they were in opposition. This is also the model they deepened when they took office.

Politically, Lula's government was very smart, since it promoted an association between the very poor, who were turned into clients of the state through social and compensatory income programmes, and the extremely rich, who figure among the largest *rentiers* group. This is certainly one of the main reasons explaining Lula's re-election. In the long run, however, these policies are perverse, because although they seem to take care of inequality, in reality they perpetuate the social chaos in the country. There are no indications that this situation will change in the second Lula administration because, even though the President has said that faster growth will be his main priority, he simultaneously stated that the macroeconomic policy framework will be maintained. It seems that Brazil will have another four years of neoliberal policies in command of the material life of the country.

Notes

1   This section and the following summarize the arguments in Paulani (2003).
2   It is worth emphasizing the positive role played by the large devaluation of the Real in this outcome, given that there is a lag between the sudden oscillation of the price of the currency and its consequences for the trade balance.
3   The expression is attributed to Paulo Arantes (2003), in an article about the first months of Lula's government, published in the magazine *Reportagem*.
4   All headlines reproduced here come from *Folha de São Paulo*, one of the country's leading newspapers; they appeared between January and May 2004.

5 Preliminary estimates suggested that Brazilian GDP had declined by 0.02 per cent in 2003. Revised data indicated that GDP had grown by 0.5 per cent.

6 During Lula's first administration, 2004 was the year in which the economy performed best, with GDP growth reaching 4.9 per cent. This was partly due to the recovery from the dismal performance in 2003, and to the export boom, which increased revenues by 32 per cent.

7 See Unctad Reports 2003 and 2004.

8 The Unctad categories are, first, mature industrial economies (including Korea and Taiwan); second, rapidly industrializing countries (such as China and India); third, countries with industrial outposts (e.g., Mexico), and deindustrializing countries (among them, Brazil).

9 This change was implemented in 1992, when Francisco Gros was president of the Central Bank and Armínio Fraga was the international director. However, the market remained incredulous until the Bank published (in November 1993) a guide explaining what the financial market operators could see but not believe. This guide, published under Gustavo Franco's directorship, became known in the market as the 'cartilha da sacanagem cambial' [guide of exchange wickedness].

10 Federal prosecutors Valquíria Nunes and Raquel Branquinho filed a suit against 15 directors of the Central Bank and the Bank of Brazil in December 2003. They argued that this transformation of the CC-5 accounts was irregular because the Central Bank cannot regulate a federal law through a circular letter.

11 In contrast with the FHC administration, which included a set of transition rules into its reforms, the initial proposal of the PT government went to Congress without them. Another 'radical' measure of the new administration was to impose pension contributions *for pensioners*, which FHC had failed to achieve. It should be remembered that the main reason for the failures of the previous administration was the fierce opposition of the PT.

12 '*Fome Zero*' was the initial name of the compensatory income programme of the Lula administration. Several months later the name of the programme changed to '*Bolsa Família*' [Family Support]. Philanthropic programmes of this type have existed since the previous administration. Lula's government extended it to a larger number of families and raised the value of the transfers. Even with these innovations in the administration is spending only R$ 9 billion (US$ 4 billion) per year with it, in contrast to R$ 150 billion (US$ 67 billion) per year servicing the domestic public debt.

13 The funded regime is worse than procyclical: it is neutral when the tide is favourable, but has a completely destabilizing impact when the economy moves downhill. The greater the weight of the assets held by the pension funds, the more adverse is this effect.

14 It is often claimed that funded regimes create much-needed savings incentives. However, the pensions reform did not create structures to channel savings into investments, which would generate an increased flow of goods and services. Quite the contrary, they become merely another element pushing the economy towards income generation without the mediation of material production.

15 The expression, extremely appropriate in referring to real interest rate paid to the creditors of the state, is attributed to João Sayad in an article in *Folha de São Paulo*, 24 April 2000.

16 See Chesnais (1998).

17 It could be argued that the wealth effect produced by the guaranteed income growth offered by the financial sector would provide incentives to consumption as well as investment, returning to the sphere of productive accumulation with

one hand what it takes out with the other. Even if this were true for consumption, it does not hold for investment because, with lower public sector spending and high real interest rates, the expected return from productive investment will remain depressed.

18 See Oliveira (1998).

19 The recalling, very appropriate and inspired by Fernand Braudel, of the illusory character of the conflict between productive and financial-speculative capital, especially if we are considering big capital, is attributed to José Luiz Fiori in an interview to *Folha de São Paulo*, 9 May 2004.

20 It must be added that, in the present context of an international fiduciary monetary system, the secutitization of public debts of the emerging countries and the positive interests that they pay, as well as the arbitrage gains that the fluctuating exchange rate makes available, due to the difference in strength between the many domestic currencies, are an indispensable accessory for guaranteeing of the rent of finance capital when, for its own reasons, the hegemonic country is not disposed to furnish that guarantee.

References

Arantes, Paulo Eduardo (2003). 'Beijando a Cruz'. In: *Reportagem*, 44, May.

Chesnais, François (1998). 'Introdução Geral'. In: Chesnais, François (ed.) *A Mundialização Financeira*. São Paulo, Xamã.

Fiori, José Luiz (2004). 'Para Fiori, "revolta social" será crescente'. Interview given to Claudia Antunes, *Folha de São Paulo*, 9 May.

Frontana, Andrés V. (2000). *O Capitalismo no fim do século XX*. São Paulo, IPE/USP, PhD thesis.

Oliveira, Francisco (1998). *Os Direitos do Anti-Valor*. Petrópolis, Vozes, Coleção Zero à Esquerda.

Paulani, Leda M. (2003). 'Brasil *Delivery*: razões, contradições e limites da política econômica nos seis primeiros meses do governo Lula'. In: Paula, João Antonio de (org.), *A Economia Política da Mudança*. Belo Horizonte, Autêntica.

Pereira, Raimundo Rodrigues (2004). 'Uma Manipulação Extraordinária'. In: *Reportagem*, 53, February. Sayad, João (2000). 'Taxa de Juros'. In: *Folha de São Paulo*, 24 April.

5

The Twilight of Lula's Government: Another Failed Experiment with Left-Wing Administrations?

*Fernando Cardim de Carvalho**
Federal University of Rio de Janeiro

*Fernando Ferrari-Filho***
Federal University of Rio Grande do Sul and Researcher at CNPq

1   Introduction

As Lula's (maybe first) presidential term draws to a close[1], assessments of his administration are bound to diverge. A few analysts, mostly those connected to the Workers' Party (PT), consider it to have been an unqualified success so far. A few others, in contrast, evaluate Lula's policies in an extremely rash way, a betrayal of his past promises and commitments. In-between, the mainstream seems to be very uncomfortable with the corruption charges levelled against the federal government, somewhat critical of its social policies, considered to be paternalistic, but mostly happy with its conservative economic policies despite their poor overall achievements so far.

In fact, no matter how sensible or misguided one judges the policies defended by Lula and PT in the past to have been, only a few analysts (or voters) would have thought that Lula would actually follow former President Fernando Henrique Cardoso's (referred to from here as Cardoso) economic strategy so closely. During his electoral campaign Lula refused adamantly to give any details of his actual intentions. As late as his inauguration, the incoming President was still signalling his willingness to change the direction Cardoso had imprinted on economic policy. In fact, his inaugural speech opened with an emphatic cry for *Change!*, which was generally interpreted as heralding some dramatic reorientation of policy, away from the stagnationist strategy followed by Cardoso.

It did not take long for many people to realize that the policy shift one associated with the election of Lula would never materialize. To the great disappointment of his followers on the left and the happy surprise of financial markets, Lula never even tried to change the basic pillars of Cardoso's second-term policies, combining high interest rates, high primary fiscal surpluses, and low growth rates. In his first months in government, Lula attributed his inability to reorient policies to the 'damned legacy' (*herança maldita*) of Cardoso's administration, that, in its last year, was the combination of rising inflation, capital flight, rising interest rates, and, of course, low growth and rising unemployment. Enthusiastically supported by conservative economists and politicians, not to mention bankers and financial investors in general, what passed initially as emergency policies quickly became the main pillar of Lula's own administration. In fact, Lula himself forcefully dispelled misunderstandings when he dismissed his past views as bragging (*bravatas*, in Portuguese), and explained that actually exercising power in the real world required maturity. By the end of his third year as president, and preparing to run for re-election, Lula's new-found maturity (that is, his willingness to follow orthodox policies to the letter) seems to be his strongest lever, at least until the disappointing economic results of late 2005 were revealed.

Lula was certainly not the first politician elected on the basis of a left-wing or progressive past to follow orthodox policies with fervent faith. In fact, recent experience in Latin America abounds in similar examples, as in the cases of former Presidents De La Rua, in Argentina, Alvarez in Ecuador (among the ones that ended up being ousted by popular revolts), or the Chilean socialists, and, so far, Vazquez in Uruguay (among others that are still in power). A few cases stand out as exceptions, notably Argentina's President Kirchner and even President Chavez in Venezuela.

Why is it so common that politicians elected on the expectation of promoting swift shifts in policy choices end up becoming icons of political and economic conservatism? This is definitely a difficult and complex question, and in this chapter we want to use Brazil's example to explore two possible hypotheses. The first has to do with subjective factors such as the *quality* of political leadership, the evaluation of the relevant correlation of forces, the existence of a clearly outlined project for the country and strength of belief in it by the governing cadres. Some parties and/or individual politicians are simply unable to pursue policies that demand depth of understanding or firmness of commitment in the face of strong opposition. The second has to do with objective factors, among which the *institutional arrangements* that may or may not facilitate dramatic shifts in policy orientations are prominent. The weight of institutional arrangements is felt in the degree of vulnerability of political authorities to extra-political forms of pressure that can neutralize political initiatives taken by elected political leaders. In this chapter, we start from a critical description of the policies pursued by Lula's government in the first three years of its term, in section 2. Section 3 will discuss the subjective and objective factors that may have conditioned policy-decision in the period to examine if they are useful in explaining Lula's failure to promote any significant change of course in Brazil. Section 4 concludes.

2   President Lula's economic policies and results

2.1   Has fear defeated hope?

A few months before the 2002 elections, the Brazilian economy began exhibiting signs of an approaching currency crisis. The apparent causes for the crisis were the persistence of macroeconomic imbalances and uncertainties about Lula's future economic policies, since he seemed to be consolidating his position as front-runner in the presidential elections. Among the causes for concern one could include: (i) the monthly inflation rate (measured by the IPCA[2]) had increased from 0.5 per cent in January to 1.3 per cent in October; (ii) the Real weakened from R\$ 2.38 per US dollar in January to R\$ 3.81 in October; (iii) the demand for Brazilian securities decreased rapidly and, as a consequence, the 'Brazil risk', measured by JP Morgan, increased from almost 600 basis points, in the beginning of the year, to about 2400 basis points in October 2002; and (iv) capital outflows intensified and, as a result, foreign reserves fell.

In this context, two important related developments took place. A new rescue package from the International Monetary Fund (IMF) was sought by Cardoso, which Lula was strongly urged to support. In fact, the pressure led Lula's campaign managers to prepare a 'Letter to the Brazilian People', where, although in very vague terms, the candidate announced to financial markets, rather than to the Brazilian people, his willingness to abide by the rules set by these markets. Thus, Lula's speeches in the electoral campaign became richer and richer in promises but shorter and shorter in definitions. In the end, he was supported by the voters' memory of what he stood for in the past, rather than by any definite plan of government, which he in fact never announced.

Immediately after his election, Lula nominated for the Finance Ministry an unknown politician from the right wing of PT and a former chair of BankBoston, who had run for Congress by Cardoso's political party (PSDB), was named chairman of the Brazilian Central Bank (BCB). As a result, since taking office in January 2003, Lula's economic policies have been marked by the continuation, and in some aspects radicalization, of Cardoso's second-term economic policies, that is to say, inflation targeting, primary fiscal surplus targeting and flexible exchange rates.[3]

Monetary policy, following orthodox guidelines, has been explicitly recessive, since it is only by choking aggregate demand that rising interest rates can keep inflation under control. As is well known, in Brazil rising interest rates have some perverse effects. Most of the financial wealth detained by the private sector is in the form of public debt securities paying interest rates indexed to the overnight interest rate. A rising interest rate punishes firms, that need credit to operate, and workers, who lose their jobs when firms face difficulties, but richly rewards the *rentiers* who hold public securities. Moreover, high interest rates cause fiscal expenditures to rise, deepening any fiscal imbalance that could already be present.

Fiscal Policy has been less obviously recessive. Dominated by the goal of obtaining a primary surplus of 4.25 per cent of Brazilian GDP, from 2003 to 2006, to guarantee the service of the public debt outstanding, Lula's fiscal policy does not really pursue *austerity*. In fact, in all these years that the federal government has been setting targets for primary surpluses, budget deficits have opened widely. Primary surpluses are little more than tricks of rhetoric that try to disguise redistribution policies under the cloak of a pretense of fiscal austerity. Overall public expenditure is not cut to reach these targets, but redistributed in favour of the payment of interest on public debt. In other words, the government is not really saving anything, it is thwarting expenditures in, say, investments towards the payments of the interest bill. Moreover, it is important to add that, as Table 5A.1 shows, the relation between general government revenues and GDP increased in the last three years: in 2003, it was 34.9 per cent, while, in 2005, this relation reached 37.7 per cent.

Nevertheless, the impact of Lula's fiscal policy on the economy is recessive because it substitutes payments for *rentiers* for public investment. One should expect that *rentiers* will not spend the money they get from the government (compared with the impact of public investments on aggregate demand). Besides, it is a deeply regressive policy when considered from an income distribution standpoint. Again, job-creating expenditures are sacrificed to remunerate debt that is held by high- and middle-income groups.

At the same time, liberalizing reforms were promoted, such as social security reform, in 2003, and tax reform, in 2004. At the beginning of 2005, new steps to further capital account liberalization were taken, and an additional liberal agenda of reforms has been proposed, including giving independence to the BCB.[4]

To sum up, when Lula decided to adopt orthodox fiscal and monetary policies and implement liberal reforms, he turned drastically to the right. In a parody of his own victory statement one can say that Lula's government has shown that 'fear has defeated hope'.

2.2   The economic results from 2003 to 2005

In 2003, the increase in the primary surplus target from 3.75 per cent in 2002 to 4.25 per cent of GDP and the institutional improvements to ensure financial discipline at all levels of government and a high average basic interest rate (Selic)[5] (around 23 per cent) allowed Brazil to reach policy credibility with the IMF, and with domestic and international financial investors. Accordingly, there was a significant improvement of the risk premium charged on Brazilian bonds: in 2002 the average EMBI for Brazil was 1380 basis points, while in 2003 it was reduced to 830 basis points[6] and an increase in the value of Brazilian bonds in the international secondary market. In addition to this, two important points that strengthened the market's 'confidence' concerning Lula's economic policy were the fact that the inflation rate, despite having reached 9.3 per cent in 2003 (1.3 per cent above the target proposed by BCB), was kept under control and the trade balance increased from US$ 13.1 billion, in 2002, to US$ 24.8 billion. To sum up, according to the multilateral organisms and international and domestic financial markets, the Lula administration has done a 'good job' in restoring confidence.

Nevertheless, the results were far from bright with regard to real economic activity. The economic policy mix led to poor economic growth in 2003 – the GDP increased only 0.5 per cent – with the productive capacity declining in several strategic sectors because of the continuing lack of investments. The average rate of unemployment was 12.3 per cent and the distribution of income deteriorated: according to the Central Statistical Office (IBGE), in general workers' average income decreased almost 15 per cent in 2003.

To sum up, the economic policy strategy based on an increased primary surplus target, inflation targeting and flexible exchange rates resulted, in the first year of Lula's term, in (i) restoration of 'confidence' by economic agents, especially the IMF and international and domestic financial investors, with the priority of monetary stabilization, and (ii) an economic stagnation.

In 2004, following a few years of poor growth, the GDP increased 4.9 per cent, the fastest expansion in five years. The domestic demand picked up, consumers and business also increased and private investments were recovered. The inflation rate was 7.6 per cent, 0.4 per cent below the inflation target proposed by BCB. Moreover, the average unemployment rate decreased (from 12.3 per cent in 2003 to 11.5 per cent in 2004) and the workers' average income dropped only 0.75 per cent. At least two reasons can explain the Brazilian economic performance in 2004: on the one hand, the average basic interest rate dropped from 23.0 per cent in 2003 to 16.4 per cent; on the other hand, due to the record trade and current account surpluses (the trade balance was around US$ 33.5 billion – built, basically, by robust export growth rather than a fall in imports – and the current account balance was US$ 11.6 billion), the Brazilian economy became less vulnerable to external shocks and to changes in global market mood. Thus, the main indicator of vulnerability, that is to say, the ratio of external indebtedness to exports, improved notably. As a result, the average country risk dropped to 542 basis points.

In conclusion, according to Lula and the monetary authorities, 2004 was a very positive year for Brazil because the conditions for ensuring sustainable economic growth had been created, such as (i) the completion of the reform agenda; (ii) the passing of legislation on public–private partnership; (iii) the improvement of fiscal conditions and the reduction of public indebtedness to almost 52.0 per cent of GDP; (iv) the country was better prepared to resist reversals in international conditions; and finally (v) the expansion of public social spending. At that time Lula stated that, at last, 'recovery was to last and the "amazing growth" (*espetáculo do crescimento*) had started'.

However, 2005 showed us that the sustained recovery of Brazilian economy was not really under way. According to the Brazilian Institute of Geography and Statistics (IBGE), GDP increased only 2.3 per cent in 2005[7]. It is possible to identify at least three reasons for this poor rate of GDP growth: first, to aim at keeping the inflation on target (5.1 per cent),[8] BCB was too conservative and, as a result, the basic interest rate was very high (the annual average overnight interest rate (Selic) in 2005 was around 19.2 per cent); second, fiscal adjustment – predominantly by raising taxes and cutting back public investments – was too tight (the relation between primary fiscal surplus and GDP reached 4.8 per cent); and third, the exchange rate dramatically appreciated – in 2003 the annual average exchange rate was a R$ 3.01 per US dollar, while in 2005 the annual average exchange rate had dropped to R$ 2.43 per US dollar. It is important to emphasize that the economic growth rate estimated by BCB will materialize only due to the fact that the international scenario[9] has been so favourable to the Brazilian economy; in this context, the trade balance and the surplus current account reached US$ 44.8 billion and US$ 14.2 billion, respectively. As a result of this external performance, the average country risk was 313.8 basis points.

To conclude, despite the fact that inflation is under control and the external front has improved, the result of GDP in the third quarter (GDP has decreased 1.2 per cent) and its estimation for 2005 showed us that the performance of Brazilian economic growth is still exhibiting a *stop-and-go* pattern.

2.3   What is expected for 2006?

The last year of Lula's first term began with some signs of a pick-up in activity, in comparison with the poor results of 2005. The most important factor to support these expectations is the fact that, since the third quarter of 2005, a gradual reduction of the basic interest rate (Selic) has been observed. This has been cause for no more than moderate optimism since inflation expectations have also fallen, as we will see below. With the fall of expected inflation the reduction of nominal interest rates translates into the necessary strong reduction of real interest rates. The federal government has also been less keen to maintain primary fiscal surpluses above target. It is expected to decline in 2006 to 4.25 per cent from 4.8 per cent of GDP in 2005. Perhaps more effective than these two factors, credit has grown steeply, particularly to consumers, the real minimum wage was raised, and money has been distributed to the poorer strata of the population through the Family Grant programme (*Bolsa Familia*). As a result, domestic demand has been more robust with private consumption and industrial production increasing and investment showing some recovery. The fragility of the activity pick-up, however, has prevented investments from growing more strongly.

Two other factors may give support to a better performance than that of 2005. First, amidst strong rumours of corruption scandals, Lula's first Finance Minister, Antonio Palocci, was replaced at the beginning of 2006 by the former president of the Brazilian Development Bank (BNDES), Guido Mantega. Mantega had been a moderate critic of Palocci's policies, raising the possibility that in 2006 some flexibility in fiscal policies may be introduced. This optimism should be tempered, however, by the strengthening of Central Bank Governor Henrique Meirelles, to whom all power over monetary policy was conceded by President Lula. The second element acting in favour of a pick-up is the presidential election in October, when President Lula seeks a second term. Monetary and, especially, fiscal policies have relaxed a bit to support Lula's bid for a second term in office.

In this context, according to the weekly report of BCB (21 August), the expectations for the main indicators of Brazilian economy for 2006 are: GDP will increase by 3.5 per cent,[10] the average interest rate and the average exchange rate are expected to be around 15.2 per cent and 2.19 per US dollar, respectively, the inflation rate is expected to reach 3.8 per cent, slightly less than the centre of the target inflation rate (4.5 per cent). Net exports are expected to reach around US$ 41.2 billion (see Table 5A.1).

Be that as it may, assuming that, by the end of 2006, the main indicators of the Brazilian economy are close to the BCB expectations, Lula's economic performance, from 2003 to 2006, could exhibit the following characteristics: (i) despite the fact that the inflation rate would be kept under control, its average rate would still be relatively high at 6.6 per cent per year on average since the introduction of inflation targeting; (ii) the average annual nominal interest rate would be around 18.4 per cent, while the average real interest rate would reach 11.1 per cent; and (iii) the average growth rate of GDP would be only 2.8 per cent. It will be a very poor performance when one remembers that Lula's first term of office has been spent under exceptionally favourable external conditions. The results of the Brazilian economy, when compared with other emerging economies, strongly suggest that poor domestic policies have prevented the country from taking advantage of the opportunities this unusually stable external environment has offered.

2.4 How to ensure price stabilization, economic growth and full employment?

What is macroeconomic stability? President Lula and the economic authorities he nominated seem to believe that inflation stabilization should be the only goal of macroeconomic policy. From the fiscal side, all that matters is building credibility with financial agents. As John Maynard Keynes, an economist apparently unknown to political leaders of the country, once suggested, macroeconomic stability should mean a combination of full employment and stable prices. For developing countries, we should add, macroeconomic stability also means long-term economic growth and social development.

Accordingly, many critics have advanced proposals to change the course of economic policies, especially because the main results of the Lula's economic policies, based on inflation targeting, primary fiscal surplus and flexible exchange rate regime, show that the chosen policies are not in fact consistent.

Table 5A.1 in the Appendix shows the following:

(i) It is notable that over the period 1999–2005 actual inflation rates in Brazil were within the targeted range in three out of the seven years of operation of this monetary policy strategy (it is important to say that in 2004 the inflation target was raised from 6.25 per cent to 8.0 per cent midway). The targets were missed in 2001, 2002 and 2003 by a substantial margin, especially in 2002. On one different occasion (2004), the inflation target was met (it was 0.4 per cent below the inflation target proposed by BCB) only after the target itself had been raised. It may, thus, be concluded that inflation targeting in Brazil was not completely successful over the first seven years of its implementation.

(ii) Despite the fact that the relation between primary fiscal surplus and GDP has been increased in the last seven years, the net public debt/GDP ratio increased from 46.9 per cent to 51 per cent. In 2004, this ratio decreased for two reasons: on the one hand, the average interest rate dropped to 16.4 per cent and the average exchange rate was appreciated; on the other hand, the GDP increased 4.9 per cent. In 2005, the net public debt/GDP was kept under control. As a conclusion, primary fiscal surplus is not creating conditions to reduce the relation between net public debt and GDP.

(iii) Looking at the evolution of the exchange rate from 1999 to 2005, it is possible to note that the real exchange rate is not stable, and the exchange rate elasticity of exports has been relatively low – that is to say, exports in the last years are increasing due to the fact that the main trade partners of Brazil have presented a robust economic performance.

In this context, some economists argue that monetary policy is too rigid and insensitive to the need to grow. As a result, to create conditions for reducing interest rates it is essential to expand private consumption and investment. Other economists, even if agreeing with the point just raised about the need to reduce interest rates more boldly, insist that it may not be enough. Thus, they defend the view that capital controls should be also adopted to protect the Brazilian economy against future external shocks. The strategic need for the strong growth of exports, preserving at the same time the feasibility of implementing active development policies, give trade negotiations, including the Free Trade Area of the Americas (FTAA) and at the World Trade Organization (WTO), dramatic importance. In addition, fiscal policy should be made more flexible in order to make room for badly needed investments in public utilities.

In fact, the conditions favourable to the promotion of full employment and the recovery of investments largely overlap. On the macroeconomic side, it is necessary to wake up the *animal spirits* of entrepreneurs, by signalling that policies supporting aggregate demand, rather than the opposite, will be pursued. This means not only that monetary policies should explicitly consider the goal of maintaining employment stability along with price stability, but also that fiscal policy would be reoriented to privilege public investment rather than debt service or even current expenditure.

Monetary policies should be oriented by employment *and* inflation targets. There is nothing particularly revolutionary about that. It is in fact precisely the way the Federal Reserve Bank sets policy rates. Unfortunately, the BCB, committed to the inflation targeting regime, seems to follow some form of the so-called Taylor rules.[11] However, the BCB could aim at minimizing what was in the past called a *misery rate*: the sum of the unemployment and the inflation rates. This is, of course, based on the existence of a short-term Phillips-curve-type of relationship between unemployment and inflation. When interest rates were set too high, in such a way that the decrease in the inflation rate would be paid for a disproportionate increase in the unemployment rate, the misery rate would increase and the BCB would revert its policy. The opposite would happen in the converse case.

Fiscal policy, on the other hand, should not sacrifice all other objectives simply to guarantee the service of public debt at any cost. There are many ways to try to reduce the burden of debt on fiscal expenditures, ranging from the more market-friendly use of options to reduce interest rates, to more aggressive initiatives of debt restructuring, involving replacing the securities currently in circulation by securities with different clauses. Bonds indexed to the rate of growth of GDP would align incentives for the financial sector with the larger interests of society to promote growth. One would not need to violate contracts to promote such a change: the short maturity of a large share of the total stock of public securities would allow the substitution to take place at the redemption of outstanding securities.

Expansive fiscal and monetary policies should strengthen *animal spirits* by pointing to the profits that could be earned by satisfying the increasing aggregate demand. The new mix of policies, however, wouldn't stand a chance if the current degree of capital account liberalization was maintained allowing residents to promote capital flight as easily as is the case presently. The reinstatement of capital controls would be necessary to give the time the government would need to show that the policy could work, generating a situation where even financial investors could profit from, mostly from the increasing demand for financial resources that would come from firms and consumers.

Reaching full employment, on the other hand, can be easier than recovering growth. Active industrial policies would be necessary to coordinate private and public efforts in accumulating capital at the necessary rate. One should mention that the lines of industrial policy announced in 2004 by the administration met with general approval. It would certainly be more plausible to assume that growth policies would have a higher probability of success in situations where aggregate demand was not maintained at low levels by macroeconomic policies, as is the current practice.

In this scenario, maintaining and expanding external trade is a strategic element. Resisting the demands of industrial countries to liberalize non-traditional sectors, such as government procurement, is essential to make any efficient industrial policy feasible. The position of the Ministry of Foreign Affairs, giving priority to trade and financial partnerships with Mercosur bloc countries and other emergent countries, is important in increasing the bargaining power of Brazil and other bloc countries in trade talks, such as the FTAA.

To sum up, to address the objective of expanding effective demand and stabilizing the inflation process, it is necessary to establish economic growth targeting. Thus, the government should (i) operate fiscal policy to implement social programmes and to promote investments, in particular to rebuild public utilities in energy production and road construction, among others; (ii) ensure that monetary policy has a significant positive impact on the level of economic activity; (iii) direct financial markets toward financing development;[12] (iv) operate an industrial policy aimed at inserting the Brazilian economy in the international scenario in a context where Brazil can incorporate the technological and structural revolutions occurring in the world, and at attracting international investments that would add aggregate value to exports;[13] (v) revise its trade policy, reducing tariffs on the importing of capital goods, and increasing tariffs on the importing of durable goods; (vi) implement trade and financial agreements with other developing countries, such as Mercosur countries, Latin American countries and emergent countries in Asia; (vii) create efficient anti-speculation mechanisms to control (or regulate) movements of capital in order to prevent monetary and exchange rate crises and augment the autonomy of domestic decision-makers; and (viii) adopt incomes policies to regulate wages and prices.[14]

3   Why Lula failed

Having a nominally left-wing government let down its supporters by adopting orthodox conservative policies that result in low growth and high unemployment is certainly not news. In fact, the opposite would be more surprising over the last two decades. The wholehearted and seemingly enthusiastic acceptance of Thatcherite theses by Tony Blair's 'New Labour' as well as the complete surrender of Spain's PSOE to neoliberalism, under the leadership of Felipe Gonzalez should serve as a warning against having too high expectations as to the willingness of left-wing political groups to promote structural changes once in government. Lula was certainly the first politician to disqualify his *own* past rhetoric as *bragging*, but not the first to renege on ideas used to win votes, perhaps only the crudest one so far.

If one looks at the recent experience of governments led by reformist left-wing organizations all over the world, one can identify three different types of behaviour. In the first we find those leaders and parties converted to neoliberal ideologies *before* their rise to power. These groups actually ran their electoral campaigns under the flag of the renewal of the left, whose ideas they argued to have become obsolete. In this first group we could place Blair's New Labour, Gonzalez's Spanish socialists and perhaps Schroeder's German Social Democrats. The second group comprises those left-wing parties and leaders that seemed to have been pushed into accepting neoliberal policies after trying to implement progressive policies and running into insurmountable difficulties. The leading example in this group is certainly the French Socialist Party after Mitterrand's rise to power in 1981. Finally, we find those parties and leaders that broadly maintain their allegiance to a reformist left-wing platform, even if under diminished expectations, as it seems to be the case in the Scandinavian Social Democratic parties, with some success in at least partially advancing progressive initiatives. In the case of left-wing parties in developing countries the situation does not seem to have been essentially different, the most emblematic cases currently being the current Argentine government in the third group and the Brazilian experience with Lula in the first.

As suggested in the introduction to this chapter, there seems to have been both subjective and objective factors orienting the choice made by each political group or leadership. Naturally this is not the place to try to develop any kind of general theory to explain the actual evolution of modern left-wing reformism. Nevertheless, some comparison with other countries' experiences may serve to enlighten us as to the reasons explaining a performance as disappointing as has been the case of Lula's government in Brazil.

3.1 Subjective factors

Perhaps the most surprising element to define PT's first tenure in power was the complete absence of a project for the country.[15] This should have been clear from the electoral campaign rhetoric, where then-candidate Lula offered mostly vague ideas, such as the goal to have every Brazilian enjoy 'three hot meals a day' by the end of his term, but it was generally believed that a political group so richly supported by influential intellectuals, as was the case of PT, would be able to present to the country a coherent vision for the country's future as well as the means to achieve it when needed.

This vision, if ever there was one, was never presented. When substantive ideas were actually presented, as was the case with industrial policies, they were not implemented, facing in fact active opposition from influential circles in the government itself (mostly from Finance Ministry officials who share strongly liberal views, similar to those of the Cardoso administration).

Without a vision of what to transform (and how to transform it), Lula government mostly drifted between vague statements of intentions and inaction. Short-term economic policies were mostly reactive, and long-term policies non-existent. To a large extent, what seemed to be an efficient campaign slogan, the 'three hot meals a day' promise, actually became the central feature of government's policy, through the program of income transferences known as Family Grants (*Bolsas Família*).

As argued in the preceding section, with hindsight, we can state that the character of the incoming Lula government was actually defined in the presidential campaign itself, when a balance of payments crisis erupted in mid-2002, fed mostly by capital flight. Up to that moment, Lula the candidate had benefited from the privilege of being the front runner, carefully dodging all situations where a precise definition of what his plans were for the future. The public (and the financial markets) could only guess what would be his policies by examining his past ideas (the ones he was to renege on after the inauguration). The best clues to his actual intentions, of course, were given by his party's programme and the statements of its leaders. Lula himself would not commit to the programme or the statements but would not disavow them either. It seems that the candidate wanted to have his cake and eat it. The mid-2002 crisis forced Lula to clarify his intentions and the result was the 'Letter to the Brazilian People', where, despite the mostly empty rhetoric that characterizes such documents, the candidate committed himself to maintaining the policies he would inherit from Cardoso. Lula's surrender meant that the macroeconomic policy would remain giving absolute priority to controlling inflation rates at very low levels through high-interest monetary policies, with fiscal policies playing primarily a supporting role of generating resources to service public debt. As a result, active policies to promote full employment and income redistribution would be limited to the amount of resources left after reaching the primary surplus targets that signaled to the 'markets' that Lula's government would play by the same strict rules that characterized the second Cardoso term.[16]

The first and foremost subjective factor to explain the performance of Lula's government is, thus, the lack of a clear and coherent vision, or of a definite project, for the country. It is probably undeniable that President Lula and many or even most of his advisers are well-intentioned. However, one cannot expect somebody to exhibit the courage of convictions when there are no clear convictions to defend courageously. On this particular, it may be illustrative to offer a contrast between the choices made by Lula and PT in 2002 and the choices of Franklin Delano Roosevelt and the US Democratic Party in 1932. As in Brazil of 2002, the US was suffering a serious crisis in 1932, in fact, a much deeper crisis that what happened in 2002 in Brazil. Capital flight, a banking crisis, the collapse of confidence of markets in government policies, etc., were all similar, if much deeper, problems to what happened in Brazil. Roosevelt, as Lula, was President elect, to be inaugurated the following year. As the crisis evolved, President Hoover sent a letter to Roosevelt, explaining that the policies he was implementing were correct, but that Roosevelt's election had unsettled the markets (an amazingly similar speech to those delivered by President Cardoso in 2002). Hoover ended his letter demanding that Roosevelt should make a public statement to the effect that he would not sponsor any kind of 'experiment' in policy-making so markets could calm down and confidence be restored. Roosevelt did not oblige, despite Hoover's new attempts to extract commitments from the President-elect as the situation deteriorated during 1932. Roosevelt did not bulge. As the historian David Kennedy observed, '[Roosevelt's] own studious refusal to make any policy commitments during the interregnum [between election and inauguration] meant that the field of political action lay before him [in 1933] swept of all obstructions' (Kennedy, 1999, p.111).

Of course, a price was paid so that Roosevelt could keep his options open. The economic situation in the United States did seriously deteriorate during 1932. But the decision to stand firm and avoiding the commitment to maintain Hoover's policies can only be explained by the clarity with which Roosevelt believed alternative policies existed and the courage of his conviction. Unfortunately, in the case of Lula in 2002, it seems that neither a plan, nor the courage of conviction existed, so the surrender was unavoidable.[17,18]

3.2 Objective factors

Although it would be a mistake to play down subjective elements like the ones just discussed, the defensiveness of left-wing governments, however, has been a much more widespread phenomenon than could be reasonably explained by factors such as the quality of leadership or the clarity of ideas. There must also be objective barriers to the implementation of programmes giving priority to the standard goals of the democratic left, such as maintaining full employment, promoting redistribution of income and wealth, and empowering the citizens. Moreover, these barriers cannot be local in nature since, as already mentioned, the phenomenon we discuss is pretty general.

If one examines the fate of centre-left parties and coalitions, ranging from the Democrats in the US, to the social democrat and labour parties of Western Europe, to the left-wing movements and parties of developing countries, one major common element stands out as the possible culprit: financial deregulation coupled with the liberalization of capital movements (in fact, they may be seen as one and the same phenomenon, the first related to domestic financial markets, and the second related to the international circulation of financial capital).

Financial deregulation makes governments dependent on financial markets since the latter set the terms in which public debt is placed and thus the costs of running fiscal deficits. Secondary markets for public securities also work as thermometers to measure the support the government may expect from financial investors.

Even more problematic for left-wing reformist governments, however, is the liberalization of the capital account of the balance of payments. More immediately, freedom of international circulation of financial capital gives wealth-holders the possibility of arbitraging between interest rates in the world economy, substantially reducing the effectiveness of domestic monetary policy.[19] In fact, capital account liberalization is much more limiting because it gives holders of financial assets the power *to vote with their feet* against any initiative that they may dislike by simply withdrawing their resources from a given economy thereby causing a balance of payments crisis.[20]

The fear of inducing capital flight was the common element between the failed experiences with left-wing reformism. One can, of course, debate whether some of the left-wing leaders that have pointed out the danger of balance of payments crises as a reason to retreat from reformist electoral platforms were plain opportunists disguising their unwillingness to move on with their promises. It does not make the difficulty any less real though.[21]

Lula faced a balance of payments crisis caused by capital flight even before he was elected. Unwilling to reintroduce the capital controls that were dismantled (but not outlawed) in the 1990s, Lula had no choice but to bow down to financial markets, which he did in unambiguous fashion, by appointing an economic team that had the complete confidence of 'the market' and placing the strength of his own post behind it.

Once Lula accepted paying the price the market demanded to allow him to govern, which was to make sure that the economy would continue to be managed by basically the same staff as before, according to the same principles set in the preceding period, there was not much one could expect from his administration and, in fact, not much happened. Orthodox economic policies coupled with more active income transferences described the limited horizon of Lula's government even before the devastating corruption scandal erupted in 2005.

4 Conclusion

Three-quarters of Lula's term are already gone. Not much is expected of the last year given the paralysing effect of the political crisis resulting from the investigation of corruption charges against the government. Nevertheless, very little was accomplished before the scandal came to light. The economic record is mediocre, as it was in the Cardoso years before him. The same stop-and-go pattern, rooted in the macroeconomic policy regime defined by the combination of inflation targeting, floating exchange rates and primary surpluses targeting, is repeating itself under Lula. On the social policy front, income transferences are certainly more generous than in the Cardoso years, but no structural change has been promoted and the factors that explained the exceedingly high concentration of income and wealth are still in operation.

Lula's failure to promote the type of change in Brazilian society that voters expected when he was elected in 2002 should probably be explained by a multiplicity of factors. In this chapter, we advanced two hypotheses. The first refers to subjective limitations of the political leadership offered by Lula and PT. They did not seem to have any real vision or project for the country other than being elected and clinging to power. Once the election was over, and even before that, Lula made a clear choice to accept whatever limitation to his authority as could be demanded to guarantee his inauguration. It is not clear whether Lula and PT ever developed any definite ideas about an alternative to the prevailing ways of the Brazilian society, but if they did they did not seem to have had any qualms in abandoning them. The second hypothesis advanced in this chapter was that there were objective barriers to policy reorientation, represented most importantly by the liberalization of the capital account pursued in the 1990s. By choosing not to challenge the freedom of circulation of financial capital, Lula, to all intents an purposes, forsook any possibility of governing the country in any other way than previously.

Notes

* Financial supports from CNPq and FAPERJ are gratefully acknowledged.
** I would like to thank Felipe Garcia and Priscila Oliveira for providing data relevant to Table 5A.1.
1 At the time this work was being written, Lula was going to run for a second term (Brazilian law allows sitting presidents to seek re-election once). In fact in the election of 29 October 2006, Lula was re-elected in the second round for a new term, 2007–2010. Despite some allegations of corruption and his orthodox economic policies, Lula managed to get 60.8 per cent of the votes.
2 IPCA covers a sample of families with a multiple of up to 40 times the minimum wage, which is determined every year by the Brazilian federal government. The sample covered by IPCA has a broad geographical basis that includes families in the biggest cities of Brazil. IPCA is calculated by IBGE (National Bureau of Geography and Statistics).
3 IT is a monetary policy framework whereby public announcement of official inflation targets, or target ranges, is undertaken along with explicit acknowledgement that price stability, meaning low and stable inflation, is monetary policy's primary long-term objective. Targets for primary fiscal surplus aims at stabilizing or reducing the relation between net public debt and GDP. In a floating exchange rate regime, there are two objectives of the exchange rate: on the one hand, it aims at equilibrating the balance of payments; on the other hand, it tries to stabilize the exchange rate according to the purchasing power parity.
4 It is important to say that all these items are not part of the traditional agenda of PT.
5 This is the interest rate equivalent to the *Federal Funds* rate in the United States.
6 Note that, during the presidential election, on October 2002, the risk premium had reached the 2400 point mark.
7 Despite this poor GDP performance, the average unemployment rate decreased (from 11.5 per cent in 2004 to 9.8 per cent in 2005) and the workers' average income increased 5.8 per cent.
8 The inflation rate in 2005 was 5.69 per cent.
9 The international prices of Brazilian commodities are still high, the growth rate of its main trade partners (United States, Argentina and China) are higher than the world average growth and foreign investment – direct and portfolio – are 'flying' to Brazil.
10 One should be careful, however, to remember that the Brazilian economy has been very volatile so that every expectation is formed under substantial uncertainty. Worse than expected results of GDP growth in the second quarter of 2006 (in the first quarter of 2006 the growth rate of GDP was 1.3 per cent, while in the second quarter it was 0.5 per cent) have already clouded even the moderate optimism shown in these data.

11 According to the Taylor rules, the nominal interest rate is increased more than one-to-one with respect to any increase in inflation. This policy reaction ensures that the real rate of interest will act to lower inflation. Given inflation, the real rate of interest is also increased as a result of output-gap positive changes. Taylor rules, therefore, require monetary policy to act automatically to inflation and output.

12 For instance, the Banco Nacional de Desenvolvimento Econômico e Social (BNDES) could increase its role in financing investments.

13 In sum, industrial policy should be used both to increase and change the composition of Brazil's exports, in order to incorporate other products with high levels of aggregate value.

14 In addition to this, fiscal initiatives, such as introducing really progressive income tax schedules and capital levies, guaranteed minimum income and social expenditure to improve the standard of living of poor people are required to promote personal income redistribution.

15 Tsakalotos (1998, p. 134)) observed that 'PASOK (the Greek Socialist Party) never had a clear conception of a coherent and implementable alternative' to neoliberal policies. This seems to have been precisely the same case as Lula's PT.

16 It is interesting that although Lula has many times made public his discomfort with being called a left winger, the PT has always resisted being seen as a social democratic organization, considered too committed to 'managing capitalism' instead of superseding it. Be this as it may, Glyn (1998, p. 2) observed, 'maintaining full employment has been the centre-piece of social democratic programmes since the 1930s'. Even mildly progressive parties, such as the Democratic Party in the Kennedy years, considered that 'taming the business cycle and maintaining full employment were the first priorities of macroeconomic policy' (Tobin and Solow, 1988, p. 5). Full employment, however, is a conspicuous absence in the language of Lula's government and more particularly from the language of macroeconomic policy-makers in the Finance Ministry and the BCB.

17 In some cases, beliefs were given up as a result of failed attempts to implement the desired policies. The perception of inexistence of alternatives results from the attempt to understand why the desired policies failed. The paradigmatic example of such a situation is the French Socialist Party retreat in 1983 from the leftist programme it had implemented in the first two years of Mitterrand's presidency. The acceleration of inflation and the emergence of balance of payments problems caused the attempt to reflate the French economy to fail, at least to the extent that pursuing the process of European integration showed itself to be a higher priority. Abandoning the policies of 1981/83 in favour of the so-called *désinflation competitive* seemed at first to be little more than an adjustment of short-term policies. However, as noted by Lordon (1998, p. 101) '[w]hat the choice of the *désinflation competitive* fundamentally means is nothing other than the acceptance of the rules of the game of an opened-up and internationalized economy.' In Mitterrand's France, as in Lula's Brazil, it took some time for supporters to realize that what seemed to be a short-term concession to the 'markets' was actually a complete turn-around.

18 In fact, Lula may have been disfavoured by his own background of personal experience. As is well known, Lula was a successful union leader. His political experience, however, was limited to an undistinguished term as Congressman. As President Lula himself has insisted a number of times, his *modus operandi* is still that of a union official, that instead of actually leading and pointing to larger goals, tries to promote consensus among the constituencies represented in his administration.

19 It is conventionally argued that this is so only under fixed exchange rate regimes. For a criticism of this view, see Carvalho and Sicsú (2004).
20 See Carvalho and Sicsú (2004).
21 The external context was clearly the major element to explain the changes in socialist policies in Mitterrand's France. It was also probably an important factor in the case of countries under socialist governments aiming at joining the European Community, as in the case of Spain or Greece. According to Stiglitz (2003), it was a major consideration in the policy debate within the Clinton administration.

References

Banco Central do Brasil. www.bcb.gov.br. Accessed in August 2006.
Carvalho, F. and Sicsú, J., 'Controvérsias Recentes sobre Controles de Capitais', *Revista de Economia Política*, 24 (2), April/June, 2004.
Glyn, A., 'The assessment: economic policy and social democracy', *Oxford Review of Economic Policy*, 14 (1), 1998.
Instituto Brasileiro de Geografia e Estatística. www.ibge.gov.br. Accessed in August 2006.
Instituto de Pesquisa Econômica Aplicada. www.ipeadata.gov.br. Accessed in August 2006.
Kennedy, D., *Freedom from Fear. The American People in Depression and War, 1929–1945*, The Oxford History of the United States, New York and Oxford: Oxford University Press, 1999.
Lordon, F., 'The logic and limits of *désinflation compétitive*', *Oxford Review of Economic Policy*, 14 (1), 1998.
Stiglitz, J., *The Roaring Nineties*, New York: W.W. Norton and Company, 2003.
Tobin, J. and Solow, R., 'Introduction to the Kennedy Economic Reports', In: Tobin, J. and Weidenbaum, M. (eds), *Two Revolutions in Economic Policy*, Cambridge (Mass): MIT Press, 1988.
Tsakalotos, E., 'The political economy of social democratic economic policies: the PASOK experiment in Greece', *Oxford Review of Economic Policy*, 14 (1), 1998.

Appendix

Table 5A.1 Some macroeconomic indicators of the Brazilian economy

Macroeconomic Indicators/Year	1999	2000	2001	2002	2003	2004	2005	2006[3]
IPCA (%)[1]	8.94	5.97	7.67	12.53	9.3	7.6	5.69	3.8
GDP growth (%)	0.8	4.4	1.3	1.9	0.5	4.9	2.3	3.5
Unemployment rate (%)[2]	8.3	7.9	6.8	7.9	12.3	11.5	9.8	10.2[4]
Interest rate (Selic), average (%)	25.5	17.4	17.3	19.2	23.0	16.4	19.2	15.2
Exchange rate, average (R$/US$)	1.815	1.829	2.35	2.926	3.077	2.922	2.43	2.19
Exports (US$ billion)	48.0	55.1	58.2	60.4	73.1	96.5	118.3	n.a.
Imports (US$ billion)	49.2	55.8	55.6	47.2	48.3	63.0	73.5	n.a.
Trade balance (US$ billion)	-1.2	-0.7	2.6	13.1	24.8	33.5	44.8	41.2
Current account (US$ billion)	-25.3	-24.2	-23.2	-7.6	4	11.6	14.2	8.0
Foreign debt (US$ billion)	241.5	236.2	209.9	210.7	214.9	201.4	168.8	n.a.
Foreign reserves (US$ billion)	36.3	33.0	35.9	37.8	49.3	52.9	53.8	n.a.
Country risk/EMBI, average	1030.0	730.0	890.0	1380.0	830.0	542.0	313.80	n.a.
Fiscal surplus/GDP (%)	3.2	3.5	3.6	3.9	4.3	4.6	4.8	4.25
Net public debt/GDP (%)	46.9	49.9	53.3	56.5	58.7	51.8	51	50.5
Investment rate (% of GDP, 1980 prices)	14.8	14.8	14.8	13.9	13.1	13.8	13.8	n.a.
General government revenues/GDP	31.7	32.6	34.0	35.6	34.9	35.9	37.4	n.a.

Notes: (1) The targets of inflation from 1999 to 2005 were the following: 1999 = [6.0%, 10.0%]; 2000 = [4.0%, 8.0%]; 2001 = [2.0%, 6.0%]; 2002 = [1.5%, 6.5%]; 2003 = [1.5%, 6.5%]; 2004 = [3.5%, 8.0%]; 2005 = [2.6%, 7.6%]. For 2006, the tolerance interval is [2.5%, 7.0%].
(2) Unemployment rate according to the IBGE methodology. (3) BCB expectations based on weekly report of 21 August 2006. (4) Average rate from January to July 2006.
Source: IBGE, IPEADATA and BCB.

6
Lula's Social Policies: New Wine in Old Bottles?

Alcino Ferreira Câmara Neto
Federal University of Rio de Janeiro

Matías Vernengo[1]
University of Utah

1 Introduction

It has become commonplace in the debates about economic and social policies in Brazil in the Washington Consensus era, that is, during the administrations of Fernando Henrique Cardoso and Luiz Inácio Lula da Silva, to emphasize that social indicators (poverty, life expectancy, literacy rates, infant mortality, fertility rates, etc.) have shown marked improvement. However, the main complaint is that inequality levels have remained high, and that social policies are unable to eliminate inequality without being complemented by more efficient use of public money, in particular, better targeting to the poor. The superficial conclusion is that there is something right about social policies from the 1990s onwards, since after the 1988 Constitution there has been a certain amount of social progress (Schwartzman, 2000; Almeida, 2004; Barros and Carvalho, 2004).

Also, it has been argued by critics of Luiz Inácio Lula da Silva's (from now on simply Lula) social policies that his approach to social policies has marked a shift from the conventional emphasis on universal policies (Almeida, 2004). In this view, Lula's social policies have emphasized targeted programmes in order to increase the efficiency of social spending, even though the debate on whether targeting has been efficient is still open.

This chapter suggests that both propositions – that the reforms of social policies after the 1988 Constitution were somehow instrumental in explaining social progress, and that Lula's policies mark a break with the 1988 Constitution – are misleading. The rise in life expectancy, the fall in illiteracy rates, the fall in infant mortality and the reduction of fertility rates have a long history, and have coexisted with one of the highest levels of inequality in the world. Recent social policy reforms have a limited role in explaining the evolution of social indicators. Even if Lula's policies put more emphasis on targeting, a controversial proposition that we do not try to sort out, it seems that both Lula's social policies and those of his predecessor are secondary to the macroeconomic policies which promote the reproduction of financial wealth, in an environment of increasing inequality.

We believe that the Cardoso administration's acceptance of the Washington Consensus agenda marks in Brazil the alignment of certain groups on the left of the political spectrum to anti-Keynesian policies. Further, there is no indication of a major break between Lula's policies and those of his predecessor, although some minor differences subsist. In particular, the increase in the minimum wage accelerated in Lula's administration and the rate of expansion of the *Bolsa-Família* programme has been exponential, which may explain the notion of a break with previous policies. However, the anti-Keynesian bias of economic policies during Lula's tenure, in our view, suggests that the ability of social policies in reducing the vast inequalities in Brazilian society remain limited at best.

The remainder of the chapter is divided into three sections. The first section provides a bird's eye view of social policies in Brazil in the very long run. The following one shows the limitations of conventional wisdom arguments about recent social policies, and discusses the role of financialization in perpetuating the historic pattern of social exclusion. The last section indicates the drawbacks of the decision to abandon the Keynesian goal of full employment by left of centre administrations.

2   A long history of social exclusion

The roots of inequality in Brazil are to be found ultimately in the colonial heritage. The sugar and gold cycles of the sixteenth and seventeenth centuries – part of the Portuguese colonial venture, and essential for the colonization of the Northeastern and Southeastern regions respectively – and their need for high sums of capital, and African slaves as the primary source of labour were part of a social structure of production that implied high levels of inequality.

After independence, the elites that dominated Brazilian politics were linked to the export sectors, in particular to the rising coffee sector, and were fundamentally concerned with the maintenance of a structure of production based on the 'latifundio' – the large agrarian property – and slave labour, which was maintained by Brazil almost until the end of the Empire. The transition to wage labour and Republican governments took place hand in hand with the maintenance of an economy dominated by export interests, electoral fraud, and a system of patronage that did little to eliminate the great income inequalities accumulated in the previous centuries.

In fact, only the Great Depression and the process of industrialization led to serious challenges to the established social structures, and opened the possibilities of a more equitable and democratic society. Yet, the Brazilian experience of National-Developmental policies, although quite successful in the promotion of industrialization, fell short in terms of generating strong social coalitions capable of reducing income inequality.

It should be noted that high levels of inequality – that sometimes are assumed to be detrimental to economic growth – were not necessarily an impediment for fast increases in income per capita. Even though the Brazilian economy lagged behind during the colonial period and the nineteenth century, during the major part of the twentieth century – up to the debt crisis of the early 1980s – it caught up with the developed world. In fact, during some periods (e.g. the Economic Miracle, 1968–73), increasing income inequality might have been instrumental in producing higher rates of growth.

All in all, the institutions for social protection created during the import substitution industrialization (ISI) phase – roughly between 1930 and 1980 – were incapable of affecting positively the indicators on inequality and social exclusion. The Brazilian Welfare State, if we can speak of one in the periphery, was incomplete, fragile and circumscribed by one of the highest levels of social inequality for middle income countries in the world. Draibe and Aureliano (1989) classify the Brazilian welfare system as conservative or corporatist, one in which social protection was mainly concerned with the relations between capital and labour, and where the State socialized the costs of the reproduction of the labour force, as part of the subsidies to promote industrialization.

However, as the system incorporated increasing numbers of participants in public programmes, the quality of services decreased markedly. For that reason, the upper and middle classes reduced their use of elementary and secondary public education, and relied on privatized health and pension systems to complement the public ones. The fall of the minimum wage (Figure 6.1) – to which several benefits were tied – is indicative of the deterioration of the precarious system of welfare from the 1950s onwards.[2] Also, in contrast with most of the international experiences, in particular the Western European one, the Brazilian system of social protection was concerned with social rights and citizenship only to a minimum extent. On the other hand, the fast rates of growth of income per capita, during the ISI period, suggested that there was hope for a reduction of the worst iniquities in the system.

However, the debt crisis, the prolonged period of high inflation, and the dismal economic performance of the 1980s, the so-called 'lost decade', relegated discussions about development and inequality to secondary plane. Stabilization was the main concern for policymakers and in intellectual discussions. The 1988 Constitution – promulgated in the midst of the process of redemocratization – delineated a model for the universalization of social security, health and education rights to all citizens.[3] The Real Plan in 1994 and the resulting economic stability – which were not accompanied by higher rates of growth – reopened the discussions on strategies of development and their impact on social conditions. The consensus was that stability allowed the implementation of several of the objectives of the 1988

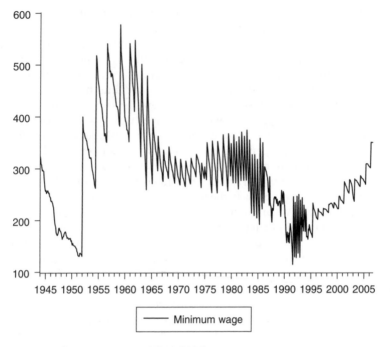

Figure 6.1   Real minimum wage (1944–2006)
Source: IPEA data.

Constitution and that there had been a significant improvement in social indicators during the Cardoso government (Almeida, 2004).

Several authors claimed that the main problem with social policies in Brazil, during the Cardoso administration (1995–2002) was the lack of targeting, usually defended by the World Bank (e.g. Schwartzman, 2000; Barros and Carvalho, 2004). However, it is clear that – beyond the philosophical question on whether social policies should be universal or targeted – the amount of social spending was insufficient during the Cardoso administration, and problems were not restricted to inefficient spending. The fundamental problem was that, with the combination of high interest rates and primary surpluses, social spending was squeezed (Vernengo, 2007).[4]

It should be emphasized that since 1994, including the four years of the Workers' Party's administration, spending on the service and amortization of public debt, that is, the interest rate bill, has oscillated around 46 per cent, with peaks of 55 per cent in 2000 and 53 in 2005, of total government spending (see Figure 6.2). In other words, on average, almost half of the federal government expenditures go to banks, corporations and wealthy individuals that hold Treasury bonds. That is the main activity of the federal government.[5] In contrast, in 2006 spending on social security, health and sanitation and

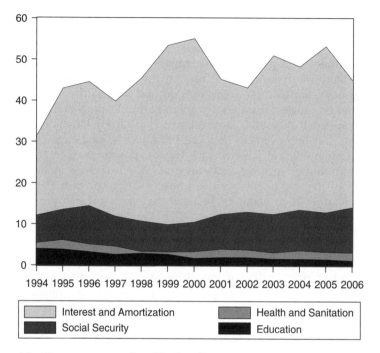

Figure 6.2 Government spending (% of total)
Source: SIAFI–STN.

education, all added up, corresponded to approximately 18.5 per cent of the total spending of the federal government.

Conventional wisdom on social policies during the Cardoso administration is that poverty, and social indicators usually improved while income inequality improved slightly at the beginning but remained at high levels (e.g. Schwartzman, 2000; Almeida, 2004). Most of the discussion on inequality is centred on Gini coefficients, but if we look at the functional distribution of income, it is clear that inequality increased, with the participation of wages in total income falling from 40.1 per cent in 1994, the year of the Real Plan, to 36.1 per cent in the last year of Cardoso's administration (Vernengo, 2007).[6] Far from reducing the high levels of inequality, the Cardoso administration was associated with a considerable compression of wages and the worsening of income distribution.

It must be noted that in addition to general efforts to enlarge access to public education and health, according to the inclusive criteria of the 1988 Constitution, Cardoso's administration created a series of programmes that complemented the welfare system and that were targeted to the poorest sectors of society. For example, the *Bolsa-Escola*, *Bolsa-Alimentação*, *Auxílio-Gás* and other cash transfer programmes were created, and the programme *Erradicação do Trabalho Infantil* (PETI) to eliminate child labour was forcefully implemented.[7] According to Almeida (2004), in spite of the creation of these complementary social protection programmes, the overall emphasis of governmental intervention during the Cardoso period remained associated to universal policies, in particular, access to education and health.

Some authors suggest that the effects of those transfer programmes, although positive are small at best (e.g. Bourguignon et al., 2003). Others suggest that the significant improvement in social indicators is, to a large extent, the result of more efficient targeted cash transfer programmes, in addition to higher minimum wages (e.g. Kakwani et al., 2006). The argument is ultimately about the size of the positive impact of targeted cash transfer programmes rather than about the general usefulness of such programmes. Critics of cash transfer programmes – like Almeida (2004) – suggest Lula's administration emphasized the relevance of cash transfer programmes, in particular the *Bolsa-Família* – after his election, and that this was a substantial break with the previous emphasis in universal social programmes. The following section discusses whether there has been a significant rupture in social policies during the Workers' Party (Partido dos Trabalhadores, PT) administration, and the reasons for the improved social indicators in both Cardoso and Lula's administrations.

3 Lula's social policies

The Workers' Party acceptance of the macroeconomic strategies adopted during the Cardoso administration should be seen as part of the general move of left of centre parties to repudiate the Keynesian policies that served as the pillars for the development of the limited Brazilian welfare state (Câmara and Vernengo, 2006). However, it would be incorrect to assume that the role of the state has been reduced. The most important change is in the way the state intervenes rather than a considerable reduction of its impact on social and economic outcomes.

Lula's government was initiated with great expectations and the belief that his administration would have a foundational character in promoting significant reductions in the secular problem of social exclusion. However, very few proposals for social policies were discussed before the election and fundamental emphasis was accorded to the necessity of generating higher rates of employment. After the election, however, the question of stability became central, and fiscal restraint was seen as an essential part of the anti-inflationary programme. In fact, as part of the strategy to obtain long-term fiscal sustainability a reform of the pension system was implemented. The main social programme – which was seen by many as the emblematic programme of the incoming government – was the so-called *Fome Zero* (or Zero Hunger). By the end of 2003 *Fome Zero* was demoted from its position of flagship of social programmes, and partially integrated into the *Bolsa-Família*, which had incorporated several of the Cardoso social programmes.[8]

The origins of *Bolsa-Família* are deeply rooted in the Workers' Party views on social policy, favouring cash transfers over other developmental programmes. Eduardo Matarazzo Suplicy, a Workers' Party Senator from São Paulo advocated a reverse income tax policy programme, which he first presented to the Senate in 1991.[9] Later those ideas led to the *Bolsa-Escola* implemented in Brasília by Cristovam Buarque and the *Programa de Garantia de Renda Familiar* in Campinas, both during Workers' Party administrations.

The main rationale for the integration of the several conditional cash transfer programmes (*Bolsa-Escola*, *Bolsa-Alimentação*, *Fome Zero* and *Auxílio Gás*) into *Bolsa-Família* was to provide a more capable administration, and to target the poor more efficiently. Almeida (2004) argues that the emphasis on *Bolsa-Família* led to a marked break with the Cardoso administration's position on social policies, and a new emphasis on targeted instead of universal programmes. This view is to some extent supported by the fast-paced increase in the extent of coverage of *Bolsa-Família*. In January 2005 it covered six million families and accounted for around 1 per cent of government spending, while by the end of 2006 it is expected to cover 11 million families and correspond to 2.5 per cent of total expenditures. However, the distinction between Cardoso's and Lula's administration social policies is minor at best. In fact, both are similar to several cash transfer programmes in Latin America.[10] The question of whether targeting of universal programmes are central is unable to shed light on the essential modification of social policies in both periods.

It is true that central to both Cardoso and Lula's social policies is the idea that cash transfer – that is, direct monetary transfers to poor families – are essential to reduce poverty and inequality. Also, the fact that most cash transfers have been conditional, depending on the commitment by poor families to send their children to school or to health centres, for example, indicates that the reduction of poverty and inequality are seen to be connected to human capital, a Chicago doctrine that became popular in development circles, in particular at the World Bank.[11] However, the fundamental change in social policies has been caused by the process of financialization.

In fact, after the Real Plan in 1994 real interest rates have been high in real terms, and that has implied that the number one expense of the central government has been the service of the debt. Public debt holders are ultimately banks, corporations, and a tiny minority of the population. The process of financialization that started with the debt crisis in the 1980s achieved its high point after stabilization. Financial transfers in the form of interest payments on domestic public debt became the central 'social programme' of both Cardoso and Lula's administrations, consuming close to 50 per cent of all spending. Not surprisingly the fall in wage participation in total income was matched by an increase of the operational surplus from 38.4 per cent in 1994 to 42.9 per cent in 2003 (Vernengo, 2007).

In other words, if the pattern of social policies that led to the corporate welfare system developed during the ISI period was fundamentally associated with the socialization of labour costs for the industrial sector, then in the post-liberalization and stabilization period social policies have become secondary to the process of financial accumulation (Pochmann, 2004). The question, then, is how social indicators (life expectancy, illiteracy rates, infant mortality, and fertility rates are displayed below, but alternative indicators like United Nations Development Programme (UNDP) Human Development Index (HDI) would show similar improvement) did actually improve during the Washington Consensus era (Table 6.1).

The conventional view, which suggests that social programmes alleviated the worst effects of economic downturns and were central in the progress of social indicators, seems misplaced considering that those indicators have improved since the 1940s, at least. Output growth is not a likely explanation of social improvement either, because the record during the 1980s and 1990s has been dismal.

The most likely explanation is that the progress in social indicators was a result of the process of industrialization, and the consequent migration from rural to urban areas. Urban areas provide greater access to electricity, treated water, medical care and public schools. In other words, urbanization, the extension of social benefits to rural workers, and the relative fall of the cost of food rather than a reduction of inequality are the most likely driving forces of social progress in Brazil (Vernengo, 2007).[12] The urbanization process that resulted from industrialization transformed the country from one in which 70 per cent of the population lived in rural areas in 1940, into one, in which more than 80 per cent of the population live in urban areas in 2000. The underlying process was one of fast rural modernization, with an intense process

Table 6.1   Social indicators (1940–2004)

	Life expectancy	Illiteracy rate	Infant mortality	Fertility rate
1940	43	56	158	6.1
1950	46	50	138	6.2
1960	52	40	118	6.3
1970	54	30	117	5.5
1980	60	25	88	4.4
1990	65	19	50	2.7
1996	67	17	41	2.1
1998	68	14	36	NA
2004	71	12	27	1.9

Sources: IBGE, and Schwartzman (2000).

of capitalist expansion in agriculture without land reform. The migration from rural areas was fast paced and in the short span of three decades nearly 40 million people migrated to cities, 24 per cent of the whole population in the 1950s, 36 per cent in the 1960s and 40 per cent in the 1970s (Cardoso de Mello and Novais, 1998).

We believe that the process of industrialization during the 1930–80 period was the force behind social progress, and that it was the success of that process that allowed the continuous improvement in social indicators long after the process of import substitution industrialization lost dynamism. The process of industrialization was so successful that urban areas remained an important outlet for rural workers that were not absorbed in the modernized agribusiness sector. Therefore, alternative macroeconomic policies, which put a lesser burden on social spending, might in fact accelerate social progress. For that reason it is hard to believe that social indicators would not have improved even more, and more importantly, that inequality would not have been reduced, if a larger share of government spending was diverted from interest payments to social programmes.

Pochmann and Amorim (2004, p. 73) note that the map of social exclusion has a clear regional pattern, with incredibly high concentration of the worst social indicators in the north and northeast regions, which they attribute to 'old causes', linked to the pattern of land tenure, the reduced bargaining power of the labour force and represented by reduced access to education, food, health and the formal labour market. On the other hand, they find that in the south and southeast regions, in the 1990s, a new form of social exclusion has emerged, one that exists despite greater access to education, food and health, and even some experience with formal labour markets. The new social exclusion is basically associated with higher levels of unemployment and labour market informality.

Further, it should be emphasized, as noted by Lessa et al. (1997), that the extension of the social safety net implicit in the 1988 Constitution never made it completely into the budgets implemented by several administrations. In fact, in 2002 the Cardoso administration spending on social programmes (excluding social security payments) corresponded to 73.9 per cent of its expenses on debt servicing (Pochmann, 2003, p. 5). Total social spending, excluding social security, as a share of GDP in 1998 was 12.2 per cent which corresponds to around half of what was spent in OECD countries in the same year (ibid., p. 6).[13] The same limitations broadly apply to Lula's social policies.[14]

The idea that social spending was high and not properly targeted on the poor is clearly out of place. Additionally, whether Lula has tried to target social policies on the poorest sectors of society seems irrelevant as an explanation of recent social progress. It seems, on the contrary, that the financialization of government expenditures has led to worsening income distribution, and by limiting the ability of the state to increase social spending it has limited the ability of the state to reduce social inequalities. The main cause of the expansion of social exclusion is the inability to create decent (i.e. well paid) employment. In the past, income inequality went hand in hand with high rates of growth and the expansion of consumption to relatively large shares of the population. During the Cardoso administration a new pattern of income concentration has emerged and has been maintained in Lula's administration, one that is inimical to growth, and relies exclusively on financial transfers towards the wealthy.

4 Brazil interrupted

The Workers' Party emerged from the so-called new unionism of the 1970s, which was rooted in the successful process of import substitution industrialization. In that sense, the emergence of the Workers' Party in 1980 gave voice to middle income and lower middle income groups that demanded higher salaries, adequate housing, education, health and social security, in other words, better social protection. That is, the classical agenda of social inclusion of the Western European left was central to the political project of the Workers' Party. However, an important feature of the new unionism was its autonomy from the state and its critical stance on the state relationship with unions and the corporatist labour regulation implemented during the so-called Vargas era. Fiori (2006) suggests that the Workers' Party's – as much as Cardoso's *Partido da Social Democracia Brasileira* (PSDB) – dislike of National Developmental policies of the Vargas era opened the opportunity for the acceptance of the neoliberal policies of the Washington Consensus agenda.

In this sense, a contradiction between the Workers' Party social policy objectives and the party's economic strategies become apparent. In particular, the emphasis on anti-inflationary policies at the beginning of Lula's administration, and the relegation of employment creation to a secondary role, indicated that according to the Workers' Party logic full employment was not central for its strategy of social inclusion. More importantly the secondary role given to employment generation by the Workers' Party may be seen as the consolidation in Brazil of a general movement of the left in the direction of anti-Keynesian policies, including the Western European left that usually was the main intellectual reference of Latin American left of centre parties (Câmara and Vernengo, 2006).

In this respect, it is interesting to note James K. Galbraith's (2003) re-evaluation of the American system. Usually the American or Anglo-Saxon model is seen as more market oriented than its Western European counterpart, which in part explains why it has often been neglected by the Latin American left. However, Galbraith notes the United States has relied heavily on government intervention in housing, health care, pensions, and education, and that, not only have these programmes been largely successful and popular, they also provide a Keynesian stimulus to spending that help account for the strength of the US economy. In other words, a greater commitment to full employment, reflected for example in the behaviour of the Federal Reserve Board when compared with the European Central Bank, seems to be a characteristic of the American model that should appeal to the left in Brazil, and Latin America in general.

The Workers' Party, as much as the social democrats, has relegated Keynesian ideas as old-fashioned, and has embraced the notion that fiscal austerity is essential for economic progress. For that reason, and in contrast to Keynesian policies, interest rates have been maintained at record levels, and primary fiscal surpluses have been the norm. Primary surpluses have been even hiked with respect to Cardoso's administration, and proposals of zero nominal deficits have become popular, implying that even higher primary surpluses are seen as acceptable and desirable. Also, exchange rates have been considerably appreciated in real terms. This macroeconomic policy mix has, not surprisingly, led to the maintenance of relative high levels of unemployment. Figure 6.3 shows that the average rate of unemployment in the Workers' Party administration remains high at roughly double the average of the 1980s level.[15]

Figure 6.3   Unemployment rate
Source: DIEESE.

Further, higher levels of unemployment have been accompanied by a significant reduction of the average real wage (Figure 6.4).[16] The benefits of stabilization that allowed average wages to increase moderately in the mid-1990s have been eroded by now, and wages remain broadly at half their 1980s level. Note that a rising minimum wage was, in part, instrumental in improving social indicators since several benefits are tied to the value of the minimum wage, though only a minority of the labour force actually receives a minimum wage, which is incredibly low.[17] Hence, the average real wage provides a better picture of the labour market conditions. Also, the fall in the average real wage is compatible with the squeeze of the share of wages in total income that fell around 10 per cent since the early 1990s.

Employment and real wage data makes it difficult to defend any claims that the Workers' Party is committed to reducing social exclusion as a central element of its agenda. Social spending cannot compensate for the lack of decent jobs and adequate compensation. Decent work should be at the heart of a national strategy for economic and social progress. As noted by Bresser-Pereira (2005) social spending alone cannot reduce the increasing income inequality, and the absorption of surplus labour should be central to any strategy of social inclusion. Further, Celso Furtado (1992) suggested that the

Figure 6.4   Average real wages
Source: DIEESE.

only possibility of reinvigorating the construction of the Brazilian economic system – interrupted since the early 1980s – would be to reinvigorate the domestic market and reverse the process of patrimonial concentration that, for him, was central to understand the social malformations in Brazilian society.

Interestingly enough, social spending is not disconnected from employment generation policies. In fact, lower rates of interest, which would stimulate consumption and employment generation, would also allow for reduced fiscal effort for debt servicing and the expansion of social spending. The main conundrum in Brazilian economic policies, then, is the high interest rate level, which impacts both employment generation and squeezes social spending. The following section discusses the causes of high real rates of interest in Brazil after stabilization in 1994.

5 Tropical casino capitalism

Our discussion suggests that central to understanding the limitations of Brazilian social policies, as well as its economic performance, is the persistence of high real rates of interest since the Real Plan. In fact, Brazil has had the highest real rate of interest in the world for most of the period. Figure 6.5 shows that the high rate of interest is a Brazilian phenomenon, with almost no parallel in recent times among Latin American countries. For the whole period nominal interest rates remained higher than the average for the Latin American economies. While nominal rates have fallen in the whole region, including Brazil, the fall was not sufficient to lead to a marked fall in the real rate of interest, because inflation also fell significantly.

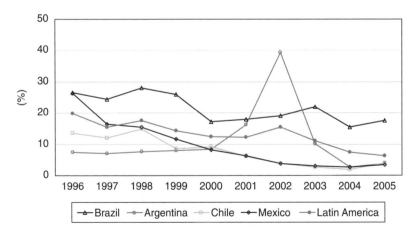

Figure 6.5 Nominal interest rates (19 Latin American countries)

Figure 6.6 shows that Brazil has had one of the lowest rates of inflation over the whole period. Also, Figure 6.7 shows that there is a clear negative correlation between high rates of interest and economic growth, which explains the relative poor performance of the Brazilian economy during Lula's administration when compared to other Latin American economies. The persistency of the high rates of interest throughout the whole period, even compared with Latin American economies that share similar problems, indicates that the

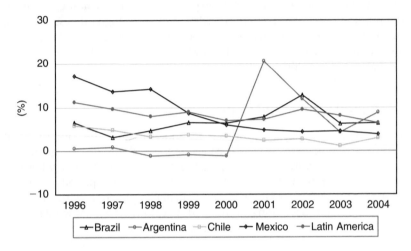

Figure 6.6   Inflation rates (19 Latin American countries)

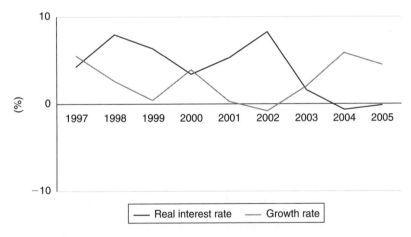

Figure 6.7   Real interest rate and growth (19 Latin American countries)
Source: International Financial Statistics, IMF.

Brazilian situation results from a conscious policy decision. Furthermore, there is no evident break in policy management in Lula's administration. Over the whole period nominal interest rates fell only as inflation fell, and the real rate of interest has been around 10 per cent, which is, as noted, among the highest in the world.

According to conventional wisdom interest rates are high in Brazil because of the lack of credibility that results from absence of fiscal responsibility. This is not verified empirically in the Brazilian case. Before discussing the effects of deficits on interest rates, the proper definition of the deficit must be clarified. If one argues that deficits lead to higher interest rates, one must not use the nominal definition of the deficit, which includes all revenues and all expenses, including interest payments. The reason for not using the nominal deficit is that if the interest rate rises the nominal deficit also increases, because it includes the interest payments on accumulated debt. Thus, the proper measure is the primary deficit, which excludes interest payments, and is the non-financial difference between spending and revenue.

In general, those who believe that lack of credibility is at the root of high rates of interest in Brazil argue that primary deficits have reduced the credibility of monetary policy in Brazil after 1999. However, the Brazilian government has had primary surpluses since 1999. In fact, since 1985 only in four years were there primary deficits, and none above 1 per cent of GDP. All in all Brazilian governments have been remarkably fiscally responsible.

A variation of the lack of credibility explanation is exposed by Arida et al. (2005). The authors note that there is no long-term credit market in Brazil, but there is 'a large long-term credit market open to Brazilian debtors where the jurisdiction is foreign' (2005, p. 268). The authors conclude that jurisdictional uncertainty associated with the settlement of contracts explains the lack of long-term credit markets in Brazil and the extraordinarily high rates of interest since 1994. There are two problems with the jurisdictional uncertainty hypothesis. First, it would be better as a theory of high long-term rates, since there is no reason why a policy variable determined by the Central Bank should respond to jurisdictional uncertainty. Yet, the base rate determined by the Central Bank has been on average close to 15 per cent since 1995. Jurisdictional uncertainty cannot explain high short-term rates. Second, and more importantly, jurisdictional uncertainty is not a new phenomenon in Brazil, and yet real rates on interest were not high before the Real Plan. In fact real rates were negative before 1994.

The alternative explanation may be termed the external financial fragility hypothesis. In this view, the main change that occurred in the Brazilian economy in the early 1990s was the liberalization of the capital account of the balance of payments. In this context, if the administration wanted to avoid the inflationary pressures caused by depreciation, as it did after 1994, the main policy instrument was to increase the rate of interest to avoid capital flight and stimulate capital inflows. High interest rates to control capital flows became central once the capital account was open. Thus, the fragility of the balance of payments situation in which inflows and outflows can lead to severe crises, which was created by external liberalization, is the main cause of permanently high rates of interest.[18]

High interest rates also play an important role in changing income distribution. Although Brazil has maintained primary surpluses above 3 per cent of GDP since 1999, nominal deficits have been around 5 per cent. The difference corresponds to 8 per cent of GDP and is made of interest payments to the owners of government bonds, including banks, pension funds, corporations and wealthy individuals. The share of wages in GDP has been compressed from 45.4 per cent in 1991 to 35.6 per cent in 2003 while the operational surplus, which includes profits, rents and interest payments, increased from 32.5 per cent to 42.9 per cent in the same period. Capital controls – that were widely used in the past, and have been used by several developing countries recently – would allow for lower rates of interest.

Capital controls reduce the pressure to use the interest rate as an instrument to avoid capital flight, and to manage the exchange rate. Lower rates of interest would translate directly into a reduced debt servicing burden for the federal administration, and would allow for the expansion of social spending. Contrary, to most authors who suggest that reduced interest rates should be used to promote a fiscal adjustment, we believe that nominal and primary fiscal deficits are necessary when the levels of unemployment are high. As we argued elsewhere,[19] one of the perverse legacies of the Washington Consensus agenda was that counter-cyclical fiscal policies were eliminated, and permanent fiscal adjustment became the norm.

In addition to increasing the fiscal space for social spending, lower interest rates would lead an environment in which income distribution might improve. Reduced income inequality, and expansion of credit would allow for the effective development of a more inclusive mass consumption society. The revitalization of domestic demand is central to promote a more equalitarian society.

In other words, to reverse the long cycle of social exclusion higher levels of social spending and more importantly higher levels of decent work should be created. The latter would only be possible in an environment that resembles what Keynes referred to as the euthanasia of the rentier, that is, capital controls and relatively low rates of interest. This would require also dismantling the financial process of capital reproduction and income concentration that has emerged after the 1980s lost decade and consolidated after the Real Plan under both the social democrats and the Workers' Party.

6   Concluding remarks

Brazilian society has a long history of social inequities that are ultimately connected to its colonial past, and the form in which the economy was integrated into mercantile capitalism. The long period of development that started with the Great Depression was unable to eliminate some of the major inequalities, and despite the improvement in social indicators, the Brazilian society remained essentially unequal. There was an incredible hope that redemocratization, that started in 1985, would lead to a considerable reduction of social and economic inequalities.

Conventional wisdom suggests that the reforms of social policies after the 1988 Constitution were somehow instrumental in explaining social progress. Yet, the rise in life expectancy, the fall in illiteracy rates, the fall in infant mortality and the reduction of fertility rates have a long history of improvement, and have coexisted with one of the highest levels of inequality in the world. Hence, recent social policy reforms have a limited role in explaining the evolution of social indicators. The election of Lula led many to believe that Brazil was mature enough to start paying its overwhelming social debt.

However, some authors put forward the notion that Lula's social policies mark a break with the 1988 Constitution emphasis on broad universal social policies. In our view, even if Lula's policies put more emphasis on targeting – something that is far from clear – it seems that the crucial element in both Lula's social policies and those of his predecessor is that social spending has been squeezed by the financial needs of the state and that employment generation has been insufficient to eliminate the enormous inequalities of Brazilian society. The problem with Lula's social policies, in our view, is that they do not break with the secular pattern of income inequalities, and, in fact, stimulate increasing social injustice.

It is true that cash transfer programmes like *Bolsa-Família* have been expanded exponentially and that the minimum wage increases have accelerated somewhat, and that may, in part, explain the relatively easy re-election of Lula for a second term starting in 2007. Yet, high rates of interest, which imply high remuneration for the wealthy, have become the hallmark of the post-liberalization period, and Lula's macroeconomic policies have been a continuation of those of Cardoso. Social policies have been confined to a secondary role, and are absolutely incapable of eliminating the vast inequities of Brazilian society. If the long history of social exclusion was associated for a long time to the type of integration with international markets – one that implied that land tenure would be unevenly distributed and one that would use forced labour – the new inequality is also directly connected with the form of integration to international markets. Inequality now results from an open financial account and the highest real rates of interest in the world. A perfect match for one of the highest levels of inequality in the world![20]

More significantly the social policies of Lula's administration are, as much as those of his predecessor, envisioned as handouts for the needy, and are disconnected from the creation of decent employment and redistribution of income. The hallmark of left of centre governments, historically, had been the integration of universal social policies tied with full employment policies, and the search of a more equalitarian income distribution. To the extent that the Workers' Party broke off with its preoccupations with full employment and income distribution it has become more attuned with the movement of several left of centre parties – like the New Labour rejection of the socialist elements of its platform in the United Kingdom or the New Democrats rejection of some of the policies associated with the New Deal in the United States – which accepted Thatcher's motto according to which 'there is no alternative'.

The key for more efficient social policies is, then, a more closed financial environment that would produce the Keynesian 'euthanasia of the rentier'. To guarantee the euthanasia of the rentier, Keynes pointed out that the central bank should be able to set the rate of interest independently from any international pressures. Hence, capital controls are the necessary complement to Keynes's fiscal policy proposals for full employment generation, and unless Lula and his Workers' Party[21] reverses the anti-Keynesian bias of their policies there is little chance of a more equitable and civilized society in Brazil. Only then, Brazilian society might reduce 'the disparity between what we are and what we hoped to be', which as Furtado (1999, p. 26) suggested 'has in no other period of our history been so large'.

Notes

1 We thank Marcia Pressentin for comments to an earlier version, and Carlos Schonerwald da Silva for his research assistance.

2 It is important to note that after the 1994 stabilization plan the real minimum wage increased steadily. Some authors suggest that, in part, the improvement in social indicators is related to the evolution of the minimum wage (e.g. Kakwani et al. 2006). Yet, it is clear from Figure 6.1 that the minimum wage only recovered the level of the late 1970s, and is far below its 1950s peak.

3 For a discussion of the social policy reforms of the 1990s, which followed the 1988 Constitution, see Draibe (1999).

4 This type of macroeconomic policy mix was typical of the Washington Consensus policies and was imposed in agreement with the International Monetary Fund (IMF) (Câmara and Vernengo, 2004–5).

5 Schumpeter (1918, p. 3) suggested that 'public finances are one of the best starting points for an investigation of society'. Fiscal spending shows, without the veil of ideology, what the real priorities of a government are. If the fundamental beneficiaries of government spending are rentiers, living from high remuneration of financial assets, it is hard to defend the notion that such administration prioritizes the poor and dispossessed.

6 They also continued to fall in the first year of Lula's administration – the only one for which there is data – with the participation of wages in total income reaching only 35.6 per cent.

7 In 1960 22.15 per cent of children between 10 and 14 worked, while the same figure in 1990 was 17.8 per cent. In the first year of Cardoso's administration the number was already 16.15 and was reduced to 14.43 by the year 2000 (World Bank, 2002).

8 Rocha (2005) suggests that the impact of *Fome Zero* and *Bolsa-Família* on social indicators might be bigger than the effects of the Cardoso programmes – *Bolsa-Escola*, *Bolsa-Alimentação* and *Auxílio-Gás*.

9 Silveira (1975) provided the original proposal for a negative income tax.
10 *Bolsa-Família* provides around 25 dollars to more than 10 million families, the *Oportunidades* programme are in Mexico gives between 100 and 170 dollars to 5 million families, and the *Plan Jefes y Jefas de Hogar*, in Argentina, provides around 50 dollars to 1.8 million people, to name the more prominent cash transfer programmes in Latin America. Of these, the *Plan Jefes*, introduced in the midst of the worst crisis in Argentinean history, is the only one that tries to integrate the recipients into the labour market, and, at least conceptually, subscribes to the notion that social policies should be centred on the generation of decent employment. *Bolsa-Família* is, in terms of coverage, the largest cash transfer programme in the world.
11 For the pioneers of development education and health were as much, if not more, a result of economic progress. For a critique of human, and the even more encompassing view of social, capital see Fine (2001).
12 These factors are also behind the fall in poverty rates (Vernengo, 2007).
13 Brazil ranks as a high social spending country within Latin America, together with Argentina, Chile, Mexico, and Uruguay. In 1998, social expenditure was about 22 per cent of GDP, more than a half corresponding to social security, while the education share was 3.9 per cent, health 3.4 per cent, housing 1.2 per cent and training programmes around 1 per cent.
14 Bresser-Pereira (2005) suggests that there has been a considerable effort since redemocratization in expanding social spending. The data presented by Pochmann (2003) suggests that the effort falls short of the Herculean task of reducing Brazilian social exclusion.
15 Figure 6.3 shows the unemployment rate for the São Paulo metropolitan area, the main industrial region of the country. Numbers for the five largest metropolitan areas would display similar results.
16 Figure 6.4 also uses the data for the metropolitan area of São Paulo, with 1985 being equal to 100.
17 It must be noted that the rate of increase of the minimum wage accelerated in Lula's administration with respect to Cardoso's administration.
18 For an explanation along those lines see Bresser-Pereira and Nakano (2002).
19 See Câmara and Vernengo (2004–5).
20 If the book by Gilberto Freyre (1933) *Masters and Slaves (Casa Grande & Senzala)* was the classic description of the inequalities of the colonial plantation society, even if it understated racial conflict, a fitting title for the portrayal of the current inequalities should be *Financial Masters and Slaves (Conta de Juros Grande & Senzala)*.
21 At the time of writing Lula has just obtained his re-election in 2006, which guarantees another four years of Workers' Party administration.

References

Almeida, Maria Hermínia Tavares de (2004), 'A Política Social no Governo Lula', *Novos Estudos CEBRAP*, vol. 70, pp. 7–17.
Arida, Persio; Edmar Bacha, and André Lara-Resende (2005), 'Credit, Interest, and Jurisdictional Uncertainty: Conjectures on the Case of Brazil', in *Inflation Targeting, Debt, and the Brazilian Experience, 1999–2003*, edited by Francesco Giavazzi, Ilan Goldfajn, and Santiago Herrera, Cambridge: MIT Press.
Barros, Ricardo Paes, and Mirela de Carvalho (2004), 'Desafios para a Política Social Brasileira', in *Reformas no Brasil: Balanço e Agenda*, Fabio Giambiagi, José G. Reis and André Urani (eds.), Rio de Janeiro, Nova Fronteira.

Bourguignon, François, Francisco H.G. Ferreira and Phillippe G. Leite (2003), 'Conditional Cash Transfers, Schooling, and Child Labor: Micro-Simulating Brazil's Bolsa-Escola Program', *World Bank Economic Review*, 17(2), 229–54.

Bresser-Pereira, Luiz Carlos (2005), 'IDH, Concentração e Desenvolvimento', *Folha de São Paulo*, 12 de setembro.

Bresser-Pereira, Luiz Carlos and Yoshiaki Nakano (2002), 'Uma Estratégia de Desenvolvimento com Estabilidade', *Revista de Economia Política*, 22(3), July, 146–77.

Câmara Neto, Alcino F. and Matías Vernengo (2004–5), 'Fiscal Policy and the Washington Consensus: A Post Keynesian Perspective', *Journal of Post Keynesian Economics*, 27(1), Winter, 333–43.

Câmara Neto, Alcino F. and Matías Vernengo (2006), 'Uma Nota sobre o Fim do Ciclo da Esquerda Brasileira'. Available at: http://www.desempregozero.org.br.

Cardoso de Mello, João Manuel and Fernando Novais (1998), 'Capitalismo Tardio e Sociabilidade Moderna', in *História da Vida Privada no Brasil*, Lilian M. Schwarcz (ed.), São Paulo: Companhia das Letras.

Departamento Intersindical de Estatistica e Estudios Socíoeconômico, various years.

Draibe, Sônia (1999), 'As Políticas Sociais nos Anos 90', in *Brasil: Uma Década em Transição*, Renato Baumann (ed.), Rio de Janeiro: Campus.

Draibe, Sônia and Liana Aureliano (1989), 'A especifidade do Welfare State brasileiro', *Economia e Desenvolvimento*, No 3.

Fine, Ben (2001), *Social Capital versus Social Theory: Political Economy and Social Science at the Turn of the Millennium*, London and New York: Routledge.

Fiori, José Luis (2006), 'A Esquerda e o Desenvolvimentismo.' Available at: http://www.desempregozero.org.br.

Freyre, Gilberto (1933), *Casa-Grande & Senzala: Formação da Família Brasileira sob o Regime da Economia Patriarcal*, Rio de Janeiro: Record, 1992.

Furtado, Celso (1992), *Brasil: A Construção Interrompida*, São Paulo: Paz e Terra.

Furtado, Celso (1999), *O Longo Amanhecer: Reflexões sobre a Formação do Brasil*, São Paulo: Paz e Terra.

Galbraith, James K. (2003), 'What is the American Model Really About? Soft Budgets and the Keynesian Devolution', The Levy Economics Institute, *Public Policy Brief* No. 72, August.

Instituto Brasileiro Geográfico e Estatístico (IBGE), *Indicadores Sociais Mínimos*. Available at: http://www.ibge.gov.br.

International Monetary Fund (IMF), *International Financial Statistics*, several issues.

Instituto de Pesquisa Econômica Aplicada (IPEA), IPEA Data. Available at: http://www.ipeadata.gov.br/ipeaweb.dll/ipeadata?83137703.

Kakwani, Nanak, Marcelo Neri and Hyun Son (2006), 'Ligações entre Crescimento Pró-Pobre, Programas Sociais e Mercado de Trabalho: A Recente Experiência Brasileira', UNDP, Poverty Centre, Brasília, processed.

Lessa, Carlos, Claudio Salm, Laura Tavares Soares and Sulamis Dain (1997), 'Pobreza e Política Social: A Exclusão dos Anos 90,' *Praga*, 1(3), 63–87.

Pochmann, Marcio (2003), *Desigualdade de Renda e Gastos Sociais no Brasil: Algumas Evidências para o Debate*, São Paulo, Secretaria Municipal do Desenvolvimento, Trabalho e Solidariedade.

Pochmann, Marcio (2004), 'Proteção Social na Periferia do Capitalismo: Considerações sobre o Brasil', *São Paulo em Perspectiva*, Apr./June, 18(2), 3–16.

Pochmann, Marcio and Ricardo Amorim (2004), *Atlas da Exclusão Social no Brasil*, São Paulo: Cortez Editora.

Rocha, Sônia (2005), 'Impacto sobre a Pobreza dos Novos Programas Federais de Transferência de Renda', *Revista de Economia Contemporânea*, 9(1), 153–85.

Schumpeter, Joseph A. (1918), 'The Crisis of the Tax State', *International Economic Papers*, 4, pp. 5–38, 1954.

Schwartzman, Simon (2000), 'Brazil: The Social Agenda', *Daedalus*, 129(2), Spring, 29–56.

Silveira, Antonio Maria da (1975), 'Moeda e Redistribuição de Renda', *Revista Brasileira de Economia*, Apr./June.

Sistema Integrado de Administração Financeira do Governo Federal (SIAFI), Secretaria do Tesouro Nacional (STN). Available at: http://www.tesouro.fazenda.gov.br/.

Vernengo, Matías (2007), 'Fiscal Squeeze and Social Policy during the Cardoso Administration (1995–2002)', *Latin American Perspectives*, forthcoming.

World Bank, (2002), *World Development Indicators*, Washington DC, CD-Rom.6

7

Assessing the Empirical Evidence on Inflation Targeting and Possible Lessons for Brazil

Alvaro Angeriz, Philip Arestis and Tirthankar Chakravarty
University of Cambridge

1 Introduction[1]

The purpose of this chapter is to prepare the ground for the chapter that follows immediately. We assess the empirical evidence on Inflation Targeting (IT), a new policy framework designed to tame inflation, and consider whether the assessment can be helpful in studying the experience in Brazil with such strategy. This policy framework has been with us since the early 1990s and given that IT was introduced in Brazil in 1999, lessons for the latter can be ascertained. Recent work makes the point that a significant number of countries adopted this strategy, and the number is growing. For example, Sterne (2002) suggests that 54 countries pursued one form of IT or another by 1998, compared with only 6 in 1990. A more recent study (IMF, 2005) suggests that 21 countries (8 developed and 13 emerging) are now clear inflation targeters, pursuing a full-fledged IT strategy (FFIT in short). IMF (2006) has recently reported that there are 17 countries that have sought technical assistance to be able to introduce it. A number of studies have attempted to examine empirically the degree and extent of the impact of IT on inflation. We review this literature in what follows and conclude that the available empirical evidence produces mixed results. In pursuing an IT strategy, countries commit themselves to price stability as the main objective of monetary policy, along with stipulating that medium-to-long-term inflation is the nominal anchor where an inflation target is set.

There are, of course, varying degrees of commitment to IT amongst countries. In more general terms, one may distinguish between three types of inflation targeting: the FFIT as suggested above, the 'Inflation Targeting Lite' (ITL) type, and the 'Eclectic Inflation Targeting' (EIT) type.[2] The main distinguishing feature is the degree of clarity and institutional commitment to price stability[3] along with an explicit inflation targeting (either point- or range-inflation target), absence of other nominal anchors, policy instrument independence and absence of fiscal dominance, transparency, accountability and credibility of the commitment to IT by the central bank (Mishkin and Schmidt-Hebbel,

2001; Stone, 2003; Carare and Stone, 2003; Kuttner, 2005: see, also, Porter and Yao, 2005). In this chapter we focus on those countries that pursue a FFIT strategy, but we refer to the other two categories as necessary in what follows. The FFIT strategy dictates that countries commit themselves to achieving a targeted inflation rate and announce a relevant framework to achieve the set target. This approach is based on the belief that inflation is negatively related to economic growth in the long run, and, also, that high inflation is associated with high inflation variability, which is harmful to the economy. If authorities are allowed discretion in monetary policy, they produce 'surprise' inflation especially so for electoral benefits, which leads to the well known by now time-inconsistency problem. Such a problem, though, can be avoided if the government delegated to an independent central bank the role of monetary policy, based on a principal–agent relationship between the government and the central bank. The government sets the broader goal of monetary policy, while the central bank has complete discretion to use its instrument to achieve the target in view of its goal. The new monetary policy framework thereby gives 'constrained discretion' to the independent central bank to respond to new information, an important dimension of the new framework given information asymmetries and policy lags, while at the same time putting in place rules in the conduct of monetary policy.[4]

We proceed by reviewing the existing empirical evidence and by identifying a number of questions that emerge from this inevitably short review. We examine these questions subsequently, all in section 2. Section 3 deals with problems that are more specific to the emerging countries. Section 4 summarizes and concludes.

2   Empirical evidence

In the mid-1990s, Leiderman and Svensson (1995) reviewed the early experience with IT, with, however, rather a limited number of relevant cases. Later studies (Bernanke et al., 1999; Corbo et al., 2001, 2002; Clifton et al., 2001; Arestis et al., 2002; Johnson, 2002, 2003; Neumann and von Hagen, 2002; Scott and Stone, 2005) inevitably afforded longer periods and more data. Overall, this evidence supports the contention that IT matters.

This evidence, however, is marred by the fact that the empirical studies reviewed fail to produce *convincing* evidence that IT improves inflation performance and policy credibility, and lower sacrifice ratio. After all, the environment of the 1990s was in general terms a stable economic environment, 'a period friendly to price stability' (Neumann and von Hagen, 2002, p. 129), and inflation was on a downward trend in many countries, especially developed countries, prior to the introduction of IT. Despite the problem of lack of convincing evidence, the proponents argue very strongly that non-adoption of IT puts at high risk the ability of a central bank to provide price stability (for example, Bernanke et al., 1999, 'submit a plea' for the Fed to adopt it; also

Alesina et al., 2001, make the bold statement that the European Central Bank could improve its monetary policy by adopting IT; both studies do not provide any supporting evidence, though). And yet, both the Fed and the European Central Bank remain highly sceptical (Gramlich, 2000, and Duisenberg, 2003, do not actually regard IT appropriate for the US and the euro area, respectively).

2.1   Evidence of IT impact on level and persistence of inflation

2.1.1   *Level*

Studying the first of these two issues, Mishkin and Posen (1997) find that IT has proved an effective 'strategy' in the fight against inflation, especially in maintaining the benefits of registering low inflation levels. These authors base their argument on the premise that whenever IT was adopted, the countries experienced inflation rates and interest rates that were lower than the magnitudes simulated with unrestricted VARs, while no major effect is apparent on the output. Besides, in the three IT countries considered, New Zealand, Canada and the UK, disinflation had largely been completed when IT was adopted, but inflation did not bounce back as expected in view of previous relevant experience. The evidence produced by the same study, however, does not enable the authors to support the contention that IT is superior to money supply targeting (for example, the Bundesbank monetary targeting between 1974 and 1998), or to the Fed's monetary policy in the 1980s and 1990s (which pursued neither a monetary nor an inflation targeting policy). Similar results are provided by Debelle (1997), who compares average inflation levels for seven IT countries with G7 countries excluding non-ITers. This contribution finds a much steeper decline in inflation in the case of the former group, concluding that IT is useful for countries facing lack of anti-inflation credibility. Newmann and von Hagen (2002) interpret similar results as a process of 'convergence', in that on average IT countries converge to the inflation rates of the non-IT countries in the targeting period. Corbo et al. (2002) are able to conclude that IT countries have been able to meet their inflation targets and reduce inflation volatility. Country-specific evidence also abounds; for example, for New Zealand, Choi et al. (2003) estimate a two regime Markov Switching model using the Hamilton Filtering technique and arrive at the conclusion that the structural break is at 1989Q4, where IT most likely began for New Zealand. They also find statistically significant (at 1 per cent level) the hypothesis that inflation volatility was considerably reduced after this date, and that the unconditional mean for the inflation process reduced considerably (from 7.5 to 0.41). They report a conclusive change in the inflation dynamic in 1989Q4.

Ball and Sheridan (2003) produce evidence that is not quite supportive of these conclusions. They study the effects of IT on macroeconomic performance in the case of 20 OECD countries, seven of which adopted IT in the 1990s. After controlling for the effect of regression to the mean, they conclude that they are unable to find any evidence that IT improves economic performance as measured by the behaviour of inflation, output and interest rates. According to these authors, the apparent success of IT countries is merely due to having 'high initial inflation and large decreases, but the decrease for a given initial level looks similar for targeters and non-targeters' (Ball and Sheridan, 2003, p. 16; see, also, Angeriz and Arestis, 2005, 2007b, 2007c). In view of this evidence, the authors are suspicious of the results reported in the rest of the literature.[5] Furthermore, the evidence collected by Pétursson (2004) for the Longest History IT Countries (LHITCs), which includes New Zealand, Canada, UK, Sweden and Australia, reaches similar conclusions, producing only a marginally significant or non-significant effect of IT adoption on inflation level. According to the author, this is due to the fact that IT countries had accomplished a substantial part of the disinflation process before adopting IT.

Chortareas et al. (2002) and Rochon and Rossi (2006) make the important point that central bank transparency and accountability are not unique to IT regimes. Further evidence for this is provided by Fatas et al. (2006), who compare quantitative target regimes (which they call transparent regimes) targeting exchange rates, money growth rates and inflation rates. By using a 40 country sample for the period 1960–2000, they conclude on the basis of least-squares estimation of the panel of these countries that the presence of a quantitative target reduces annual inflation and actually hitting the target lowers it further.[6] While this result is statistically and economically significant across all forms of quantitative targets, IT performs slightly better on being adopted that the others.

2.1.2 *Persistence*

IT may also have an impact on the relationship between current inflation and its past history. Using univariate time series, Sikklos (1999) finds that the autoregressive coefficients show a noticeable drop in the strength of the relevant relationship for countries such as New Zealand, Canada, Spain, Finland, Spain, Sweden and Spain. Similarly, Levin et al. (2004) find that actual inflation exhibits lower persistence in IT countries, and that the total variance of actual inflation is only slightly higher than the variance for shocks to the autoregressive model, whereas it is twice as big or higher in the case of non-IT countries, thereby exposing a substantial degree of propagation in the latter. They conclude that, as the variance of inflation is roughly the same in both groups, low levels of inflation persistence prevented higher levels of inflation volatility in IT countries.

Benati (2006) visits the theoretical underpinnings of the models of inflation persistence. She rejects the hypothesis that persistence is hardwired into or structural to the macro model of the economy in the sense of Lucas (1976), i.e. that it is invariant to changes in monetary regime. Benati quotes Coenen and Levin (2004), in that 'backward-looking price setting behaviour (such as indexation to lagged inflation) is not needed in explaining the aggregate data, at least in an environment with a stable monetary policy regime and credible inflation objective' and provides evidence by looking at reduced-form evidence of statistical persistence across monetary regimes and by looking at the results from models which aim to model inflation persistence structurally. The extent of serial correlation for each country and monetary regime is based on fixed coefficient AR(p) models. Here, the results indicate that inflation in the UK, Canada, Sweden and New Zealand under IT is almost white noise. Further, to test whether the structural component of inflation persistence captured by the hybrid Phillips curve changes across monetary regimes or not, Benati (op. cit.) uses Bayesian estimation of a sticky-price DSGE model of the economy with a hybrid Phillips curve. The results indicate that inflation persistence is not intrinsic in the sense of Lucas. For example, UK and Canada show the same kind of inflation persistence in the post Second World War period as the US in the post-Bretton Woods period. And following Coenen and Levin (2004), under stable monetary regimes, backward indexation is not needed to fit the data and a New Keynesian Phillips curve is almost a perfect fit for the data.

Lendvai (2006) also evaluates a New Keynesian macroeconomic model (for the USA, 1970–2005) where monetary regime shifts are allowed and inflation is not structurally persistent; however, there is imperfect information on part of private agents with regard to the credibility of the central bank. To account for this firms have staggered price contracts and also follow a Bayesian learning scheme about the current regime. Lendvai (op. cit.) shows that while in a stable monetary policy regime the role of learning reduces and inflation persistence recedes, agents behave as if they observe the regime directly. It is also shown that this could be drastically altered in the case of a regime shift and the concomitant uncertainty about the regime. Cecchetti and Debelle (2006) note that the inflation mean and persistence are linked and claim that allowing for a break in the inflation mean, inflation has not been a highly persistent process. Thus, persistence depends crucially on the sub-sample under consideration. On the basis of univariate modelling of data from 19 countries they find that inflation is a fairly stable process with little persistence but punctuated by large shifts in levels; on other occasions persistence is kept in check by the credibility of the monetary policy working through the inflationary expectations.[7] However, this also means that the decline in persistence previously reported in empirical work (across IT and non-IT countries) is reduced, making it secondary to change in the inflation mean.[8]

Ball and Sheridan (2003), also, as mentioned earlier, report no significant improvements regarding inflation persistence after the adoption of IT. Further results on inflation persistence are reported in Vega and Winkelried (2005), who find that persistence depends on the measure selected to detrend the series of inflation.

2.2   Evidence of IT impact on inflation expectations

The evidence on this front is as unclear as on the aspect under section 2.1. Gurkaynak et al. (2006) use long-term bond yields data to test whether IT helps anchor inflation expectations. They propose that if differences in survey forecasts of macroeconomic statistics and actual data do not lead to differences between long-term yields on government bonds and government bonds indexed for inflation (which can be seen as a market expectation of inflation – the forward inflation compensation), this could be seen as an indicator of a belief in the inflation-fighting objectives of the central bank. They use data (1999–2005) from Sweden and UK, and compare it with data from a non-IT country – the USA. They find that only in the USA are bond yields sensitive to economic surprises which would indicate that near term economic fluctuations are not expected by market participants to be resolved in the long term. The UK behaved similarly to the USA before it gained central bank independence in 1997. They do not differentiate between a change in mean and the other moments of the distribution of inflation expectations, instead claiming the results as consistent with IT anchoring the entire distribution of inflation expectations.

For variability of inflation expectations, evidence along the lines of Johnson (2003) comes from Erturk and Ozlale (2004) who use a GARCH specification to model inflation uncertainty. Furthermore, they use time varying parameters (estimated using a Kalman Filter) to allow for structural changes. They, thus, distinguish between structural (due to changes in the model) and impulse uncertainty (arising out of shocks and unexpected developments)[9]. They also use parametric and non-parametric tests to test for breaks in the levels and variability of inflation expectations. On the basis of a non-parametric test they find conclusive evidence of a drop in the mean of inflation expectations in New Zealand, Sweden and the UK, but not so for Australia and Canada. They next test for structural breaks in the inflation expectations data as a result of introduction of IT, where they test for breaks without specifying a date a priori and they also differentiate between a shift in the mean and a shift in the trend of the process. They find no change in trend for the two types of uncertainty; however, a shift in trend for the level of inflation expectations is observed for Australia and Sweden (in 1994Q1 and 1993 Month 2 respectively). However, they find no change in the mean for structural uncertainty: a change in the mean of impulse uncertainty is observed for Australia, New Zealand and Sweden but only in the case of New Zealand does this break occur after IT is introduced. They also find a break in the mean of the inflation expectations and in all cases these occur after IT is introduced. Thus results are fairly clear cut for inflation expectations but not so for inflation uncertainty.

Dotsey (2006) points out that some economists prefer survey based methods of deriving inflation expectations than those derived from financial market data.[10] However as Gurkaynak et al. (2006) point out, survey-based empirical studies like Ball and Sheridan (2003) and Levin et al. (2004) lead to weak support for the hypothesis that IT anchors inflation expectations – Ball and Sheridan (op. cit.) are unable to differentiate between IT and non-IT countries and Levin et al. (op. cit.) suffer from scarcity of data points.

Johnson (2002) provides evidence that shows significant impact on inflation expectations following the adoption of IT regimes in developed countries. Controlling for the business cycle and for the ongoing fall in inflation rates, the author reports a substantial reduction in the private expectations of inflation levels after IT announcements. In the exercise undertaken by Johnson (2003), own forecasts are compared with forecasts undertaken by professional forecasters, for five consecutive 12-month periods after the announcement of inflation targets. This study isolates the additional effect of the announcement of inflation targets on the level of expected inflation in the case of Australia, Canada, New Zealand, Sweden and the UK (where most of the responses on expected inflation come from professional forecasters). Immediate reduction in expected inflation is registered in New Zealand and Sweden with a smaller effect and slower impact in Australia and Canada; inflation targets do not appear to have a significant impact in the UK.

The possibility of IT anchoring significantly long-run expectations is studied in Levin et al. (2004). Private sector inflation forecasts of horizons of 5 to 10 years are uncorrelated with previous records of inflation in IT countries, while this is not the case for the US, Japan and countries from the European Union (EU). Variability of expectations, however, does not decrease according to the evidence produced by Johnson (2002). This author controls for past level and variability of inflation, finding that neither the variability of expected inflation nor the average absolute forecast error present significant additional reductions, beyond the effect through the drop in inflation. By contrast, Corbo et al. (2001) find that IT has reduced inflation uncertainty and inflation forecast errors towards the low level prevalent in non-targeting industrial countries. A clear success for the IT strategy is recorded in Levin et al. (2002) regarding the objective of de-linking expectations from realized inflation. Their reported estimations suggest that long-term expectations have been less responsive to recorded patterns of past inflation in IT countries than in non-IT countries. In the latter case, the relevant estimates are insignificant at a 6-to-10-year horizon. This finding implies that long-term expected inflation rates are related to shifting views of the long-term course of monetary policy (see, also, Ball and Sheridan, 2003). Finally, Pétursson (2004) finds that interest rates have fallen significantly and more than inflation for all countries and in particular for the LHITCs, where controls for business cycles and the general global fall in world interest rates are included. This suggests that more weight is placed on long-run developments in expectations in IT countries, and that IT is interpreted with flexibility, considering also real and financial stability as determinants of interest rates. Increased credibility is not, however, immediate. The 'announcement' effect is shown not to be enough and only when real progress and the will by central banks to accept a temporary contraction became apparent was credibility achieved.

2.3   Evidence of IT impact on disinflation costs

Bernanke et al. (1999) produce an assessment of the real output costs related to disinflation, using sacrifice ratios[11] and parameter instability tests. Following the method suggested by Ball (1994), they use a moving average process with nine lags to compute a trend in inflation and assume an *ad hoc* method to compute the GDP trend.[12] They then compute the sacrifice ratio and find that disinflation does not appear to be less costly than it would have been the case, had IT not been adopted. They also estimate Phillips curves for the periods before and after IT, rejecting the hypothesis of instability in the parameters estimated for these functions. Corbo et al. (2001) calculate the sacrifice ratios as the cumulative GDP variation to a trend utilizing the Hodrick – Prescott filter, divided by the corresponding inflation change in any period. Inflation targeting improvements are registered with important decreases in sacrifice ratios in Canada, Australia and the UK, but also a relevant deterioration is reported in New Zealand and Sweden. Corbo et al. (op. cit.) are able to conclude that sacrifice ratios have declined in emerging IT countries, with output volatility having fallen in both developed and emerging countries after their adoption of inflation targeting. The fall has reached levels similar, if not lower, to those of non-IT developed countries.

Durham (2001) estimates sacrifice ratios (univariate specification and multivariate specification with common control variables using OLS and FGLS), with a view to assess the effects of monetary and fiscal policy in 19 high-income countries and 59 low-income countries, using annual data from 1957–2001Q1. He finds that there is little evidence that targeting reduces sacrifice ratios. Regression analysis and results produce reductions in sacrifice ratios, some lower-income countries exhibit higher sacrifice ratios after targeting; this is true for each of the three different specifications used (after Mahadeva and Sterne, 2000; Mishkin and Schmidt-Hebbel, 2001; Corbo et al., 2001). Similar results are obtained when the dummy is changed from a dichotomous variable of IT to one, which includes the importance of inflation in the reaction functions of central banks. A dummy which registers whether or not the government has an explicit inflation target and whether it has any inflation-indexed debt outstanding, which seeks to measure optimal monetary and fiscal policy when included, has a negative coefficient for sacrifice ratios. Clifton et al. (2001) estimate Phillips curves that incorporate inflation expectations. They conclude that IT enhanced the credibility of central banks, which adopted IT. In IT countries and in the pre-IT periods, inflation expectations were backward looking, but after the IT adoption expectations turned both backward- and forward-looking. They also find that the unemployment-inflation trade-off improved in OECD countries after IT. This is not clear, however, in the period immediately after its implementation, but it improves over time as monetary policy gains in credibility. According to the authors, this pattern could explain the Bernanke et al. (1999) earlier results. This result is corroborated by Razzak (2001), who considers the case of five IT countries. This is attempted by using a Lucas type aggregate supply equation (Lucas, 1973) to check if credible monetary regimes improve the macroeconomic trade-off between nominal income and inflation.[13] In the case of Australia, New Zealand and Sweden the regimes are unambiguously 'credible'; this is not clear in the case of the UK and Canada, where an increase in the variability of relative prices might have counteracted the effects of stable inflation.

IT and increase in credibility in particular improve the trade-off between inflation and output losses resulting in the aftermath of a disinflationary shock – where a low credibility central bank might have to face higher output and real exchange rate fluctuations. And as Diana and Sidiropoulos (2004) show, central bank independence (CBI) negatively affects inflation persistence. Inflation persistence and the sacrifice ratio are positively correlated; thus CBI leads to a faster speed of disinflation.

2.4   Evidence of IT impact on the conduct of monetary policy

The evidence as to whether IT changed the way in which monetary policy is conducted is analysed in a number of ways and the outcome is mixed. In a review of the evolution of IT regimes over 1990–2006, Paulin (2006) condenses the changes in the conduct of IT into changes in key parameters (conditioned on learning and experience), the numerical target (points and ranges), the target itself, the policy horizon, supporting institutional and policy structures and communication, as well as the publication of forecasts.[14]

The numerical target, defined with a tolerance band around it, is an important influence on the credibility of the central bank. Most practitioners have refrained from lowering the target despite considerable success in inflation control. This has been due to a fear of deflation (especially in the case of the zero lower limits on nominal inflation) and measurement errors. Paulin (op. cit.) also points out that transgressing these tolerance bands is not associated with a hard response from policy makers. Taylor and Davradakis (2006) test for asymmetry in central bank behaviour in the case of the Bank of England by estimating non-linear Taylor rules.[15] They model the Bank of England behaviour as a 3-regime model according to whether inflation is in a band around the target or substantially different from the target. They find that when inflation is about a half point lower than the declared target of 2.5 per cent, interest rate response behaves like a random walk with some correlation to the output gap. However, when inflation is a half point above the target, the Taylor rule begins to bite with statistically significant coefficients. This implies nonlinearity in the conduct of monetary policy by the Bank of England despite the announced symmetry.

The target variable should have the property that it should be a visible and easily understood index from the communications perspective; it should also exclude price movements, which do not have a medium-term impact on inflation (i.e. transitory effects), as they might strain credibility. Rich and

Steindel (2005) delineate the properties of an ideal price index to be used for IT and then compare several price indices of core inflation (for the US). Such properties are ease of construction, similarity in mean and trend to the goal inflation measure and its forecasting ability. However, their results as to which is the best forecaster of inflation are inconclusive. Armour (2006) conducts a similar exercise for Canada, using the following criteria: lack of bias, low volatility with respect to CPI inflation and the ability to forecast the mean and trend of CPI inflation. Again, the results are inconclusive, with CPIW (CPI inflation with components weighted by a factor proportional to the inverse of their volatility) emerging as an uneasy winner.

The policy horizon can be seen as the monetary policy lags or the period over which it is desirable to bring inflation back to its target. Coletti et al. (2006) report the outcome of two studies about optimal target horizons conducted at the Bank of Canada. Dynamic Stochastic General Equilibrium (DSGE) models of the Canadian economy were subjected to a combination of shocks in the presence of nominal, real and financial frictions and parameters of the monetary policy rules, which were varied in order to minimize the loss due to a too rapid or a too slow adjustment. The policy horizon is then seen to depend on the nature of the shock; however, in most cases a 6-8 quarter policy horizon is seen as adequate.

Several reviews have concentrated on the transparency and communication aspect of the practice of monetary policy.[16] Crowe (2006) assesses the joint hypothesis that IT enhances transparency and that transparency impacts the accuracy of private sector inflation forecasts. Transparency (better understanding of central bank's objectives and decision-making process and access to its forecasts and analysis) should increase the accuracy of private-sector forecasts of those variables over which the central bank has any control.[17] However, Morris and Shin (2002) claim that an opposite effect is possible; when the private sector second guesses itself, then public information can crowd out high quality private information, thereby increasing variability. Crowe (op. cit.) estimates both these effects in 11 IT countries and their non-IT counterparts selected on the basis of score matching strategies. The author finds evidence that private forecasts are indeed better as a result of IT, but there is no evidence of an effect of the kind proposed by Morris and Shin (2002). Faust and Leeper (2005) make the case for communication strategies, which involve unconditional forecasts of policy interest rates and goal variables. They claim that the path of the interest rate variable is important from the welfare perspective and should be announced. While acknowledging that communications are crucial to transparency, they claim that only the path independent instrument forecasts as produced by Norges Bank and the Reserve Bank of New Zealand can lead to complete transparency.

Mishkin (2002) finds that the results of estimating Taylor rules suggest that central banks focus more on the control of inflation after IT adoption, in their attempt to achieve price stability. His results supported by VAR evidence, indicate that the relative importance of inflation shocks as a source of the variance of interest rates rises after IT adoption.[18] Cecchetti and Ehrmann (1999) and Corbo et al. (2001) also assess changes in central bank aversion to inflation, delivering mixed results. Cecchetti and Ehrmann (1999) find that, where an increase in central bank aversion to inflation is apparent, both for IT countries and non-IT countries, it is within the group of IT countries that it has increased the most. UK is an exception, not registering significant changes in these magnitudes.

Corbo et al. (2001) elaborate on these measures, discovering that inflation aversion increased among the non-industrialized countries, which applied IT, but the same cannot be said for the industrialized ones. Corbo et al. (2001), also find that the strength in the reaction of interest rate changes to both inflation and output shocks, decreased significantly among IT countries but these reductions were weaker or non-existent among non-IT industrial countries. Ball and Sheridan (2003), instead, conclude that IT does not affect output growth or output variability, nor does it affect interest rates and their variability. Pétursson (2004), however, shows that (unconditional) growth rates are sensibly higher in the year following IT adoption than the five-year average of records previous to the IT. Output fluctuations are also shown to decline, in line with findings of Corbo et al. (2001), Neumann and von Hagen (2002) and Truman (2003).

A different approach to dealing with the question of whether improved results in inflation are due to the way monetary policy responds to inflation, is to examine the official short-term interest rates. Kahn and Parrish (1998), for instance, collect high and stable values for real official short-term interest rates, which are associated with tight monetary policies. In order to account for changes to policy due to incoming information, they estimate policy reaction functions, which regress the interest rate against several explanatory variables. The results are mixed. On the one hand, they find structural breaks in New Zealand and the UK. The former presents a stronger reaction of official rates to lagged inflation and unemployment, and a weaker reaction to exchange rate. UK registers a loss in significance for the exchange rate, most likely reflecting the changing role of the exchange rate after the break away from the ERM. These results are, however, not clearly attributable to IT. On the other hand, Canada, Sweden and the US (the latter, considered as a benchmark) show no significant changes.

2.5   Evidence of IT impact on macroeconomic variables

Cohen et al. (2003) consider the response of exchange rates (both nominal and real) to real and nominal shocks in order to assess IT benefits and sacrifices. They point out that IT regimes developed as a way of moving away from exchange rate targets. Increased flexibility in nominal exchange rates should, therefore, be considered as a benefit, since it would smooth out real shocks, acting as a type of shock absorber for the rest of the economy. In assessing the impact of IT they compare the effect that real shocks have on nominal exchange rates both after and before IT, and hypothesize a smaller impact as credibility is built. IT may, instead, imply a sacrifice if real exchange rates became more volatile with nominal shocks and purchasing power parity deviations being more severe. If IT regimes build up credibility, however, it is expected that nominal shocks would only have small and non-persistent effects on nominal exchange rates after IT, and hence real exchange rates would not be excessively affected. For LHITCs they produce evidence that overwhelmingly supports a positive evaluation of IT strategy. First, sacrifice ratios expressed as percentage changes in nominal exchange rates due to nominal shocks, are negative in most countries except for Australia (where no difference is registered), Chile and Brazil (where positive sacrifice ratios are registered). Second, benefit ratios, defined as the increase in the percentage of real exchange rate explained by real shocks, increase in all LHITCs, but not for all cases examined. The benefit ratio is negative in the case of Israel, making the case for IT in general more dubious according to this criterion.

Dissent comes from Uhlig (2004) when commenting on Levin et al. (2003). For IT to be a successful strategy it has to reduce inflation and its volatility, reduce output volatility and increase the rate of economic growth. However, inflation volatility as reported by Levin et al. (op. cit.) was higher for IT-ers, and the output volatility is essentially the same when compared to non-IT economies. Following Ball and Sheridan (2003), if we assume that this is due to larger shocks or adverse initial conditions in IT countries then we have no evidence of a difference in economic activity among IT and non-IT countries. Dehejia and Rowe (2000) put fixed exchange rates against inflation and price-level targeting to test their relative performance in the face of disinflationary shocks. They claim that price-level targeting is best for stabilizing output, real exchange rates and real interest rates relative to their natural rates. However, as they recognize, in their model (a Mundell–Fleming demand-side type with 'outside' lags to account for the transmission lag) the cards are stacked in favour of price-level targeting. This is so because deviations from natural output occur when price deviates from its expected level. Tucker (2006) questions this claim in a speech delivered to the Chicago Graduate School of Business. Price-level targeting would accomplish stabilization by allowing near-term inflation expectations to rise a little above its average. However, this would involve communicating a price target, which fluctuates in the short-term depending on the recent inflation experience and the policy horizon; this might endanger the credibility of the central bank.

3   IT in emerging countries

Emerging countries have had varied experience in terms of inflation targeting. A number of them over the recent past have been targeting the money supply or the exchange rate, especially the latter. Money-supply targeting has been shown to be a rather unreliable means of controlling inflation in view of instabilities in the demand for money.[19] Theoretically, IT as a monetary policy regime in emerging economies has been criticized on two grounds: its susceptibility to shocks and limited sustainability in the presence of certain features, which are common in these economies. Kumhof (2000) claims that in emerging economies the real exchange rate remains an important additional objective of monetary policy leading to conflicts with the inflation target. Small open economies with a strong commitment to CPI inflation cannot afford to let the exchange rate be unmanaged as has been suggested, as it is an important component of the price index (exchange rate pass-through).[20] He shows, in a microfounded model, that when foreign reserves are adequately low, exchange rate depreciation tends to overshoot the inflation target in anticipation of a crisis. This leads to domestic inflation and rapid reserve losses in the final phases of the cycle, which is akin to the phase in exchange rate management (ERM). Examples of these sorts of runs are Chile and Mexico in the latter half of 1998. The greater the weight of the exchange rate in the nominal target, the greater is the risk of speculative attack. This makes it difficult to establish the credibility of the target as it depends on commitment contingent on the absence of speculative pressure. Kumhof (op. cit.) shows that in the presence of sticky prices in a small open economy, this aggravates the belief of unsustainability of inflation target arising from fiscal inconsistencies, which may be a feature of these economies. With expectations of lack of sustainability (which are assumed to be fulfilled by the central bank in equilibrium), the non-tradables inflation is deemed to remain above target causing tight monetary policy to reduce the rate of depreciation. This results in large current account deficits and real appreciation in the final phases. The welfare losses are higher the higher is the degree of price stickiness. Further to this, fiscal dominance plays its part by calling for even tighter monetary policy than under other monetary regimes like ERM, which results in more welfare losses.

Mishkin (2004) points out that IT needs to take into account certain other differences between developed economies and emerging market economies when assessing how sound policies might be. These are the nature of the fiscal inconsistencies referred to above. He points out how a weakness of institutions could lead to 'currency substitutions and liability dollarization' (due to changes in the real value of the currency) and cause 'sudden stops' (large and rapid reversals of capital inflows) especially in the presence of a weak banking system and fiscal imbalances. The lack of fiscal stability could lead to monetary policy becoming subservient to fiscal policy (fiscal dominance). This may suggest that central banks of the countries that fall within this category should target their exchange rates (the 'fear of floating' argument of Calvo and Reinhart, 2002). This, of course, would go against one important pillar of IT, namely that of 'absence of other nominal anchor' (Mishkin and Schmidt-Hebbel, 2001). There is also the further difficulty that the impact of changes in the exchange rate on inflation depends on the nature of the exchange rate change – a pure portfolio shock increases inflation, while the effect of a real shock would depend on its nature, i.e. whether it is a demand or supply shock.[21]

Theoretical arguments about fiscal 'boundedness' of price stabilizing policy are presented in Sims (2005) and Benigno and Woodford (2005). Sims claims that the intermediate target of IT – 'inflation expectations' is not directly controlled by the central bank; it could lose control of inflation. He quotes Benhabib et al. (2001) who show that a central bank can lose control of a deflation in the presence of certain kinds of fiscal policy. In the presence of fiscal policy which does not link primary surpluses to debt, any attempt by the central bank to limit the volume of nominal liabilities will be futile. Even if fiscal policy is appropriate, there are possible equilibria in which inflation causes demonetization of real balances. The dynamic response of the economy to shocks depends on their nature (real or money demand) and also their direction. According to Kumh of (2000) even under ideal conditions, the response of ERM and IT to real external shocks is the same. In a negative terms-of-trade shock, the time taken for the real exchange rate to depreciate to its steady state is the same under ERM and IT. There is some improvement under IT but this does not necessarily represent an improvement in welfare terms. IT also performs unambiguously better than ERM in the face of a foreign inflation shock, but in the face of a money demand shock, ERM and IT again perform similarly. Devereux et al. (2006) consider the effect of interest rate and terms of trade shocks on a small, open economy with capital accumulation constraints due to 'liability dollarization', financial frictions and exchange rate pass-through. They compare three different regimes (which they consider to be equally credible and fiscally dominated): fixed exchange rates, IT with CPI inflation and IT with non-traded goods' (NPT) price inflation. They show that in the presence of high inflation pass-through, constraints on capital accumulation do not affect the ranking of the alternatives and NPT with IT emerges as the best strategy. Fixed exchange rates and IT with CPI tend to stabilize inflation and exchange rates at substantial costs to the real economy. There is a definite trade-off between real stability and inflation and exchange rate stability, where NPT-based IT is the best alternative. In the presence of low levels of ER pass-through, CPI based IT is a better alternative; the policymaker can allow nominal exchange rate volatility to stabilize the real economy in the face of external shocks. In the case of very low pass-through as well, CPI-based IT emerges as the best strategy. ER is no longer an 'expenditure switching' device, causing changes in the relative prices at home and abroad, ER simply acts as a cushion for the real economy. These results are invariant to the nature of the shock.

These considerations make rationalizing and implementing IT a more challenging task for emerging economies than in developed countries. The evidence so far on the experience of these countries has not been as numerous and varied as in the case of the developed countries (Angeriz and Arestis, 2007c). Some evidence suggests that IT is a success story in emerging countries (see, for example, IMF, 2005; Porter and Yao, 2005). According to these studies, IT is associated with a statistically significant larger reduction in the level and standard deviation of inflation as compared to other regimes. It also leads to a reduction in the level and volatility of inflation expectations. It is conceded, nonetheless, that such experience 'comes against a backdrop of relatively subdued inflation worldwide', and, indeed, it is still too early to generalize, for it remains to be ascertained how 'inflation targeting [lite] regime will fare if global inflation rises significantly, although a formalization of the current regime may limit any erosion of the gains already achieved' (Porter and Yao, 2005, p. 18). An application of the Ball and Sheridan (2003) methodology (controlling for mean reversion) to 13 (five IT countries) Latin American countries by Brito and Bystedt (2006) and to 35 (11 IT countries) emerging economies by Goncalves and Salles (2005) shows IT to be successful in producing price stability without an adverse cost to growth. Evidence presented in Angeriz and Arestis (2005) though, suggests that non-IT central banks have also been successful in achieving and maintaining consistently low inflation rates. This evidence clearly implies that an emerging country central bank does not need to pursue an IT strategy to achieve and maintain low inflation.

A further comment on the experience of IT emerging countries is that whatever 'success' they may have had ought to be set against the background of the 'preconditions' that need to be met before IT adoption. IMF (2005) summarizes these pre-conditions as follows: technical capability of the central bank in implementing IT; an efficient institutional set up to motivate and support the commitment to low inflation, including institutional independence; a healthy financial system; an economic structure characterized with fully deregulated prices; and absence of fiscal dominance. On current evidence, these preconditions admittedly do not prevail in most, if not all cases (IMF, 2005). Under such circumstances, the IT framework may be highly unsuitable for these countries. Batini and Laxton (2005), however, claim that on none of the parameters deemed as 'preconditions' for adopting IT, as stated above, are there systematic differences between conditions in today's potential emerging market IT-ers and IT-ers at the time of their adoption of IT. This is substantiated by detailed questionnaires to 21 IT central banks and 10 non-IT central banks, and by econometric evidence. They also note that technical infrastructure and the banking and financial sector see greater development with the adoption of IT; indeed efforts to this end may be vital for the success of the IT regime, a view supported by Mishkin (2004, p. 11).

4   Summary and conclusions

We have reviewed in this chapter the available empirical evidence for both developed and emerging countries that adopted the IT monetary policy strategy. Our overall conclusion is that the available evidence clearly suggests that a central bank does not need to pursue an IT strategy to achieve and maintain low inflation. Non-IT countries have been as successful in achieving low inflation rates. How relevant might these conclusions be for Latin America and Brazil in particular, the focus of this book, is a particularly relevant question. It might not actually be too pejorative to suggest that all the aspects touched upon, or alluded to, in the whole chapter are important issues in the case of emerging countries and Brazil in particular. The chapter that follows vividly demonstrates this proposition, especially at the empirical level, in the case of the Brazilian economy.

Notes

1 This contribution relies on, and extends, Angeriz and Arestis (2007a).
2 Truman (2003), however, does not see much value in this classification scheme, branding it as 'dressed-up self-destruction'.
3 A widely-cited definition of price stability has been offered by Greenspan (1988): 'By price stability, I mean a situation in which households and businesses in making their saving and investment decisions can safely ignore the possibility of sustained, generalized price increases or decreases'.
4 The strategy contains the single objective of price stability for monetary policy, and not output stabilization, to avoid the time-consistency problem and thus the inflationary bias referred to in the text. This is consistent with the monetarist view that in the long run monetary policy can only affect inflation and not real variables.
5 Hyvonen (2004), however, challenges the Ball and Sheridan (2003) conclusions on the premise that mean reversion does not happen by itself. In the absence of a policy framework such reversion does not occur.
6 They are aware of the pitfalls of least-squares type estimation and perform comprehensive sensitivity and robustness analysis. They also seek to address the issue of endogeneity that is often raised, by including five Instrumental Variables (IVs) of political and institutional conditions, which might affect inflation. When augmented with the dummy variables of having and hitting quantitative targets, these IVs are highly significant and consistent with the results of the base model described above.
7 However, opposition to reduced form univariate modelling has been voiced (*e.g.* Benati, 2006).
8 Cecchetti and Debelle (2006) also survey the existing empirical literature of inflation persistence and underlying theories to explain inflation persistence. They also show that based on canonical time-dependent models of price setting (*e.g.* Calvo, 1983, and Taylor, 1980) inflation persistence is attributable to backward indexation of inflation expectations.
9 In a later paper, Berument et al. (2005) use similar methodology as above to introduce 'steady-state' uncertainty and test the effect of each of these types of inflation uncertainties on interest rates.
10 Ang et al. (2006) utilize data from asset markets, macroeconomic variables and surveys to forecast inflation and find that surveys outperform the others (see, also, Bomberger, 1996).
11 Sacrifice ratios as a measure of the cost of disinflation have been criticized in the literature for a number of reasons: for ignoring subsequent benefits of low inflation environment, ignoring the impact of other policies on output and inflation and

calculating of trend output and disinflation dating is inherently arbitrary (Mayes and Chapple, 1994).

12 A problem with the Ball (1994) approach is that the model relies on the absence of supply shocks, so that all deviations of actual output from potential output are attributed to policy-induced demand contraction (Cechetti, 1994). This could potentially have substantial effects on the results (King and Watson, 1994).

13 Razzak defines credible regimes as those that do not trade on the Phillips curve and stabilize inflation and aggregate demand shifts.

14 Some very useful tables on the evolution of these parameters in the major IT countries are to be found in Paulin (2006).

15 Taylor and Davradakis (2006) cite reasons for such asymetries: asymmetry in central bank preferences, concavity of output growth with respect to inflation and asymmetries and nonlinearities in the business cycle.

16 See Fracasso, Genberg and Wyplosz (2003) for a review of communication practices and central bank Inflation Reports.

17 Morris and Shin (2002) also point out that greater transparency in forecasts is only beneficial when the central bank's forecast is more accurate than private forecasts.

18 However, as Mishkin notes, 'the VAR evidence in the paper tells us little about the impact of inflation targeting on the conduct of monetary policy' (Mishkin, 2002, p. 150).

19 Although it is true to say, as in the text, that monetary targeting has been attempted in a number of emerging countries, Latin American countries have not used this strategy in a similar fashion, especially in the recent past. The main reason is the recognition of the serious possibility of instability in the demand for money as suggested in the text, a feature not merely of Latin American countries but other emerging and developed countries (Mishkin and Savastano, 2001). As the chapter that follows shows, Brazil has been no exception to this rule.

20 The average pass-through in emerging market economies was close to 33 per cent (47 per cent for Latin American economies) in the 1990s, while it was less than 10 per cent for developed countries (Céspedes and Soto, 2005).

21 The arguments so far in this section are applicable in the case of asset prices, such as housing and stock prices. Bernanke and Gertler (1999) suggest that IT strategy should not target asset prices directly, but should utilize the information provided by movements in asset prices. In this way the possibility of asset price bubbles is less likely thereby promoting financial stability. Arestis and Karakitsos (2005) summarize the arguments against such a thesis and propose targeting of net wealth instead.

References

Alesina, A.F., Blanchard, O., Gali, J., Giavazzi, F. and Uhlig, H. (2001), *Defining a Macroeconomic Framework for the Euro Area: Monitoring the European Central Bank 3*, Centre for Economic Policy Research: London.

Ang, A., Bekaert, G. and Wei, M. (2006), ' Do Macro Variables, Asset Markets, or Surveys Forecast Inflation Better?', *Finance and Economics Discussion Series* No. 2006–15, Divisions of Research & Statistics and Monetary Affairs, Federal Reserve Board: Washington, D.C.

Angeriz, A. and Arestis, P. (2005), 'An Empirical Investigation of Inflation Targeting in Emerging Economies', *Working Paper*, Cambridge Centre for Economic and Public Policy, University of Cambridge.

Angeriz, A. and Arestis, P. (2007a), 'Inflation Targeting: Assessing the Evidence', in J. McCombie and C.R. Gonzales (eds), *Issues in Finance and Monetary Policy*, Palgrave Macmillan: Basingstoke.

Angeriz, A. and Arestis, P. (2007b), 'Assessing the performance of Inflation Targeting Lite Countries', *World Economy*, forthcoming.

Angeriz, A. and Arestis, P. (2007c), 'Assessing Inflation Targeting Trough Intervention Analysis', *Oxford Economic Papers*, forthcoming.

Arestis, P., Caporale, G.M. and Cipollini, A. (2002), 'Is There a Trade-off Between Inflation and Output Gap?', *The Manchester School of Economic and Social Research*, 70(4), 528–45.

Arestis, P. and Karakitsos, E. (2005), 'On the US Post-'New Economy' Bubble: Should Asset Prices be Controlled?', in P. Arestis, M. Baddeley and J. McCombie (eds), *The 'New' Monetary Policy: Implications and Relevance*, Edward Elgar Publishing Ltd.: Cheltenham.

Armour, J. (2006), 'An Evaluation of Core Inflation Measures', *Bank of Canada Working Paper* No. 2006–10. http://www.bankofcanada.ca/en/res/wp/2006/wp06-10.pdf

Ball, L. (1994), 'What determines the sacrifice ratio?', in G. Mankiw (ed.), *Monetary Policy*, University of Chicago University Press: Chicago, 155–82.

Ball, L. and Sheridan, N. (2003), 'Does Inflation Targeting Matter?', *NBER Working Paper Series*, No. 9577, National Bureau of Economic Research: Cambridge, MA.

Batini, N. and Laxton, D. (2005), 'Under What Conditions Can Inflation Targeting Be Adopted? The Experience of Emerging Markets', Paper at the *Ninth Annual Conference of the Central Bank of Chile*, 20–21 October, Santiago, Chile.

Benati, L. (2006), 'Investigating Inflation Persistence across Monetary Regimes', Paper at *CREI Seminar 2006–2007*, 30 October 2006. http://www.crei.cat/activities/crei_seminar/06-07/benati.pdf

Benhabib, J., Schmitt Grohe, S. and Uribe, M. (2001), 'Monetary Policy and Multiple Equilibria', *American Economic Review*, 91, 167–86.

Benigno, P. and Woodford, M. (2005), 'Optimal Inflation Targeting under Alternative Fiscal Regimes', Paper at *Novena Conferencia Anual del Banco Central de Chile*, 20–21 October 2005. http://www.bcentral.cl/esp/estpub/conferencias/anuales/pdf/2005/Woodford_Benigno.pdf

Bernanke, B.S. (2003), 'A Perspective on Inflation Targeting', Remarks at the *Annual Washington Policy Conference of the National Association of Business Economists*, 25 March, Washington DC.

Bernanke, B.S. and Gertler, M. (1999), 'Monetary Policy and Asset Price Volatility', in *New Challenges for Monetary Policy*, Federal Reserve of Kansas City: Kansas City.

Bernanke, B.S., Laubach, T., Mishkin, F.S. and Posen, A. (1999), *Inflation Targeting: Lessons from the International Experience*, Princeton University Press: Princeton.

Berument, H., Kilinc, Z. and Ozlale, U. (2005), 'The Missing Link Between Inflation Uncertainty and Interest Rates', *Scottish Journal of Economics*, 52(2).

Bomberger, W.A. (1996), 'Disagreement as a Measure of Uncertainty,' *Journal of Money, Credit, and Banking*, 28, pp. 381–92.

Brito, R.D. and Bystedt, B. (2006), 'The Macroeconomic Effects of Inflation Targeting in Latin America,' Paper at *The 3rd Seminario de Economia de Belo Horizonte*, Brazil. http://www.eg.fjp.mg.gov.br/seminarioiii/download/brito.pdf

Calvo, G.A. (1983), 'Staggered Prices in a Utility-Maximizing Framework', *Journal of Monetary Economics*, 12, 383–98.

Calvo, G.A. and Reinhurt, C.M. (2002), 'Fear of Floating', *Quarterly Journal of Economics*, 117(2), 379–408.

Carare, A. and Stone, M.R. (2003), 'Inflation Targeting Regimes', IMF Working Paper 03/9, Washington, DC: International Monetary Fund.

Cechetti, S. (1994) 'Comment', in G. Mankiw (ed.), *Monetary Policy*, University of Chicago University Press: Chicago, 188–93.

Cecchetti S.G. and Debelle, G. (2006), 'Inflation Persistence: Does It Change?', *Economic Policy*, April, pp. 311–52.

Cecchetti, S.G. and Ehrmann, M. (1999), 'Does Inflation Targeting Increase Output Volatility? An International Comparison of Policymakers' Preferences and Outcomes', *NBER* Working Paper 7426.

Céspedes, L.F. and Soto, C. (2005), 'Credibility and Inflation Targeting in an Emerging Market: Lessons from the Chilean Experience', *International Finance*, 8(3), pp. 545–75.

Choi, K., Jung, C. and Shambora, W. (2003), 'Macroeconomic Effects of Inflation Targeting in New Zealand', *Economic Bulletin*, 5(17).

Chortareas, G., Stasavage, D. and Sterne, G. (2002), 'Does it Pay to be Transparent? International Evidence from Central Bank Forecasts', *Federal Reserve Bank of St Louis Review*, 84(4), pp. 99–117.

Clifton, E.V., Hyginus, L. and Wong, C.-H. (2001), 'Inflation Targeting and the Unemployment – Inflation Trade-Off', IMF Working Paper 01/166, Washington DC: International Monetary Fund.

Coenen, G. and Levin, A.T. (2004), 'Identifying the Influences of Nominal and Real Rigidities in Aggregate Price-Setting Behaviour', *ECB Working Paper* No. 418.

Cohen Sabbán, V., Gonzalez Rozada, M. and Powell, A. (2003), 'A New Test for the Success of Inflation Targeting', mimeo.

Coletti, D., Selody, J. and Wilkins, C. (2006), 'Another Look at the Inflation-Target Horizon', *Bank of Canada Review*, Summer 2006.

Corbo,V., Landerrretche, M.O. and Schmidt-Hebbel, K. (2001), 'Assessing Inflation Targeting After a Decade of World Experience', mimeo, Central Bank of Chile: Santiago.

Corbo,V., Landerrretche, M.O. and Schmidt-Hebbel, K. (2002), 'Does Inflation Targeting Make a Difference?', in N. Loayza and R. Saito (eds), *Inflation Targeting: Design, Performance, Challenges'*, Central Bank of Chile: Santiago, Chile.

Crowe, C. (2006), 'Testing the Transparency Benefits of Inflation Targeting: Evidence from Private Sector Forecasts', IMF Working Paper No. 06/289. http://www.american.edu/academic.depts/cas/econ/Brown%20Bag%20Seminars/Papers/fall2006/to_send_transparency.pdf

Debelle, G. (1997), 'Inflation Targeting in Practice', Working Papers Series, No. 97/35, International Monetary Fund: Washington, DC.

Dehejia, V.H. and Rowe, N. (2000), 'Macroeconomic Stabilisation: Fixed Exchange Rates vs Inflation Targeting vs. Price Level Targeting', *Carleton Economic Papers* No. 99–15, Carleton University, Department of Economics. http://www.carleton.ca/economics/cep/cep99-15.pdf

Devereux, M.B., Lane, P.R. and Xu, J. (2006), 'Exchange Rates and Monetary Policy in Emerging Market Economies', *Economics Journal*, 116(April), pp.478–506.

Diana, G., and Sidiropoulos, M. (2004), 'Central Bank Independence, Speed of Disinflation and the Sacrifice Ratio', *Open Economies Review*, 15(4), pp. 385–402.

Dotsey, M. (2006), 'A Review of Inflation Targeting in Developed Countries', *Business Review*, 3rd Quarter, Federal Reserve of Philadelphia: Philadelphia, PA.

Duisenberg, W. (2003), 'Introductory Statement, and Questions and Answers', ECB Press Conference, 8 May, Frankfurt, Germany.

Durham, J.B. (2001), 'Sacrifice ratios and monetary policy credibility: do smalller budget deficits, inflation-indexed debt, and inflation targets lower disinflation costs?',

Finance and Economics Discussion Series No. 2001-47. Board of Governors of the Federal Reserve system (US). http://www.federalreserve.gov/pubs/feds/2001/200147/200147pap.pdf.

Erturk, B. and Ozlale, U. (2004), 'Do Inflation Targeting Regimes Reduce Inflation Uncertainty? Evidence from Five Industrialized Countries', Department of Economics, Bilkent University, Turkey.

Fatas, A., Mihov, I. and Rose, A.K. (2006), 'Quantitative Goals for Monetary Policy', European Central Bank Working Paper Series, No. 615, April 2006.

Faust, J. and Leeper, E.M. (2005), 'Forecasts and Inflation Reports: An Evaluation', Paper at Sveriges Riksbank Conference 'Inflation Targeting: Implementation, Communication and Effectiveness,' 11–12 June, 2005.

Fracasso, A., Genberg, H. and Wyplosz, C. (2003), 'How do Central Banks Write?: An Evaluation of Inflation Reports by Inflation-Targeting Central Banks', Geneva Reports on the World Economy Special Report 2, CEPR.

Gonçalves, C.E.S. and Salles, J.M. (2005), 'Inflation Targeting in Emerging Economies: What Do The Data Say?', Working Paper, Columbia University.

Gramlich, E.M. (2000), 'Inflation Targeting', Remarks Before the Charlotte Economics Club, 13 January, Charlotte: North Carolina.

Greenspan, A. (1988), 'Statement before the Subcommittee on Domestic Monetary Policy', Committee on Banking, Finance and Urban Affairs, US House of Representatives, Washington DC, 28 July.

Gurkaynak, R.S., Levin, A.T. and Swanson, E.T. (2006), 'Does Inflation Targeting Anchor Long-Run Inflation Expectations? Evidence from Long-Term Bond Yields in the US, UK and Sweden', Centre for Economic Policy Research Discussion Paper No. 5808, CEPR: London, UK.

Harvey, A. and Jaeger, A. (1993), 'Detrending, Stylized Facts and the Business Cycle', *Journal of Applied Econometrics*, 8(2), 231–47.

Hyvonen, M. (2004), 'Inflation Convergence Across Countries', Discussion Paper N. 2004–04, Federal Reserve Bank of Australia.

IMF (2005), 'Does Inflation Targeting Work in Emerging Markets?', *IMF World Economic Outlook*, September 2005–09–16, Washington DC: International Monetary Fund.

IMF (2006), 'Inflation Targeting and the IMF', http: www.imf.org/external/np/pp/eng/2006/031606.pdf.

Johnson, D.R. (2002), 'The Effect of Inflation Targeting on the Behaviour of Expected Inflation: Evidence from an 11 Country Panel', *Journal of Monetary Economics*, 49(4), 1521–38.

Johnson, D.R. (2003), 'The Effect of Inflation Targets on the Level of Expected Inflation in Five Countries', *Review of Economics and Statistics*, 85(4), 1076–81.

Jonas, J. and Mishkin, F.S. (2005), 'Inflation Targeting in Transition Countries: Experience and Prospects', in B.S. Bernanke and M. Woodford (eds), *The Inflation Targeting Debate*, Studies in Business Cycles, No. 32, Part III, Chicago: University of Chicago Press.

Kahn G. and Parrish K. (1998), 'Conducting Monetary Policy With Inflation Targets', mimeo, Federal Reserve Bank of Kansas City, www.kc.frb.org.

King, R.J. and Watson, M.W. (1994), 'The post-war U.S. Phillips curve: a revisionist econometric history', *Carnegie-Rochester Conference Series on Public Policy*, 41, 157–219.

Kumhof, M. (2000), 'A Critical View of Inflation Targeting: Crises, Limited Sustainability, and Aggregate Shocks', Working Papers Series No. 00022, Stanford University, Department of Economics.

Kuttner, K.N. (2005), 'A Snapshot of Inflation Targeting in its Adolescence', *RBA Annual Conference Volume*, Reserve Bank of Australia. Available at: http://www.rba.gov.au/PublicationsAnd Research/Conferences/2004/Kuttner.pdf

Leiderman, L. and Svensson, L.E.O. (eds), (1995), *Inflation Targets*, Centre for Economic Policy Research: London.

Lendvai, J. (2006), 'Inflation Dynamics and Regime Shifts', European Central Bank Working Paper Series No. 684, October 2006.

Levin, A., Natalucci, F. and Piger, J. (2004), 'The Macroeconomic Effects of Inflation Targeting', *Federal Reserve Bank of Saint Louis Review*, 86(4), 51–80.

Lucas, R.E. (1973), 'Some International Evidence on Output-Inflation Tradeoffs', *American Economic Review*, 63(3), pp. 326–34.

Lucas, R.F. (1976), 'Econometric Policy Evaluation: A Critique', *Carnegie-Rochester Conference Series on Public Policy*, 1, 19–46.

Mahadeva, L. and Sterne, G. (eds) (2000), *Monetary Policy Frameworks in a Global Context*, Routledge: London.

Mayes, D. and Chapple, B. (1994), 'The Costs and Benefits of Disinflation: A Critique of the Sacrifice Ratio', *Reserve Bank Bulletin*, 57(4).

Mishkin, F.S. (2002), 'Does Inflation Targeting Matter? Commentary', *Federal Reserve Bank of St. Louis Review*, 84(4), 149–53.

Mishkin, F.S. (2004), 'Can Inflation Targeting Work in Emerging Market Countries?', NBER Working Paper 10646, National Bureau of Economic Research: Cambridge, MA.

Mishkin, F.S. and Posen, A.S. (1997), 'Inflation Targeting Lessons from Four Countries', *Federal Reserve Bank of New York Economic Policy Review*, 3(1), 9–117.

Mishkin, F.S. and Savastano, M.A. (2001), 'Monetary Policy Strategies for Latin America', *Journal of Monetary Economics*, 66(3), 415–44.

Mishkin, F.S. and Schmidt-Hebbel, K. (2001), 'One Decade of Inflation Targeting in the World: What do We know and What do We Need to Know?', Working Paper No. 101, Central Bank of Chile, July.

Morris, S. and Shin, H.S. (2002), 'Social Value of Public Information', *American Economic Review*, 92(5), 1521–34.

Neumann, M.J.M. and von Hagen, J. (2002), 'Does Inflation Targeting Matter?', *Federal Reserve Bank of St. Louis Review*, 84(4), 127–48.

Paulin, G. (2006), 'Credibility with Flexibility: The Evolution of Inflation-Targeting Regimes, 1990–2006', *Bank of Canada Review*, Summer 2006.

Pétursson, T. (2004), 'The Effects of Inflation Targeting on Macroeconomic Performance', mimeo, Central Bank of Iceland: Reichvick, Iceland.

Porter, N. and Yao, J.Y. (2005), ''Inflation Targeting Lite' in Small Open Economies: The Case of Mauritius', IMF Working Paper 05/172, International Monetary Fund: Washington, DC.

Razzak, W.A. (2001), 'Are Inflation-Targeting Regimes Credible? Econometrics Evidence', *Reserve Bank of New Zealand Working Paper*. http://www.geocities.com/razzakw/paper8.pdf

Rich, R. and Steindel, C. (2005), 'A Review of Core Inflation and an Evaluation of Its Measures', *Federal Reserve Bank of New York Staff Reports*, No. 236.

Rochon, L.-P. and Rossi, S. (2006), 'Inflation Targeting, Economic Performance, and Income Distribution: A Monetary Macroeconomics Analysis', *Journal of Post-Keynesian Economics*, Summer 2006, 28(4).

Romer, D. (2005), 'Advanced Macroeconomics', 3rd Ed., McGraw-Hill: New York.

Scott, R. and Stone, M. (2005), 'On Target: The International Experience with Achieving Inflation Targets', IMF Working Paper 05/163, International Monetary Fund: Washington, DC.

Sikklos, P.L. (1999), 'Inflation-Target Design: Changing Inflation Performance and Persistence in Industrial Countries', *Federal Reserve Bank of St. Louis Review*, 81(1), 47–58.

Sims, C. (2005), 'Limits to Inflation Targeting', in B.S. Bernanke and M. Woodford, (eds) (2005), *The Inflation Targeting Debate*, National Bureau of Economic Research Studies in Business Cycles (NBER-BC). http://sims.princeton.edu/yftp/Targeting/Targeting FiscalPaper.pdf

Sterne, G. (2002), 'Inflation Targets in a Global Context', in N. Loayza and N. Soto (eds), *Inflation Targeting: Design, Performance, Challenges*, Central Bank of Chile: Santiago, Chile.

Stone, M.R. (2003), 'Inflation Targeting Lite', IMF Working Paper 03/12, International Monetary Fund: Washington DC.

Taylor, J.B. (1980), 'Aggregate Dynamics and Staggered Contracts', *Journal of Political Economy*, 18(1), 1–23.

Taylor (1993), 'Discresion Versus Policy Rules in Practice', *Carnegie-Rochester Conference Series on Public Policy*, 39, 199–214.

Taylor, M.P. and Davradakis, E. (2006), 'Interest Rate Setting and Inflation Targeting: Evidence of a Nonlinear Taylor Rule for the United Kingdom', *Studies in Nonlinear Dynamics and Econometrics*, 10(4).

Truman (2003), *Inflation Targeting in the World Economy*, Institute for International Economics, Washington DC.

Tucker, P. (2006), 'Reflections on Operating Inflation Targeting', Speech at the Chicago Graduate School of Business, 25 May, 2006. www.bankofengland.co.uk/publications/speeches/2006/speech274.pdf

Uhlig, H. (2004), Comment on *'The Macroeconomic Effects of Inflation Targeting'*, by A. Levin, F. Natalucci, and J. Piger, written for the 'Inflation Targeting: Prospects and Problems', 28th Annual Economic Policy Conference, Federal Reserve Bank of Saint Louis, October, 2003.

Vega, M. and Winkelried, D. (2005), 'Inflation Targeting, a successful story?', Working Paper, http://econwpa.wustl.edu/eps/mac/papers/0502/0502026.pdf

8
Inflation Targeting in Emerging Countries: The Case of Brazil

Philip Arestis
University of Cambridge

Luiz Fernando de Paula
University of the State of Rio de Janeiro and CNPq

Fernando Ferrari-Filho
Federal University of Rio Grande do Sul and CNPq

1 Introduction[*]

The purpose of this chapter is to examine Inflation Targeting (IT) in the case of emerging countries by concentrating essentially on the case of Brazil. IT is a new monetary policy regime (see, for example, Bernanke and Mishkin, 1997) that has been adopted by a significant number of countries (see, for example, Sterne, 2002). Brazil adopted this economic policy framework in June 1999. While the focus of this chapter is on Brazil, we also examine the experience of other countries both for comparative purposes and for evidence of the extent of success of this 'new' economic policy by other IT countries. In addition, we compare the experience of Brazil with IT and with that of non-IT countries, and ask the question of whether it makes a difference in the fight against inflation whether a country has adopted IT or not.

We proceed as follows: section 2 deals with the more theoretical aspects of the IT framework. This is followed in section 3 by an examination of recent stabilization policies in Latin America, and Brazil in particular. This enables us to demonstrate how countries, and Brazil in particular, came to implementing IT strategies. Section 4 concentrates on the Brazilian experience with IT, while section 5 compares the Brazilian IT experience with that of other 'similar' emerging countries. The latter group includes both countries within Latin America and other countries outside Latin America. A final section, section 6, summarizes and concludes.

116

2 Theoretical aspects of IT

There are a number of theoretical aspects that are the backbone of IT. We examine the following two aspects: main theoretical elements, and certain key operational aspects of IT. We begin with the first.

2.1 Main theoretical elements

This sub-section summarizes the main theoretical elements of IT. There are six such elements as follows:[1]

(i) IT is a monetary policy framework whereby public announcement of official inflation targets, or target ranges, is undertaken along with explicit acknowledgement that price stability, meaning low and stable inflation, is monetary policy's primary long-term objective (King, 2002). The price stability goal may be accompanied by output stabilization so long as price stability is not violated. Explicit numerical target for inflation is published, either as a point or a range, and a time horizon for reaching the inflation target. Such a monetary policy framework improves communication between the public, business and markets on the one hand, and policymakers on the other hand, and provides discipline, accountability, transparency and flexibility in monetary policy. The focus is on price stability, along with three objectives: credibility (the framework should command trust); flexibility (the framework should allow monetary policy to react optimally to unanticipated shocks); and legitimacy (the framework should attract public and parliamentary support). In fact, credibility is recognized as paramount in the conduct of monetary policy to avoid problems associated with time-inconsistency (Barro and Gordon, 1983). It is argued that a policy, which lacks credibility because of time inconsistency, is neither optimal nor feasible (Kydland and Prescott, 1977; Calvo, 1978; Barro and Gordon, 1983).

(ii) A further role of IT is to 'lock in' the gains from 'taming' inflation. Bernanke et al. (1999) are explicit on this issue, when they argue that 'one of the main benefits of inflation targets is that they may help to "lock in" earlier disinflationary gains particularly in the face of one-time inflationary shocks' (p. 288). In an important contribution, though, Johnson (2003) finds rather mixed results for this contention. Johnson (op. cit.) compares actual forecasts with predicted forecasts undertaken by professional forecasters for five consecutive 12-month periods after the announcement of inflation targets. The study isolates the additional effect of the announcement of inflation targets on the level of expected inflation in the case of Australia, Canada, New Zealand, Sweden and the UK. Immediate reduction in expected inflation is registered in New Zealand and Sweden with a smaller effect and slower impact in Australia and Canada; inflation targets do not appear to have a significant impact in the UK.

(iii) In this framework, monetary policy is taken as the main instrument of macroeconomic policy. Fiscal Policy is no longer viewed as a powerful macroeconomic instrument (in any case it is hostage to the slow and uncertain legislative process); in this way, 'monetary policy moves first and dominates, forcing fiscal policy to align with monetary policy' (Mishkin, 2000, p. 4). Monetary policy is a flexible instrument for achieving medium-term stabilization objectives, in that it can be adjusted quickly in response to macroeconomic developments. Indeed, monetary policy is viewed as the most direct determinant of inflation, so much so that in the long run the inflation rate is the only macroeconomic variable that monetary policy can affect. Monetary policy cannot affect economic activity, for example output, employment, etc., in the long run.

(iv) Monetary policy should not be operated by politicians but by experts (whether banks, economists or others) in the form of an 'independent' central bank. Politicians would be tempted to use monetary policy for short-term gain (lower unemployment) at the expense of long-term loss (higher inflation), the time-inconsistency problem (Kydland and Prescott, 1977). An 'independent' central bank would also have greater credibility in the financial markets and be seen to have a stronger commitment to low inflation than politicians do. There is also the question of instrument independence, when the monetary policy instrument is under the control of the independent central bank, and goal independence, when the independent central bank sets the goal of monetary policy (Debelle and Fischer, 1994; Fischer, 1994). It is argued that instrument independence is preferable to insulate the independent central bank from time-inconsistent policies. However, in terms of the goals of monetary policy, it is thought that an independent central bank should be goal dependent so that its long-run preferences coincide with society's preferences, i.e. elected government's (Bernanke et al., 1999).

(v) A mechanism for openness, transparency and accountability should be in place with respect to monetary policy formulation. Openness and transparency in the conduct of monetary policy improve credibility. IT central banks publish inflation reports that might include not only an outlook for inflation, but also output and other macroeconomic variables, along with an assessment of economic conditions. There is also some accountability mechanism: if the inflation target is not met, there should be specific steps in place for the central bank to follow; this may include publishing an explanation, or submitting a letter to the government explaining the reasons for missing the target and how to return to it. Furthermore, transparency reduces uncertainty about the central bank's preferences, which is expected to lead to lower expected rate of inflation.

(vi) In the case of inflation targeting in an open economy, exchange rate considerations are of crucial importance, and we highlight this aspect in the case of emerging countries, and Brazil in particular in what follows in this chapter. They transmit both certain effects of changes in the policy instrument, interest rates, and various foreign shocks. Given this critical role of the exchange rate in the transmission process of monetary policy, excessive fluctuations in interest rates can produce excessive fluctuations in output by inducing significant changes in exchange rates. This may suggest exchange rate targeting. However, the experience of a number of developing countries, which pursued exchange rate targeting but experienced financial crises because their policies were not perceived as credible, is relevant to the argument. The adoption of IT, by contrast, may lead to a more stable currency since it signals a clear commitment to price stability in a freely floating exchange rate system. This, of course, does not mean that monitoring exchange rate developments should not be undertaken. Indeed, weighting them into decisions on setting monetary policy instruments is thought desirable. Such an approach is thought to make undesirable exchange rate fluctuations less likely, thereby promoting the objective of financial and price stability (Bernanke and Gertler, 1999).

2.2 Operational aspects

In terms of the operational framework of IT, a number if issues suggest themselves. To begin with, there is the establishment of inflation targets. This is the setting of a point target or a band and choosing the time period over which the target is expected to be achieved. It is important to note that the target horizon (over which the central bank is expected to achieve its inflation target) cannot be shorter than the control horizon (over which the policy is expected to affect the target variable). Clearly, choosing a range as opposed to a point for the inflation target contains a great deal of flexibility, not only for output stabilization but also for accommodating large movements in the nominal exchange rate; this is a particularly thorny issue in the case of emerging countries, and Brazil in particular as shown below. In those cases where a range is chosen, there is the question of symmetrical/asymmetrical response with respect to the central target. Symmetrical behaviour purports to show equal concern for both inflation and deflation. Such an approach reduces the likelihood of output declines and deflation, and indicates that the central bank cares about output fluctuations; this helps to maintain support for its independence. An asymmetric approach to inflation targeting may be advantageous when high inflation rates threaten credibility. This is often the case for developing and emerging countries adopting inflation targeting. A greater weight on overshoots than undershoots in the loss function is suggested under these circumstances.

IT also requires the setting up of a model or methodology that can provide information on future inflation, an issue that relates to the necessity of forecasting inflation. There is also the key issue of how to measure inflation. A relevant question in this context is whether the chosen price index should reflect the prices of goods and services for current consumption only, or for both current and future consumption. In the latter case constructing such a price index is, of course, not feasible. Then there is the problem of noisy or erratic short-run movements in prices, which suggests that an adjusted or core (long-term) price index should be used. Such an index might exclude from the general or headline price index items such as food and energy prices, shocks to the exchange rate, indirect tax or regulated prices on the assumption that such changes are the result of temporary and self-correcting short-term shocks that contain very little information on long-term price movements. Another important excluded category of items relates to changes directly associated with the policy change. Items, which vary directly with the policy instrument, such as mortgage payments, may be excluded from the definition of the targeted price index. Such effects, however, may contain significant and protracted second-round effects. For example, a rise in indirect taxes that lowers inflation temporarily, can affect aggregate demand, which may lower prices in the long run, thereby implying important loss of information on future price developments.

There is still the question of the trade-off between reducing deviations of inflation from target, and preventing a high degree of output variability. This is particularly pertinent in the case of supply shocks that cause inflation to exceed the target and are associated at the same time with lower output. Monetary authorities have a serious dilemma in these circumstances: the quicker the disinflation, the shorter the period of actual inflation being above its target. But then the quicker disinflation is, the greater the potential output variability. Policy preferences is an important determinant of this trade-off in addition to the magnitude of the supply shock. Flexibility is required in this context, which, however, may conflict with credibility if agents interpret it as reluctance by the central bank to deflate. There is, thus, another trade-off in this case between credibility and flexibility (Garfinkel and Oh, 1993).

This discussion highlights another important operational aspect. This relates to the question of monetary rules. Central banks on the whole are assumed to follow one form or another of Taylor Rules (Taylor, 1993). In its original formulation this monetary rule took the ad hoc formulation as shown in equation (1):

$$R_t = RR^* + p^T + d_1 Y_t^g + d_2(p_{t-1} - p^T) \tag{1}$$

where the symbols are as follows: R is the rate of interest used for monetary control purposes, p^T is desired inflation in the original Taylor (op. cit.) formulation (in current parlance it is the inflation target set by the central bank), Y^g is output gap (i.e. the difference between actual and potential output), and p is actual inflation. Equations of the type depicted in (1) are what is called Taylor rules, since Taylor (1993) who showed that a simple equation of this form, with $d_1 = 0.5$ and $d_2 = 1.5$, captures surprisingly well the behaviour of the US federal-funds rate and the Federal Reserve System (Fed) monetary policy. The nominal rate is increased more than one-to-one with respect to any increase in inflation. This policy reaction ensures that the real rate of interest will act to lower inflation. Given inflation, the real rate of interest is also increased as a result of output-gap positive changes. Taylor rules, therefore, require monetary policy to act automatically to inflation and output. These Taylor-type rules have been criticized (for example, Svensson, 2004) in terms of the possibility of real indeterminacy: if the rise in the nominal rate of interest in response to a rise in expected inflation is not high enough, then the real rate of interest falls raising demand which fails to check inflation. *Mutatis mutandis*, an excessive rise in the nominal rate of interest in response to a rise in expected inflation would also cause indeterminacy. However, indeterminacy can be avoided if monetary authorities respond rather aggressively, that is with a coefficient above unity to expected inflation, but not overly higher than unity. This result has been demonstrated in the closed-economy case (Clarida et al., 2000) as well as in the small open-economy case (De Fiore and Liu, 2002).

3 The Brazilian experience: from the exchange rate anchor to IT

Stabilization policies in Brazil, and more generally in Latin American countries, in the 1990s were based on some form of exchange rate anchor. Liberalization of the trade, financial and capital accounts was thought paramount. The experience with those programmes showed that although they were successful in ending the history of chronic high inflation, they showed, nonetheless, that local currency appreciation as a result of favourable differentials between domestic and foreign prices, was causing balance of payments disequilibria. A new problem emerged, which was closely related to the endeavour to achieve and maintain balance of payments equilibria. That was the use of high interest rates by monetary authorities to attract foreign capital. The need to maintain high interest rates in order to attract foreign capital increased public internal debt (monetary authorities had to sterilize the inflow of foreign capital), which deteriorated economic performance and fiscal balances. Under those conditions in a global world where financial and productive capital are mobile, the successful application of an internal stabilization policy generated an endogenous process of deteriorating economic conditions. That, then, left Latin American countries vulnerable to speculative attacks on their currencies, and thus subjected them to currency crises (Kregel, 1999). The currency crises in Mexico (1994–95), in Brazil (1998–99, and 2002), and in Argentina (2001–02), are some good examples of this dynamic process. That unhappy experience of some Latin American countries with pegged exchange rate regimes, and the associated era of deep financial crises in the 1990s, led them to search for alternative nominal anchors. Since at the same time more or less several industrial countries adopted the IT as a new monetary policy framework, it became an alternative policy regime for countries in Latin America. In fact, IT was adopted by Chile in 1990, Mexico in 1999, Colombia in 1999, Brazil in 1999, and Peru in 2002.

The Real Plan, in Brazil, was created on the same basis as the stabilization programmes applied all over Latin America over the period of late 1980s to late 1990s. That system was characterized by a fixed or crawling-peg exchange rate, in combination with a more open trade policy. The exchange rate was the price anchor utilized throughout that period.[2] During the exchange rate anchor period, very high interest rates were targeted designed to attract short-term foreign capital for balance-of-payments purposes. The volume of those capital flows was many times greater than the volume required for the needs of the balance of payments, thus raising the level of foreign reserves and leading to a real appreciation of the exchange rate.[3] That appreciation resulted in significant balance of trade deficit. The effect of that liberal economic policy arrangement aggravated Brazil's external fragility and, consequently, the country had three speculative attacks on its currency over the three-year period 1995 to 1998. Furthermore, the Brazilian economy, from the third quarter of 1998 to the first quarter of 1999, was characterized by macroeconomic instability, resulting in a sharp outflow of short-term capital. Thus, repeated financial crises in a very short period of time, i.e. the South East Asian crisis and the Russian crisis along with the international recession of 1997–98, contributed to deteriorating the Brazilian economy. In fact, as a result of the effects of the Russian crisis in particular, Brazil was forced to abandon its crawling-peg exchange rate and adopted a floating exchange rate regime. The exchange rate depreciated as a result, thereby producing significant price pass-through effects with the inevitable adverse consequences on the inflation front.

Following the transition to a floating exchange rate, in January 1999, Brazil adopted an IT regime, in June 1999, to keep inflation under control. At the same time, the Central Bank of Brazil raised the basic short-term interest rate to accommodate the currency depreciation shock. As a result, an appreciation to the exchange rate occurred very fast and inflation, despite the huge devaluation in the beginning of 1999, ended the year in single figures.

4　The Brazilian experience with IT

4.1　The institutional dimension

The Brazilian IT monetary policy regime is modelled on the basis of the British IT model. The National Monetary Council (CMN)[4] sets the inflation targets, which are proposed by the Minister of Finance. The Central Bank of Brazil Monetary Policy Committee (COPOM)[5] has to achieve the inflation target through the use of the short-term interest rate. In fact the Central Bank of Brazil makes use of the Taylor rule as its reaction function. The relevant relationship is:

$$R_t = RR^\star + p^T + g_1 Y_t^g + g_2 (p_{t-1} - p^T) + g_3 (er_t - er_{t-1}) + g_4 R_{t-1} \qquad (2)$$

where the symbols are as above, with the exception of er which stands for the exchange rate. The Brazilian Taylor rule relates the interest rate to deviations of expected inflation from the target, allowing also for some interest rate smoothing (R_{t-1}) and reaction to the output gap as well as movements in the exchange rate (Minella et al., 2003, p. 11). The Brazilian IT regime sets year-end inflation targets for the current and the following two years. Inflation targets are based on the headline inflation index, i.e. extensive national consumer price index (IPCA).[6] A certain degree of flexibility is introduced through defining IT within a range, which has varied between 2.0 or 2.5 percentage points above and below the central point target. The other main reason for the introduction of this flexibility is that it helps the Central Bank of Brazil to achieve its inflation target in view of the serious supply shocks to which the Brazilian economy is exposed.

The inflation target is fulfilled when yearly variation of the inflation index is inside the set range. If inflation breaches the target set by the CMN, the Governor of the Central Bank of Brazil is required to write an open letter to the Minister of Finance explaining the reasons the target was missed, as well as the measures proposed to bring it back to target, and the time period over which these measures are expected to take effect. The interest rate target set by the COPOM is the target for the Selic interest rate, the interest rate for overnight interbank loans, collateralized by those government bonds that are registered with and traded on the 'Sistema Especial de Liquidação e Custodia' (SELIC). The Selic target is fixed for the period between its regular meetings. The Governor of the Central Bank of Brazil, though, has the right to alter the Selic interest rate target anytime between regular COPOM meetings (once per month). This is made possible by the COPOM, which has the right to introduce a monetary policy bias at its regular meetings, where the bias refers to easing or tightening of monetary policy outside meetings. The COPOM authorizes the Governor of the Central Bank to alter the Selic interest rate target in the direction of the bias at anytime between regular COPOM meetings. Eight days after each meeting, the Committee releases the minutes on the Central Bank of Brazil website and to the press through the Central Bank of Brazil press officer. The minutes provide a summary of the COPOM's discussion and decisions. At the end of each quarter (March, June, September, December), the COPOM publishes the Central Bank of Brazil Inflation Report, which provides detailed information on economic conditions, as well as the COPOM's inflation forecasts upon which changes in the Selic interest rate are determined. The objective of this report is to inform the public and the market about the goals, design and implementation of monetary policy.

4.2 Brazil's experience with IT

Table 8.1 shows actual inflation and the targets for 1999–2005. From 1999 (when IT was introduced in Brazil)[7] to 2002, the tolerance intervals were 2 percentage points above and below the central target; for 2003 and 2004 the intervals were enlarged to 2.5 percentage points. The inflation rate was 8.9 per cent and 6.0 per cent for targets of 8 per cent and 6 per cent in 1999 and 2000, respectively. The targets were within the acceptable range. However, in 2001 and 2002, several external and domestic shocks – such as domestic energy crisis in Brazil, effects of 11th September 2001, the Argentine crisis, and the confidence crisis related to the presidential election in 2002 – hit the Brazilian economy with significant impacts on inflation. Indeed, the inflation rate reached 7.7 per cent in 2001, 1.7 per cent above the target's upper range, and 12.5 per cent in 2005, more than 5 percentage points above the upper range. According to Minella et al. (2003, pp.6–8), the exchange rate rose 20.3 per cent and 53.5 per cent in 2001 and 2002, respectively. As a result, in 2001, 38 per cent of the inflation rate can be explained by the exchange rate depreciation, whereas for 2002 the contribution of the exchange rate stood at 46 per cent.[8] In 2003 the inflation rate was 9.3 per cent above the adjusted target of 4.5 per cent, and outside the range of 2.5 per cent tolerance interval.[9] The high inflation in 2003 was due mainly to the inertial effect of 2002 high inflation, in spite of the maintenance of the conservative economic policy with very high interest rates by the new President, Lula da Silva, from the Workers' Party. In 2004 IPCA was 7.6 per cent, only slightly less than the upper range of the inflation target (8.0 per cent).

Examining Table 8.1 more closely, further comments are in order. It is notable that over the period 1999–2005 IT targets in Brazil were within the set range in three out of the seven years of the operation of this monetary policy strategy. The targets were missed in 2001, 2002 and 2003 (despite raising the inflation target to 6 per cent from 4 per cent) by a substantial margin, especially in 2002. On one different occasion (2004), the inflation target was met only after it had been raised in early 2003 (note 9). It may, thus, be concluded that IT in Brazil was not completely unsuccessful over the first seven years of its implementation. This begs the question of comparing Brazil's IT

Table 8.1 Brazil – inflation targets and headline consumer price index (IPCA)

Year	Inflation target (%)	Tolerance intervals +/− (%)	IPCA (%)
1999	8.0	2.0	8.94
2000	6.0	2.0	5.97
2001	4.0	2.0	7.67
2002	3.5	2.0	12.53
2003	6.0*	2.5	9.30
2004	5.5*	2.5	7.60
2005	5.1	2.5	5.69

Note: *The original inflation target was 3.25% (tolerance interval of 2%) in 2003 and 3.75% (tolerance interval of 2.5%) in 2004. Later BCB decided to change again to inflation target in 2003 to the maximum limit of 8.5%, that was known as 'adjusted target.'
Source: Central Bank of Brazil.

performance with that of other emerging countries both within Latin America and outside it, and also both with IT and non-IT countries. Section 5 is designed to conduct this exercise, and we turn our attention to it next.

5 Comparing the Brazilian experience with other 'similar' countries

This exercise is undertaken with the help of Tables 8.2–8.4, which contain data that concern inflation and GDP (average, standard deviation and coefficient of variation) of a group of emerging countries that have adopted IT and those that have not adopted IT.[10] Two groups of emerging countries are reported: the biggest Latin American countries and some other emerging countries. Long periods of high inflation (inflation above 50 per cent per year) in the data have not been included, as for example in the case of Brazil before 1995 and Israel before 1986.[11] Standard deviations and coefficients of variation can be sometimes misleading, as for example in the case of China, where a high inflation standard deviation is present, as a result of a sharp decline of high to low inflation, although this country has had very low inflation since the late 1990s. It is for this reason that we also report data on inflation in Figures 8.6–8.8 on inflation for all countries included in the sample, and separated by countries that adopt IT, and those that do not adopt IT.[12] These figures are very important for the analysis, since they report inflation trends in each country. Figures 8.1–8.5 report relevant statistics for Brazil in order to support the analysis on the recent performance of IT in this country.

The following observations are in order:

(a) Inspection of Tables 8.2–8.4 clearly shows that the fall of inflation is a recent general tendency in emerging countries, whether or not they adopt an IT regime (see, also, Figures 8.6–8.8). Although in all IT emerging countries the rate of inflation declined after the adoption of IT, in most of them the coefficient of variation increased (Table 8.2). It is also true that countries that did not adopt IT experienced improvements around the same time as IT countries (Tables 8.3–8.4). Indeed, some emerging non-IT countries, such as China, India, Egypt and Malaysia, have had inflation rates below 4 per cent per year in the last few years. For some countries, China, India and Malaysia, the stability of the nominal exchange rate has had an important role for price stabilization purposes. So, IT and non-IT countries have experienced similar reductions in inflation in recent years.[13] Theory suggests that 'flexible' IT stabilizes both inflation and output. However, there is no clear evidence that emerging countries that adopt IT have had a better performance in GDP terms (both in terms of output growth and GDP coefficient of variation) when compared with the emerging countries that do not adopt IT reported in this chapter. Indeed, China, India and Malaysia are among the countries that have

Table 8.2 Emerging IT countries

| Country | Before IT | | | | | | After IT | | | | | |
| | Inflation | | | GDP | | | Inflation | | | GDP | | |
	Average	SD	CV	Average	SD	CV	Average	SD	CV	Average	SD	CV
Latin American countries												
Brazil	9.71	9.06	0.93	2.58	1.76	0.68	8.88	2.42	0.27	1.78	1.56	0.88
Chile	20.45	5.94	0.29	4.50	2.99	0.66	8.01	5.83	0.73	5.64	3.56	0.63
Colombia	23.71	4.26	0.18	3.62	1.64	0.45	6.80	2.21	0.32	1.86	1.76	0.95
Mexico	20.76	9.37	0.45	3.43	3.60	1.05	8.41	4.97	0.59	2.36	2.77	1.17
Other emerging countries												
Israel	23.43	12.18	0.52	4.43	12.18	0.52	7.07	4.43	0.63	3.86	2.99	0.77
Poland	29.74	11.16	0.38	5.23	1.74	0.33	6.21	4.39	0.71	5.18	5.41	1.04
Czech Republic	13.73	16.43	1.20	n.a.	n.a.	n.a.	3.88	3.69	0.95	1.80	1.72	0.95
Thailand	4.97	2.06	0.41	5.28	6.56	1.24	1.41	0.55	0.39	4.75	2.25	0.47
South Korea	6.18	1.71	0.28	7.46	1.98	0.27	3.49	2.28	0.65	4.17	5.98	1.44

Notes: SD = standard deviation; CV = coefficient of variation (SD/average) Before IT / After IT : Brazil: 1995–98/1999–2003; Colombia; 1989–98/
1999–2003; Mexico;1989–98/1999–2003;
Chile: 1981–90/1991–2003; Czech Republic:1988–97/1998–2003 (until 1992, data from Czechoslovakia);
Israel: 1986–91/1992–2003; Poland:1992–97/1998–2003; Thailand:1990–99/2000–03; South Korea:1988–97/1998–2003.
Source: IMF (2002, 2004)/IPEADATA for Brazil's inflation/Polish Market Review, August 2003.

Table 8.3 Emerging non-IT countries

Country	1980–91						1992–2003					
	Inflation			GDP			Inflation			GDP		
	Average	SD	CV	Average	SD	CV	Average	SD	CV	Average	SD	CV
Latin American countries												
Argentina	663.56	950.55	1.43	0.82	6.18	7.56	6.02	12.23	2.03	2.09	6.41	3.07
Uruguay	65.86	26.06	0.40	1.35	5.24	3.88	26.39	21.32	0.81	1.29	5.48	4.24
Venezuela	25.42	5.33	0.21	1.55	5.33	3.44	40.15	24.48	0.61	−0.18	5.15	−29.42
Other emerging countries												
China*	10.16	7.78	0.77	9.23	3.93	0.43	6.00	8.40	1.40	9.76	2.44	0.25
Egypt**	18.19	3.27	0.18	5.14	2.26	0.44	6.69	4.71	0.70	4.62	1.37	0.30
India	9.52	2.58	0.27	5.46	2.20	0.40	7.50	3.83	0.51	6.09	1.35	0.22
Malaysia	3.63	2.78	0.77	6.44	3.35	0.52	2.96	1.33	0.45	6.02	5.61	0.93
Turkey	53.23	23.15	0.43	4.26	3.61	0.85	68.81	22.02	0.32	3.52	5.81	1.65
Russia	n.a.	n.a.	n.a.	n.a.	n.a.	n.a.	147.94	258.80	1.75	0.04	7.33	201.68
South Africa***	14.64	1.96	0.13	1.92	3.03	1.58	7.94	2.47	0.31	2.23	1.70	0.76

Notes: SD = standard deviation; CV = coefficient of variation (SD/Average) * Data for inflation: 1987–91 and 1992–2003; ** Data for inflation and GDP: 1983–91 and 1992–2003; *** Data for inflation and GDP: 1980–91 and 1992–2001.

Source: IMF (2002, 2004)/Deutsche Bank Research (www.dbresearch.de) for data on Russia.

Table 8.4 Emerging IT countries (full period)

Country	1980–91 Inflation			1980–91 GDP			1992–2003 Inflation			1992–2003 GDP		
	Average	SD	CV	Average	SD	CV	Average	SD	CV	Average	SD	CV
Latin American countries												
Brazil	534.25	645.22	1.21	2.76	4.30	1.56	383.00	766.89	2.00	2.46	2.09	0.85
Chile	21.78	6.82	0.31	5.06	3.00	0.59	6.86	4.28	0.62	5.44	3.64	0.67
Colombia	25.33	6.17	0.24	3.37	1.49	0.44	15.49	8.10	0.52	2.98	2.00	0.67
Mexico	61.65	39.07	0.63	2.64	3.84	1.45	15.02	10.52	0.70	2.72	3.61	1.33
Other emerging countries												
Israel	111.07	118.71	1.07	3.68	1.74	0.47	7.07	4.43	0.63	3.86	2.99	0.77
Poland*	104.85	164.25	1.57	-0.56	6.53	11.59	17.98	14.71	0.82	5.21	3.83	0.74
Czech Republic**	6.89	16.25	2.36	n.a.	n.a.	n.a.	7.61	5.61	0.74	2.24	2.18	0.97
Thailand	5.82	5.33	0.92	7.70	3.12	0.41	3.65	2.47	0.68	4.33	5.61	1.30
South Korea	8.49	8.24	0.97	7.82	3.62	0.46	4.34	1.87	0.43	5.40	4.39	0.81

Notes: SD = standard deviation; CV = coefficient of variation (SD/average) * Data from 1981; ** Data from Czechoslovakia for 1980–93.
Source: IMF (2002, 2004)/IPEADATA for Brazil's inflation/Polish Market Review 08/2003.

had the highest output growth in recent years, and they are non-IT countries (their growth rates are 9.8 per cent, 6.1 per cent and 6.0 per cent, respectively, in the years 1992–2003). Consequently, there is no evidence that inflation targeting improves performance in emerging economies as measured by the behaviour of inflation and output. This finding suggests that better performance resulted from something other than IT.[14]

(b) The picture in Latin American countries should be interpreted with due attention given that these countries have suffered currency crises recently: Mexico in 1994–95, Brazil in 1998–99 and 2002, and Argentina in 2001–02. Such crises have had big effects on both inflation and GDP in these countries. Argentina, after the experience of hyperinflation (1989–90), adopted a currency board in 1991 and the inflation rate declined sharply during the 1990s. In 2002 the country had a serious currency crisis and, as result, a sharp recession in 2001–02 took place, followed by a rapid recovery after the crisis. Mexico has had poor economic performance with a declining inflation after the 1994 Tequila crisis. Although general conclusions are difficult to derive in the case of Latin America in view of the fact that IT is a recent import in these countries, a general observation emerges from this experience: in three cases, Brazil, Colombia and Mexico, economic performance worsened since the adoption of IT by these countries (Tables 8.2–8.4). Chile is an exception. It is the single Latin American country that has had real GDP growth above 5 per cent on average. Non-IT countries have had similar experiences (Table 8.3).

(c) Although there is a clear downward trend in inflation in emerging countries, Brazil is an interesting case. Inflation has been maintained high in relation to other IT countries over the relevant period; but, then, the coefficient of variation is the lowest over the same period (Table 8.2). Furthermore, Brazil's GDP performance has been poor: the average growth rate of GDP from 1999 to 2003 was 1.78 per cent. During the IT regime, the interest rate has been very high in Brazil. The average nominal basic interest rate (Selic) was 19.83 per cent over the period 1999 to 2004 (Figure 8.1). The average real primary interest rate during this period was 10.2 per cent. It was so high because monetary policy aimed at keeping inflation under control, reducing public debt, and stabilizing the exchange rate volatility. Indeed, empirical studies show that monetary authorities use interest rate not only to control inflation directly but also to influence the exchange rate, trying to control exchange rate pressures, with an evident 'fear of floating'.[15] The consequences of high interest rates are: (i) serious constraint on economic growth, through the price of credit (loan rates) and entrepreneurs' poor expectations; and (ii) it increases public debt, which is formed mainly by indexed bonds or short-term pre-fixed bonds.[16] Despite the significant improvement in the balance of payment figures in 2003 and 2004, Brazil's recent experience shows that in countries with a high level of external debt and a fully-liberalized capital account, external capital

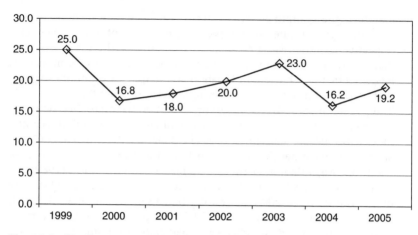

Figure 8.1   Brazil: average Selic rate from 1999 to 2005
Note: Selic rate is the Central Bank of Brazil's basic interest rate and serves as a reference for the other rates of interest. The average Selic rate for 2005 was calculated considering the first two quarters.
Source: Central Bank of Brazil.

flows can cause periods of intense exchange rate instability.[17] This can jeopardize efforts to achieve and maintain announced inflation targets. This situation has also caused low economic growth, because monetary authorities tend to increase interest rates during periods of external turbulence in order to meet inflation targets, and also stabilize exchange rates.

(d) In Brazil, exchange rate volatility has been considerable (Figure 8.2). As argued earlier, macroeconomic instability brought a strong currency devaluation of the Real (the name of the Brazilian currency), which, as a result, affected domestic prices via the exchange rate pass-through. This came about through the direct impact of devaluation on the imported inputs or indirectly through the 'monitored' prices. Monitored or administered prices are defined as those that are relatively insensitive to domestic demand and supply conditions or that are in some way regulated by a public agency. The group includes oil by-products, telephone fees, residential electricity, and public transportation. Its dynamics differ from those of market prices in three ways: '(i) dependence on international prices in the case of oil by-products; (ii) greater pass-through from the exchange rate;[18] and (iii) stronger backward-looking behavior' (Minella et al., 2003, p. 7), as electricity and telephones rates are generally adjusted annually by the General Price Index (IGP).[19] Our estimation of the percentage of monitored prices to consumer price index (IPCA) is around 28 per cent on average from April 2003 to March 2005 (Figure 8.3). Furthermore, Figure 8.4 shows that administered prices have increased more than market prices. So that, there is presence of an inertial component in the administered prices in Brazil as part of them is set by contracts to the past variation of the price index.

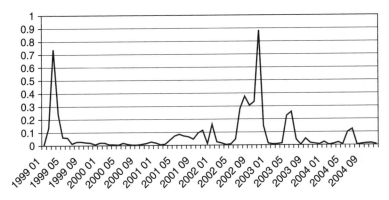

Figure 8.2   Brazil: exchange rate volatility
Note: Exchange rate volatility is calculated using a GARCH (Generalized Autoregressive Conditional Heteroskedastic) model, a non-linear model that is used to calculate the volatility of time series.
Source: Authors' calculations based on data from the Central Bank of Brazil.

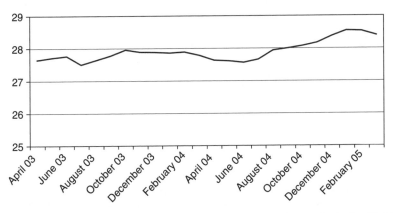

Figure 8.3   Brazil: percentage of administered prices over consumer price index (IPCA)
Note: Administered prices include: utilities services (fixed telephone fees, residential electricity etc.), oil by-products, private health plans, i.e. prices that are or determined (or authorized) directly by government (oil, private health plans) or are governmental permissions that include some sort of price indexation. See note 7 for details on IPCA.
Source: Authors' calculations based on data from IBGE (www.ibge.gov.br).

(e) A final comment on the transmission channel from exchange rate to inflation in Brazil, is in order. Exchange rate variations affect the General Price Index (IGP), which in its turn affects the index of administered prices. As administered prices change,[20] consumer price index (IPCA) is also affected. IPCA is also affected directly by exchange rate changes due to their effects on the imported inputs. Since IGP has been higher than

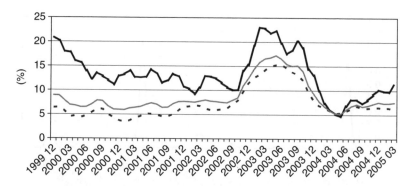

Figure 8.4 Brazil: administered and market prices in extensive consumer price index (IPCA)
Notes: ····· market prices —— administered prices —— IPCA For the definition of administered prices see note in Figure 8.3.
Source: IPEADATA (www.ipeadata.gov.br).

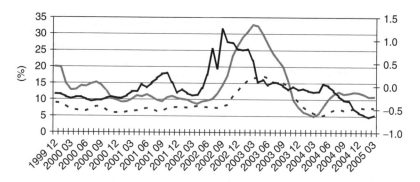

Figure 8.5 Brazil: exchange rate deviation and prices indexes
Note: ····· IPCA —— IGP —— Exchange rate deviation See note 7 for details on IPCA, and note 19 for relevant details on IGP. Exchange rate deviation was calculated as the difference between the nominal exchange rate and its linear trend.
Source: IPEADATA (www.ipeadata.gov.br).

IPCA, the latter has been influenced by the IGP behaviour through administered price adjustments (Figure 8.5).[21] On the other hand, periods of appreciation of the exchange rate, with some lag, have resulted in a decrease in the rate of inflation, after a time lag. So, inflation in Brazil is very much influenced by exchange rate movements.[22] Under these conditions, monetary policy may have some effect on market-determined prices, but it is not very effective in controlling administered prices. Consequently, in view of the importance of administered prices in the determination of the Brazilian inflation rate, inflation pressures result in the Central Bank of Brazil having to increase interest rates higher than might be necessary to restrain inflation that derives from market prices. This is so since the Central Bank has to account for the secondary effects that emanate from the shocks of monitored prices.[23] This more aggressive monetary policy generates negative effects on income and employment.

6 Summary and conclusions

We have summarized the theoretical aspects of IT, and the principles that govern its implementation in the case of Brazil. It is clear from this analysis

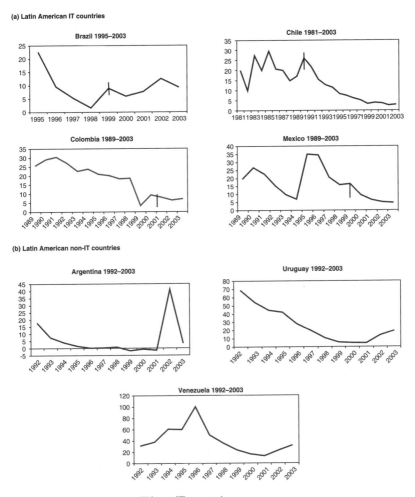

Figure 8.6   Latin American IT/non-IT countries
Sources: IMF (2002, 2004); IPEADATA for Brazil.

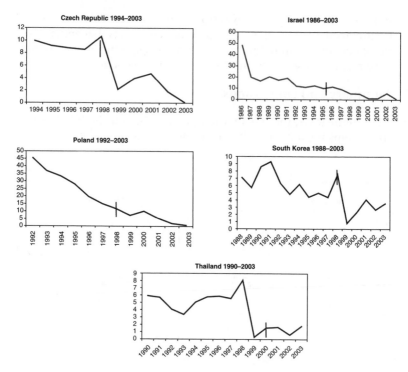

Figure 8.7   Other emerging non-Latin American IT countries
Source: IMF (2002, 2004).

that the authorities in Brazil adhere religiously to the theoretical principles of the IT framework. We have examined the experience of Brazil with IT, compared it with the experience of the pre-IT period and with the experience of other countries, IT and non-IT ones.

Two general conclusions emerge from this analysis. IT countries appear to have been successful in taming inflation. But, then, so have non-IT countries. Furthermore, although Brazil has implemented IT as the theory of the framework suggests, inflation rates over the IT period have been high. Brazil has one of the highest interest rates in the world, along with inflation, which has been maintained at a significantly high level. The Central Bank of Brazil has to maintain very high interest rates in its attempt to control inflation. High interest rates have caused poor economic growth performance, and deterioration of other macroeconomic variables, such as public debt. It appears that we have a rather bad economic scenario in Brazil: low economic growth with relatively high inflation.

Our results conform to recent contributions on the IT experience of a number of Latin American countries. Especially so with Eichengreen's (2002)

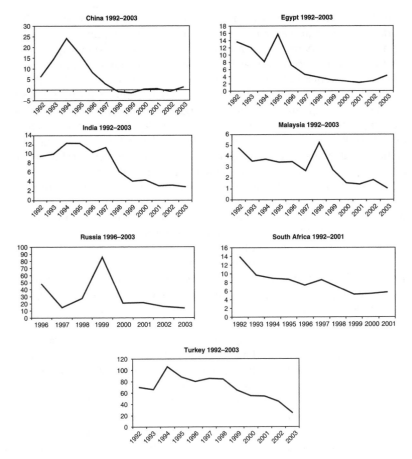

Figure 8.8   Emerging non-IT countries
Source: IMF (2002, 2004).

contention that IT is more complicated in countries like the Latin American ones, essentially for three main reasons: their economies are exposed to financial and international commodity shocks because of the liberalization of the balance of payments trade, financial and capital accounts; their liabilities are almost dollarized; and their policymakers lack credibility. The first and the second reasons are particularly pertinent in the case of Latin America countries. Openness exposes these economies to disturbances that emanate from exchange rate fluctuations that cause pass-through inflation. Liability dollarization affects financial institutions because, in general terms, the banking system of Latin America countries is weak, and as such it brings financial vulnerability when external shocks occur. However, Paula and Alves Jr. (2003) demonstrate that this is not typical of the Brazilian banking sector in recent years. Moreover, IT is too rigid for these countries essentially because it affects economic growth and exchange rate flexibility that is required under such a regime of monetary rules. The latter can cause financial instability, a very real possibility in these countries as history has demonstrated vividly. Schmidt-Hebel and Werner (2002) are very clear on the dangers of IT: 'all Latin American inflation targeters are open economies that employ floating exchange rate regimes . . . [and] are subject to large external shocks and significant exchange rate volatility, and the exchange rate may therefore play an important role in the conduct of monetary policy under inflation targeting' (p. 2). Exchange rate market volatility generates frequent changes to inflation rates and results in countries not being able to meet their inflation targets.

The larger external shocks faced by Latin America countries affect the exchange rate, and, consequently, the inflation rate, leading to higher interest rates to curb the inflationary pressures. As a result, these economies in general are confronted by higher volatility of interest rates and exchange rates. In this context, 'monetary policy in emerging economies may therefore be more sensitive to exchange rate movements both indirectly (because of pass-through effects on inflation) and directly (because the exchange rate is an additional argument in central bank objective functions, reflecting their concern for devaluation-induced bank failures and domestic recessions)' (Schmidt-Hebel and Werner, 2002, p. 15). In other words, the pass-through from exchange rate changes to inflation is larger and more significant in the Latin American economies than in industrial countries because the former have a substantially higher degree of openness, a history of high inflation, and low central bank credibility. In addition, Latin American countries present large mismatches between foreign currency assets and liabilities, which bring two adverse shocks: self-fulfilling attacks and financial crises on the country's assets and domestic recession following large exchange rate depreciations. It is the case that Latin American countries are susceptible to supply shocks, perhaps more so than many other countries, than to demand shocks. To the extent that this is validated, IT might not work as effectively as in those countries where demand shocks dominate over supply shocks.

Notes

*We are very grateful to Fabio Barcelos for generous research support in the form of collecting data on developing and emerging countries, especially on Brazil, and for producing the tables and figures for the chapter. We are also grateful to Lilian Furquim for providing data relevant to Figure 8.5.

1 Arestis and Sawyer (2005) provide an extensive discussion of the IT theoretical framework.

2 The Brazilian Real Plan differed from Argentina's Convertibility Plan in that it adopted a more flexible exchange rate anchor. At the launch of the Brazilian programme in July 1994, the government's commitment was to maintain an exchange

rate ceiling of one-to-one parity with the dollar. Moreover, the relationship between changes in the monetary base and foreign reserve movements was not explicitly stated, allowing some discretionary leeway. After the Mexican crisis, the exchange rate policy was reviewed and in the context of a crawling exchange rate range, the nominal rate began to undergo gradual devaluation. In early 1999, however, after six months of speculative pressure, the *real* was devalued and, some days later, the Brazilian government adopted a floating exchange rate. For a general analysis of the origins and development of the Real Plan, see Ferrari, Filho and Paula (2003).

3 During the pegged exchange rate period, July 1994 to January 1999, the basic interest rate (Selic) was raised and kept at high levels in order to avoid large outflow of reserves.

4 CMN has three members: the Minister of Finance, the Minister of Planning and the Governor of the Central Bank of Brazil. Besides the inflation target, CMN is also responsible for the approval of the main norms related to monetary and exchange rate policy, and to the regulation of the financial system.

5 COPOM was created on 20 June 1996, and was assigned the responsibility of setting the stance of monetary policy and the short-term interest rate. It is composed of the members of the Central Bank of Brazil's Board of Directors.

6 IPCA covers a sample of families with a multiple of up to 40 times the minimum wage, which is determined every year by the Brazilian federal government. It now stands at approximately US$ 130 per month, and it is thought to be enough to cover the basic needs of a family. The sample covered by IPCA has a broad geographical basis that includes families in the biggest cities of Brazil. IPCA is calculated by IBGE (National Bureau of Geography and Statistics).

7 For more information on the macroeconomic background that led to the shift of IT in Brazil, see Bogdanski et al. (2000).

8 Minella et al. (2003) calculations are based on the structural model of the Central Bank of Brazil and the information concerning the mechanisms for the adjustment of administered prices.

9 At the beginning of 2003 the new federal government announced a change in the inflation targets for 2003 and 2004. They were raised to 6 per cent and 5.5 per cent for 2003 and 2004, from the original inflation targets of 4.0 per cent and 3.25 per cent, respectively.

10 For most countries that do not adopt IT we use data from 1992 to 2003. Since South Africa adopted IT very recently (2002), we have included this country in the group of non-IT, but using data only until 2001.

11 The reason for excluding periods of high inflation is that during those periods the rate of inflation is so high and after the price stabilization (in general with some sort of exchange rate anchor) the rate of inflation is so low (compared with the former period), that the shift produces a huge distortion in the time series of inflation figures. This would complicate the comparison between the period before IT and after IT in Table 8.2. For Table 8.3 and Table 8.4, however, we have not excluded any data, unless they were not available.

12 Once more we have excluded periods of high inflation in Figures 8.6–8.8 as the inclusion of these periods would cause an enormous distortion in the figures.

13 Note that in our sample (Tables 8.2–8.4), Venezuela is the single exception, as average inflation increased from 1980–91 (35.4 per cent) to 1992–2003 (40.2 per cent), although since 1996 the inflation rate in this country has traced a downward trend.

14 One might argue that these findings are due to specific economic problems of emerging countries, in a way that developed countries are not faced with, and

thus IT might be better suited for these countries. However, a recent paper on OECD countries shows that this is not the case: comparing seven OECD countries that adopted inflation targeting in the early 1990s to 13 that did not, Ball and Sheridan (2003) find that on average there is no evidence that IT improves performance as measured by the behaviour of inflation, output, and interest rates. They conclude that 'the formal and institutional aspects of targeting – the public announcements of targets, the inflation reports, the enhanced independence of central banks – are not important. *Nothing in the data suggests that convert targets would benefit from adopting explicit targets*' (p. 29, italics added; see also Arestis and Sawyer, 2005).

15 Mendonça (2005), using a Taylor rule to study the determination of interest rate by the Central Bank of Brazil, over the period 1999–2004, finds that exchange rate changes explained a great deal of the variation of the Selic interest rate (around 57 per cent after one year of the exchange rate shock in 2003).

16 The behaviour of the domestic public debt in Brazil has proved particularly vulnerable to changes in the rate of interest and exchange rate (see, in this regard, Paula and Alves Jr., 2003).

17 According to data from Central Bank of Brazil, the ratio of external debt to exports declined from 3.6 in 2001 to 2.1 in 2004, due to the recent increase in exports, and the ratio of foreign reserves to external debt increased from 17.1 in 2001 to 26.3 in 2004. Although there is a significant improvement recently in the external vulnerability indicators, they are still in the range of what is considered 'danger' for the country.

18 According to Minella et al. (2003) '[t]here are three basic links (i) the price of oil by-products for consumption depends on international oil prices denominated in domestic currency; (ii) part of the resetting of electricity rates is linked to changes in the exchange rate; and (iii) the contracts for price adjustments for electricity and telephone rates link these adjustments, at least partially, to the General Price Index (IGP), which is more affected by the exchange rate than the consumer price indexes' (p. 7).

19 IGP is prepared by Getulio Vargas Foundation, a private foundation, and it is calculated through a weighted index that includes wholesale price index (60.0 per cent), consumer price index (30.0 per cent) and national index of building costs (10.0 per cent). The reason for the use of this index to adjust electricity and telephones rates (instead of IPCA) is that when these services were privatized in the second half of the 1990s, Brazilian government was interested in attracting foreign firms, and for these firms IGP is better than IPCA, as it is much more sensitive to exchange rate variations (due to the high weight of the wholesale price on it).

20 Minella et al. (2003, p. 25) estimated that the pass-through to administered prices from July 1997 until December 2002 was 25 per cent, resulting in a pass-through of about 16 per cent for the headline IPCA.

21 Figueiredo and Ferreira (2002), using a simple regression, identify the general index of prices and the index of domestic supply prices as the main components that explain the difference between movements in markets prices and administered prices.

22 Ferreira (2004), using a VAR model to evaluate the determinants of the rate of inflation in Brazil in 1995–2004, finds a positive response of inflation to shocks in nominal exchange rate, an effect that spreads over time. In the same connection, Gomes and Aidar (2005) estimate, using a VAR, a Taylor rule for the Brazilian economy from January 1999 to May 2004, and conclude that 24.4 per cent of the inflation rate (IPCA) variation is explained by the exchange rate. It is interesting

that some economists of the Central Bank of Brazil also conclude that 'exchange rate volatility is an important source of inflation variability. The design of the inflation-targeting framework has to take into account this issue to avoid that a possible non-fulfilment of inflation targets as a result of exchange rate volatility may reduce the credibility of the central bank' (Minella et al., 2003, p. 29).

23 The credit channel is also limited in Brazil since the ratio of credit to GDP has been around 24–30 per cent in 2000–04, according to data from Central Bank of Brazil, while it was 45.3 per cent in US, 84.7 per cent in Japan and 103.7 per cent in the euro area in 2000 (Belaisch, 2003).

References

Arestis, P. and Sawyer, M. (2005), 'Inflation Targeting: A Critical Appraisal', *Greek Economic Review*, (Forthcoming).

Ball, L. and Sheridan, N. (2003), 'Does Inflation Targeting Matter?', NBER Working Paper Series, 9577, 1–47.

Barro, R.J. and Gordon, D.B. (1983), 'A Positive Theory of Monetary Policy in a Natural Rate Model', *Journal of Political Economy*, 91(3), 589–619.

Belaisch, A. (2003), "Do Brazilian Banks Compete?". IMF Working Paper WP/03/113, Washington: IMF.

Bernanke, B.S. and Gertler, M. (1999), 'Monetary Policy and Asset Price Volatility', in *New Challenges for Monetary Policy*, Proceedings of the Symposium Sponsored by the Federal Reserve Bank of Kansas City, Jackson Hole, Wyoming, 26–28 August, 77–128.

Bernanke, B.S., Gertler, M. and Gilchrist, S. (1999), 'The Financial Accelerator in a Quantitative Business Cycle Framework', in J. Taylor and M. Woodford (eds), *Handbook of Macroeconomics*, Volume 1, Amsterdam: North Holland.

Bernanke, B.S. and Mishkin, F.S. (1997), 'Inflation Targeting: A New Framework for Monetary Policy?', *Journal of Economic Perspectives*, 11(2), 97–116.

Bogdanski, J., Tombini, A.A. and Werlang, S.R. (2000), 'Implementing Inflation Targeting in Brazil', Working Papers Series, Banco Central do Brasil, July, 1–29.

Calvo, G. (1978), 'On the Time Consistency of Optimal Policy in the Monetary Economy', *Econometrica*, 46(4), 1411–28.

Central Bank of Brazil (2005). www.bcb.gov.br. Accessed in June.

Clarida, R., Gali, J. and Gertler, M. (2000), 'Monetary Policy Rules and Macroeconomic Stability: Evidence and Some Theory', *Quarterly Journal of Economics*, 115(1), 147–80.

Debelle, G. and Fischer, S. (1994), 'How Independent Should a Central Bank Be?', in J.C. Fuhrer (ed.), *Goals, Guidelines, and Constraints Facing Monetary Policymakers*, 195–221, Boston: Federal Reserve Bank of Boston.

De Fiore, F. and Liu, Z. (2002), 'Openness and Equilibrium Determinacy Under Interest Rate Rules', European Central Bank Working Paper No. 173, Frankfurt: European Central Bank.

Eichengreen, B. (2002), 'Can Emerging Markets Float? Should they Inflation Target?', Working Papers Series, Banco Central do Brasil, February, 1–46.

Ferrari-Filho, F. and Paula, L.F. (2003). 'The Legacy of the *Real* Plan and an Alternative Agenda for the Brazilian Economy', *Investigación Económica*, 244, 57–92.

Ferreira, A.B. (2004). 'Metas para a Inflação e Vulnerabilidade Externa: um Estudo do Brasil'. Master Dissertation, 2005's BNDES Prize, Belo Horizonte, CEDEPLAR/UFMG.

Figueiredo, F.M. and Ferreira, T.P. (2002). 'Os Preços Administrados e a Inflação no Brasil'. Working Papers Series, Banco Central do Brasil, December, 1–32.

Fischer, S. (1994), 'Modern Central Banking', in F. Capie, C.A.E. Goodhart, S. Fischer and N. Schnadt (eds), *The Future of Central Banking*, Cambridge: Cambridge University Press, pp. 262–308.

Garfinkel, M.R. and Oh, S. (1993), 'Strategic Discipline in Monetary Policy with Private Information: Optimal Targeting Horizons', *American Economic Review*, 83(1), 99–117.

Gomes, C. and Aidar, O. (2005). 'Metas Inflacionárias, Preços Livres e Administrados no Brasil', Proceedings of X Encontro Nacional de Economia Política, SEP, Campinas/Brazil.

International Monetary Fund (IMF) (2002), *International Financial Statistics Yearbook*, Washington, IMF.

International Monetary Fund (IMF) (2004), *International Financial Statistics Yearbook*, Washington, IMF.

Johnson, D.R. (2003), 'The Effect of Inflation Targets on the Level of Expected Inflation in Five Countries', *Review of Economics and Statistics*, 85(4), 1076–81.

King, M. (2002), 'The Inflation Target Ten Years On', *Bank of England Quarterly Bulletin*, Summer, 42(4), 459–74.

Kregel, J. (1999), 'Was there an Alternative to the Brazilian Crisis?', *Revista de Economia Política*, 19(3), 23–38.

Kydland, F. and Prescott, E.C. (1977), 'Rules Rather than Discretion: The Inconsistency of Optimal Plans', *Journal of Political Economy*, 85(3), 473–92.

Mendonça, H. (2005). 'O Efeito dos Preços Administrados na Taxa de Juros Brasileira', Proceedings of X Encontro Nacional de Economia Política, SEP, Campinas/Brazil.

Minella, A., Freitas, P., Goldfajn, I. and Muinhos, M. (2003), 'Inflation Targeting in Brazil: Constructing Credibility under Exchange Rate Volatility'. Working Papers Series, 77, Banco Central do Brasil, November, 1–32.

Mishkin, F.S. (2000), 'What Should Central Banks Do?', *Federal Reserve Bank of St. Louis Review*, 82(6), 1–13.

Paula, L.F. and Alves, Jr., A.J. (2003), 'Banking Behaviour and the Brazilian Economy After the Real Plan: a Post-Keynesian Approach', *BNL Quarterly Review* no. 227, pp. 337–65.

Schmidt-Hebel, K. and Werner, A. (2002), 'Inflation Targeting in Brazil, Chile, and Mexico: Performance, Credibility, and the Exchange Rate', Banco Central de Chile, Documentos de Trabajo, No. 171.

Sterne, G. (2002), 'Inflation Targets in a Global Context', in N. Loayza and R. Soto (eds), *Inflation Targeting: Design, Performance, Challenges*, Central Bank of Chile: Chile.

Svensson, L.E.O. (2004), 'Commentary on Meyer: Practical Problems and Obstacles to Inflation Targeting', *Federal Reserve Bank of St. Louis Review*, 86(4), 161–4.

Taylor, J.B. (1993), 'Discretion Versus Policy Rules in Practice', Carnegie-Rochester Conference Series on Public Policy, December, 195–214.

9
Fiscal Policy, Credit Availability and Financing of Regional Policies in Brazil: Has Lula's Government Changed Anything?[1]

Frederico G. Jayme Jr and Marco Crocco
Department of Economics, Federal University of Minas Gerais

1 Introduction

The relationship between regional imbalances and strengthening of the financial system is not simple though it may seem so at first sight, given that developing countries have less developed financial systems. In a national financial system as in Brazil this aspect deserves special treatment, particularly if we recognize that regional development policy cannot be studied without considering macroeconomic policy, fiscal mechanisms of public financing, the nature of fiscal federalism and the Fiscal Responsibility Law.[2]

In this sense, the decentralization, the fiscal federalism as well as the autonomy of sub-national governments are crucial for articulating regional development policy in Brazil. In fact, the share of tax revenues and the autonomy of federative units are critical success factors for financing regional development. Therefore, the Constitutional Funds for regional development, created through the Constitution of 1988 in Brazil, as well as others regional development funds have an important role.

The Constitutional Funds – FNO (Constitutional Fund for the North), FNE (Constitutional Fund for the Northeast) and the FCO (Constitutional Fund for the Centre-West) – perform the function of financing economic and social development of the least developed regions. They are composed of 3 per cent of two taxes, the Income Tax and the Tax on Industrialized Products (IPI). Of the total collected, 60 per cent goes to the FNE and the remaining 40 per cent to the others funds. In order to evaluate the effectiveness and efficiency of these funds in reducing regional imbalances in Brazil it is important to analyse the evolution of their transfers and their financing sources.

The main purpose of this chapter is to analyse the conditions within which regional policies are financed in Brazil as well as the inequalities in Brazilian financial system. The starting points are the financing sources in a context of tax resources sharing and expending autonomy of the federative states. We intend to investigate particularly the role of federalism in regional financing in Brazil. We shall denote federalism as a system, which favours, not only the financing autonomy of the subunits, but also the reduction of regional inequalities through an efficient programme of tax transfers. Since the stabilization in 1994, there has been a re-centralization of the financial resources in federal government. Besides, credit supply fell until 2002. Although in Lula's administration credit supply increased sharply, there is no evidence that the political economy of regional policies in Brazil changed enough to foster growth in less developed regions in Brazil. Therefore, we also intend in this chapter to assess Lula's government with regard to credit availability to deal with regional imbalances. The analysis of credit concentration and its role in the depth of regional imbalances uses information at municipal level on credit supply and other variables obtained from the SISBACEN[3] database. As one can see, the outcome is a mixed figure: although the use of Constitutional Funds has improved during Lula's administration, the distribution of credit by the bank sector continues to be concentrated in the most developed regions.

This chapter is organized as follows. Sections 2 and 3 contain appraisals of federalism in Brazil and the Fiscal Responsibility Law. These aspects provide some empirical background for a discussion of Federal Funding and the role of credit at regional level focused on in sections 4 and 5. We close with some concluding notes and proposals for financing regional development.

2   Federalism, financing and regional development in Brazil

The Constitution of 1988 increased tax revenue of states and municipalities in Brazil, concluding a process of decentralization that started in the middle of the 1970s. The new Constitution tried to correct the distortions of the previous one and to rescue the principles of fiscal federalism lost with the tax reform of the first military government in the middle of the 1960s. With the merger of some taxes and the modernization of others, the intention was to build a modern structure, progressive and less unfair than the previous one. More than this, the chapter on taxes of the 1988 Constitution allowed for both more autonomy and an increase in the municipalities' tax revenue. It aimed also to reduce regional inequalities through the creation of special Funds for financing least developed regions (FNO, FCO and FNE). These funds would have guaranteed sources since they represented the quota-part of two important taxes, the IPI and IR.

From the viewpoint of taxes, tributes and improvements of the system, the new constitution presented few differences from the previous structure. There were no significant differences in terms of simplification and volume of tributes, but a reduction in number from 17 taxes to 15. However, the merger of six indirect taxes in one tax of enlarged base corrected some distortions and simplified collection. An important aspect concerning taxes on property, both urban and rural, was the possibility of the introduction of a progressive tax. Undoubtedly, this could have meant a great improvement compared to the previous structure, as it could have increased the fairness of the distribution of the tax onus on urban property.

As for the distribution of tax competences, the new Constitution represented an improvement in the tax revenue for the states and municipalities. According to Serra and Afonso (1992), the municipalities owned the benefits of the tax decentralization.

Regarding the states, the volume of taxes remained unchanged, except for the base of tax revenue, which was enlarged, mostly owing to the change of the ICM in ICMS (Value Added Tax – VAT). An important element in this enlargement was the possibility of an addition over the income tax due to the federal government for individual or firms. This addition amounted up to 5 per cent of the paid tax on profits and capital profits. Finally, the new Constitution enlarged the States Fund of Participation in the income tax and in the tax on industrialized products.

The municipalities, on the other hand, were the main beneficiaries in the share of the tax system, through the amplification of tax competences and transfers from the federal government and the states. Serra and Afonso (1992) notice that, even before the promulgation of the new constitution, there was already a process of increasing transfers from federal government to municipalities, besides the possibility of growing expenses through credit operations.

Regarding transfers, the most important modification was the amplification of the quota part of the ICMS (VAT) from 20 per cent to 25 per cent. It's also important to notice that this not only increased the percentage of transfers, but also enlarged the base of tax revenue. The proportion of transfers to municipalities' Fund of Participation rose from 17 per cent to 22.5 per cent, and the Tax on Financial Transactions (IOF) on the gold started was to be shared in 70 per cent on the municipalities. Finally, according to the Constitution of 1988 the federal government was prohibited from exempting municipal taxes, altering a common practice used during the military period, which severely hurt fiscal federalism.

As for the structure of expenses, the changes represented a better social control on the public budget. There were also restrictions on the public debt and on credit operations exceeding capital expenses. This process culminated in the promulgation of the Fiscal Responsibility Law (FRL) in 2000, which limits the augmentation of expenditures via debt-creation.

The period following the promulgation of the Constitution, particularly after the Real Plan, represented a decreasing capacity for financing the states and municipalities. The reasons were twofold: the rise in social demands resulting from an increase in unemployment and under-employment in metropolitan zones, and the centralizing policy implemented by the federal government. Besides, the tax competition between states and the municipalities in metropolitan regions, by increasing the unemployment, produced an elevation in demand for social expenditures, which the municipalities found difficult to afford as they were unable to increase their debt because of the constraints imposed by the Fiscal Responsibility Law.

Despite last year's economic stagnation, the tax burden in Brazil has been persistently growing since 1994. However, it is not equally distributed between the states. In fact, the federal government was the main beneficiary of taxes and federal contributions. From 1993 up to 2002, there was an elevation of almost 39 per cent, which does not find an equivalent at the international level. The main reasons for this behaviour are the policies for increasing social contributions and the positive effects of stabilization on the amount of tax revenue. Besides, this outstanding growth is also a consequence of improvements in federal tax revenue and inspection strategies.

Notwithstanding the difficulties of international comparison due to methodological differences in the measure of the tax burden, we may say that Brazil's levels of tax revenue are similar to developed countries. The largest tax burdens are those from European countries, exceeding, in some cases, 50 per cent of the GNP while USA's GTB is about 35 per cent of the GNP. In 2002, the GTB was 18.3 per cent in Mexico and 19.9 per cent in Chile.

The tax burden in Brazil can also be analysed from the point of view of distribution of tax resources and of taxes by incidence. The first case is important since despite the increase in the participation of the municipalities in the tax share following the 1988 Constitution, after the Real Plan the federal government has tried to re-centralize the distribution of tax resources and at the same time is relocating many federal expenses to municipalities.

Concerning the sharing of tributes by base of incidence, there was an outstanding increase in the share of indirect and cumulative tributes. The literature on equity of tax base demonstrates clearly that indirect taxes are easier to collect. However, it is important to note this kind of reinforcing the higher levels of income concentration in Brazil, which emanates mainly from the disregard of the consumer's distributive profile. This is precisely true in the Brazilian case. The tax incidence (direct and indirect) on income of individuals earning up to three times the minimum wage is higher if compared with individuals whose income is larger than ten times the minimum wage. This fact demonstrates the income-concentrating characteristic of the tax structure in Brazil.

The tax incidence on goods and services represents almost half of the total amount collected. It is worth while noting that the Cofins – Contribution for the Financing of Social Security – rose from 5.4 per cent, in the beginning of 1990s to around 11 per cent of the total tax revenue in 2002, more than duplicating its participation in the GNP in this period. The predominance of indirect taxes on goods and services is a typical example of the federal government strategy to speed up the tax collection. Indirect taxes are politically more viable for approval and have a high degree of productivity. This explains the increase in the participation of these taxes in the total tax revenue.

Furthermore, this strategy, when based on cumulative taxes, acts as a good mechanism to increase total tax revenue. However, this not only undermines equity principles, but also causes vertical conflicts, particularly when we observe that the cumulative taxes, mostly created in the last decade, are federal taxes. This is an important point, since the increase in gross tax burden (GTB) in Brazil, in the last ten years, came together with a tax recentralization. It is also note worthy that though the tax incidence on property and income in Brazil has increased in the last five years (particularly income tax), it is still very low, corresponding to around 8.5 per cent of the GNP and 24 per cent of the total tax revenue in 2002.

As already pointed out, the strategy of tax burden augmentation in Brazil in the last ten years decreased the share of states and municipalities over the tax allotment, resulting not only in an exasperation of the vertical and horizontal conflicts, but also in a negative impact on the ability to use tax transfers as a mechanism to reduce regional imbalances.

The share of the federal government grew from 61.7 per cent of the total in 1995 to 64.1 per cent in 2003. Nevertheless, after the voluntary transfers and other types of transfers, the municipalities' share increased to the detriment of states and federal government. Actually, an increase in the municipalities' share would not be a concern per se. The central question here is whether a great volume of voluntary transfers imposes on these sub-unities an unhealthy position of dependence on federal resources. It is important to note that the share of the municipalities in their own income revenue and in the available revenue rose after 1988, validating the argument that the Constitution of 1988 represented, particularly for municipalities, a better availability of tax resources.

For the states, however, the situation became worse, since the available revenues (in the enlarged concept) dropped from 27 per cent in 1997 to 24.6 per cent in 2003, accentuating the slow, although systematic, re-centralization process. The increase of GTB in this period obviously also represented an increase in the participation of the states in the tax revenue/GDP ratio. However, as already observed several times, an increase in public expenditure, as a result of higher social demands and relocation of more attributions to these sub-unities, acted as a counterbalance to the process of augmentation of the tax revenue. Not forgetting that we also must include the financial costs of state debts re-negotiated in the Fernando Henrique Cardoso (1995–2002) government as well as the limitations imposed by the FRL[4] on the increase of expenses.

Since the Constitution of 1988, particularly after Fernando Henrique Cardoso's (hereafter FHC) years, several tributes of strictly federal competence were created and re-articulated without a distribution sharing to the federative sub-unities. More than this, the transfers of federal attributions represented additional responsibilities of great proportions for these sub-unities, particularly the municipalities.

As a result of the policies implemented by the federal government in the last years, the decomposition of the sales tax burden into value added tributes and cumulative taxes points out to the decreasing tendency of the value added tributes, and to the augmentation of cumulative taxes, mainly the general sales taxes.

There has been excessive creation of cumulative social contributions, as they allow a rapid increase in the amount of both the tax revenue assembled and the availability of resources. The clear re-centralization of tax resources and the increase in States' and municipalities' expenses, particularly after 1995, which worsened further after 1999, has led to increased financial troubles. The result is a perverse combination: elevation of the GTB simultaneously with the collapse in the participation of the sub-spheres in resource distribution. We can add to the already tricky situation in terms of financing capacity of these federative units, an increase in expenses along with a federative horizontal competition.

3   The fiscal responsibility law and its impact on regional financing

The Fiscal Responsibility Law (FRL), from 4 May 2000, aims at a more balanced and transparent administration of public resources. The administrators of executive, legislative and judicial powers, as well as the Federal Attorney and the three spheres of government (federal, state and municipal), are now responsible for their budgets and targets, in a way to avoid unmanageable expenses without the endorsement of the federal government. As regards control and accountability of public expenses, the FRL is an indisputable advancement. However, as an instrument of demand encouragement it has clear limitations. In this sense, allocation of public expenses as an instrument of development and mitigation of regional disparities challenges the law's major objectives. Actually, the theoretical approach behind the FRL restrains (although not explicitly) the fiscal instruments needed for economic cycle stabilization in a Keynesian way.

The FRL as originally conceived (which does not mean that it could be modified), depended on several items: a government that guarantees fiscal balance as a means towards full efficiency, a debt/GDB rapport that is compatible with inter-temporal solvency, institutional reforms that should ensure property rights and legal institutional conditions to assure private investors. A detailed analysis of its costs and benefits to fiscal policies is a subject of this topic.

Undoubtedly, the Fiscal Responsibility Law (FRL) constitutes a dividing wall in Brazilian public administration. It introduces new management practices for public finances as it establishes clear and precise rules for the control of expenses and public debt. It compels rulers to account for their acts or omissions on a regular basis and values routine planning in fiscal administration.

In addition, the FRL normalizes and modernizes the federative vertical relations. In fact, despite the efforts of democratization behind the reforms in the 1988 Constitution, which provide more autonomy and a better financial structure for states and municipalities, the horizontal and vertical federative conflicts did not lessen. On the contrary, the absence of clear rules steering the relationship between federative units aggravated the conflicts. Furthermore, state budgetary deficits were transferred to the federal government, breaking a valued principle to federative systems, the independence between federative units. So, the Constitution of 1988 created a system that increased the autonomy of states and municipalities, though it was not able to guarantee responsibilities to these sub-units. The FRL tries to correct part of this problem.

Understanding the role of the FRL in public and regional development financing as well as in the allocation of public expenses is important to avoid hasty evaluations, both positive and negative ones. In addition, it is necessary to find better ways to use public resources in accordance to the limits imposed by the law. Among the important innovations brought about by the FRL we point out:

(a) limitations in the expenses with the salaries, establishing not only the amount to be spent by each level of government according to the net receipt, but also – and that's a novelty – the percentage due to the executive, legislative and judicial power, removing the previous distortions mainly in state governments;
(b) reaffirmation of more rigid limits which were already established by the federal senate for public debt, indicating that officials not behaving responsibly would be punished equally and with more rigidity;
(c) definition of fiscal annual targets and a requirement to present quarterly reports of fiscal administration, creating also other transparency mechanisms such as the Council of Fiscal Management (to be constituted);
(d) establishment of control mechanisms for public finances in electoral years;
(e) prevention of financial help amongst the federal government and subnational governments, creating a clearer relationship between the federative units and recovering the idea of fiscal federalism.

The five items quoted above are of basic importance to increase the social control on public expenses, which impose accountability, as well as strengthening the federalism. One of the points that deserves distinction is the public debt. It is well known that debt is a recognized fiscal instrument of increasing expenses, which can be used as an anti-cyclical mechanism. The federal government as well as some states and municipalities can use this instrument to increase public expenditure in order to avoid stagnation and recession. However, the FRL, by establishing excessively rigid and non-negotiable mechanisms, can lead to a fall in public investments. As a matter of fact, the monetary policy of the central bank, in order to be compatible with the rigid targets of inflation, increases the debt by issuing bonds of the federal government and some states, which – given the limits of debt – is translated into a reduction of expenses particularly investments. In this way, there is an incompatibility between monetary and fiscal policy objectives. In order to maintain the debt inside the limits of the FRL there is a reduction of non-financing public spending to levels that are incompatible with the maintenance of the administrative engine. To sum up, from a macroeconomic point of view, the FRL combined with tight monetary policy, imposes significant restrictions on federative units, making it difficult for investments and for regional development policy that is based on public expenses. It's worth noting that the Constitutional Funds of Financing are already set up as an important instrument of reduction of these imbalances, and, in theory, they are not directly affected by the FRL. However, to the extent that the tight monetary policies are associated with a restrictive fiscal policy at federal level, it will affect the short-term economic growth and consequently the revenue of taxes and the sources of financing for regional development.

However, the FRL modernizes and democratizes the instruments of fiscal management of public finances. According to Khair (2000), the FRL rely on four axes: projection, transparency, control and accountability. In other words, it affects not only the fiscal results but also the way the public finances are administered. In order to understand the impacts of the FRL in all dimensions it is necessary to consider other indicators, even those not immediately quantifiable. Hence, it is possible to connect the FRL with several axes of democratization and control of public finances.

Here we intend to emphasize the efficiency and the effectiveness of the law with respect to the four axes pointed above and to incorporate another one, which is related to the prohibition of help between governments, an essential innovation in Brazilian federative relationship. The five axes are the following: (1) plans to manage revenues, expenditures and debts; (2) publicity of the fiscal management reports; (3) control of expenditures and debt; (4) accountability, and (5) the elimination of the predatory characteristics of the financial relationship through the new rule that prohibits help between governments. To sum up, we intend to point out the necessity of valuing the FRL in a multidimensional perspective.

One of the most important aspects of this Law is article 19, which imposes limits for total personnel expenditures. If the expenses of federative units exceed the prudential limit (95 per cent of the legal limit), several actions will be prohibited. For example: the concession of advantages, raising salaries, any salary adjustment or revision; the creation of offices, jobs or functions, new admissions of public servants as well as any type of admission or employment of personnel. If the reduction does not reach the maximum limit after the legal term, the officials will not receive the voluntary transfers, credit operations will contract, and other guarantees will be suspended.

However, the FRL promotes inflexibility in the way federative units can spend their resources. Despite its importance in controlling expenditures – and we know that Brazil has a long-time practice of bad public administration of states and municipalities – the FRL restrain the use of an anti-cyclical fiscal policy. The basis of these policies is such that in periods of economic slowing down, it is convenient to the state to increase expenses to support the level of the aggregated demand. In effect, Keynesian policies use the anti-cyclical effect of public spending to moderate the harmful effects on income and GNP when the economy is slowing down. Increasing public spending (running into debt via emission of bonds) can produce a positive effect on the aggregated demand, and the rise in income allows subsequently for an increase of tax revenue. In periods of growing income, public spending can (and it must) lessen. The FRL, such as approved, does not take into account the importance of the anti-cyclical effect of expenditure. In this sense, it ends up as an additional mechanism that eventually can aggravate the fiscal and financial situation of the federation. This happens because of the iron-clad imposition of the inter-temporal budgetary balance in order to ensure primary surpluses that are compatible with the reduction of debt/GDP rapport.

From the point of view of regional imbalances, the FRL contributes to destabilization of regional development policies. In a setting of growing commercial and financial openness, market integration as well as increasing productivity, the productive activities tend to agglomerate. This happens mainly because capital tends to flow to consolidated and more lucrative sectors. The consequence is an increase in regional concentration of productive activities. In effect, without public policies favouring regional development and mitigation of income and wealth concentration, both regional imbalances and concentration of income and wealth will worsen. The FRL, despite its principles of increasing the democratization of information and budget may turn out to be another inhibiting instrument for policies aiming at moderate regional income and wealth inequalities.

4   Sources of financing regional development in Brazil

The sources of regional financing in Brazil are characterized by a myriad of instruments and institutions that do not always attain efficiency and perfectly utilize available resources. To the constitutional financing funds we add the fiscal funds for regional development (formerly linked to the SUDAM (Superintendence for the Development of the Amazonia), SUDENE (Superintendence for the Development of the Northeast) as well as some support agencies such as BNDES (National Bank for Social and Economic Development), CODEVASF (Company for the Development of Saint Francisco Valley), DNOCS (Department of Works against the Drought) and SUFRAMA

(Manaus Free-Trade Bureau), amongst others. Thus, the absence of a regional de-concentration process in Brazil, particularly after the 1988 Constitution, cannot be attributed to a lack of financial instruments. Quite the opposite, as data on financing funds can demonstrate, the variety of subsidizing instruments is possibly one of the reasons for the inefficiency of the process. Besides, one cannot disconnect financing which results from economic development.

In recent years, public financing in Brazil was limited by contracting fiscal and monetary policies. The high interest rates stimulate and support banks to apply for public titles in order to guarantee a better resource administration. As a consequence, the credit operations were affected, and so were the projects that could possibly be financed. This becomes clear when we analyse the relationship between annual transfers from the National Treasury to the funds and the amount loaned by the funds.

Table 9.1 shows the transfers from the National Treasury to Fiscal Financing Funds since 1994. It is possible to observe that the transfers to the FINAM (Investment Fund for Amazonia) did not undergo abrupt falls as did the transfers to the FINOR (Investment Fund for the Northeast) after 2001. The transfers to the FINOR and FUNRES (Investment fund for the Recovery of the Espirito Santo) showed an evolution close to the behaviour of the

Table 9.1   Transfers from the National Treasury to the investment fiscal funds

Year	FINAM	FINOR	In thousands of R$ from the year 2000
			FUNRES
1994	–	177.270	–
1995	331.836	336.079	11.897
1996	156.646	402.064	14.988
1997	257.263	468.044	22.802
1998	346.119	410.543	13.334
1999	401.930	329.595	18.576
2000	549.656	428.748	16.663
2001	(*)	119.530	(*)
2002*	440.000	174.322	(*)
2003*	465.000	(*)	(*)

Notes: * Refers to transfers to FDA
(*) Data unavailable
1. The Fiscal Funds FINAM and FINOR were closed to new projects in 05/02/2001 together with the extinction of SUDENE and SUDAM.
2. The ADA (Agency for the Development of Amazon) and ADENE (Agency for the Development of the North-east) were created.
3. The FDA and the FDN, replacing the FINAM and the FINOR respectively were also created.
4. Transfers from STN to FINOR after 2001 refers only to projects already in execution.
Sources: STN/SUDAM/BASA/SUDENE/BNB/GERES/BANDES

economy, collapsing after 1999. The same did not happen with the FINAM. According to Crocco (2003), despite the smaller share of the northern region in the GNP compared to the northeast region, this growth rate was higher in the 1994-2003 period. As a result, a vicious circle of stagnation and fall in the credit and financing to these regions was established.[5]

The transfers from the National Treasury to constitutional financing funds (FNO, FCO and FNE) – the most important financing instruments for regional development as they are linked to the IPI (Tax on Industrialized Products) and IR (Income Tax) revenues – can be examined in Table 9.2. In 17 years of the funds' existence, the total transfers exceeded the significant amount of R$ 30 billion, at December 2005 prices. Notwithstanding the relative stagnation from 1994 to 2000, after 2001 we observe a systematic elevation in the transfers. This suggests that the economic growth of the 1994–98 period was not followed by an increase in the tax revenues composing these funds. Actually, as already pointed out, the GTB remained nearly stable in the 1994–98 period (around 29.5 per cent of the GNP), presenting a systematic growth since then. The transfers to the constitutional funds can prove this fact. Despite the GNP inflections in 1999, 2002 and 2003, the transfers increased, mainly because of the tax policies implemented by federal government.[6]

Notwithstanding the increase of the transfers from the Treasury to the constitutional funds since 2001, there is a little difference between FHC's

Table 9.2 Annual transfers from the National Treasury to constitutional financing funds

Year	Fund			
	FCO	FNO	FNE	R$ mil
				Total
1994	389.810	389.810	1.169.435	1.949.054
1995	400.462	400.462	1.201.381	2.002.306
1996	376.285	376.285	1.128.858	1.881.428
1997	388.344	388.344	1.165.046	1.941.734
1998	394.829	394.829	1.184.480	1.974.139
1999	406.827	406.827	1.220.477	2.034.132
2000	453.747	453.747	1.361.262	2.268.756
2001	548.253	548.253	1.044.756	2.741.262
2002	630.393	630.393	1.891.179	3.151.965
2003	638.814	637.269	1.912.338	3.188.421
2004	722.970	722.970	2.168.907	3.614.847
2005	848.923	848.923	2.546.769	4.244.616
Total	6.199.658	6.198.113	18.594.888	30.992.660

Note: Values update by BTN and TR in December 2005 prices
Sources: National Treasury Secretary (STN) – and Ministry of National Integration

administrations and Lula's. The average growth rate of these transfers during the first three years of Lula's government was lower than that observed for the second period of FHC's administration (10.43 per cent on average for the first one compared to 12.4 per cent for the second). This happened despite the fact that the average growth rate of GDP during Lula's administration had been higher than during FHC's (2.6 per cent and 2.1 per cent, accordingly).

While transfers from the Treasury remained stable until 2000, rising significantly afterwards, the contracted values and the operations administered by the funds increased after 1994. However, as shown in Table 9.3, there is a sharp distinction between the administration of FHC and Lula's administration. During the first administration of FHC (1995–98) the annual average of operations administrated by the funds had been 117 849 (units as in table). In the second term of FHC this average had been reduced to 82 250. In contrast, during 2003 to 2005 this average was 283 517. Taking into account that the average contracted values had increased between these two periods (from R$ 1 574 750.00 to R$ 1 945 831.00 accordingly) implying a higher concentration in financing projects. In fact, this behaviour fits well into the strategy of public development banks. By increasing efficiency and reducing the leverage, they also reduce their exposure to high risk credit.

However, this pattern has been changed during the first three years of Lula's administration. As shown in Table 9.3, the number of credit operations by the funds has an annual average of 283 517, implying a growth of 244 per cent. This outcome is a result of the change in the strategy of the administration of the funds, which has been more focused in increasing the number of credit operations in contrast to the search for efficiency by applying the Funds' resource to the financial market. Moreover, the annual average contract values have also increased in Lula's administration, jumping from R$ 1 945 831 to R$ 5 273 849.

This strategy has been effected by the increase in the number of credit operations for cooperatives and small firms, especially in the northeast, the poorest region of the country. During the second term of FHC's administration the average number of credit operations for this type of firms was 76 327, increasing to 308 223 during Lula's period. The northeast region, in his term, was responsible for 78 per cent of these operations, showing a region development policy for this region based on incentives to this type of firm. However, despite this effort to improve the number of credit operations for those who are disadvantaged and searching for credit in the traditional financial systems (cooperatives and small firms), the contracted values still concentrated in operations with medium and large firms. In 2005, the latter of these were responsible for 64 per cent of the total credit supplied by the constitutional funds in Brazil.

Table 9.4 demonstrates this change in the strategy of the constitutional financing funds' administrators (Bank of Brazil, Bank the Brazilian Northeast (BNB) and Bank of the Amazonia (BASA)) after the beginning of Lula's administration. As one can see, until 2002, the FNE loans were, on average,

Table 9.3 Number of credit operations (OP) and contracted values (CV)

Year	Fund						CV in thousands of R$	
	FCO		FNO		FNE		Total	
	OP	CV	OP	CV	OP	CV	OP	CV
1989/1993	26 035	1 322 186	16 928	787 629	144 316	4 893 854	187 279	7 003 669
1994	12 825	331 235	20 674	527 878	64 652	949 708	98 151	1 808 821
1995	11 906	200 800	13 533	371 492	67 882	1 040 373	93 321	1 612 665
1996	15 179	253 874	14 486	213 036	80 616	1 303 763	110 281	1 770 673
1997	24 867	348 001	6 735	79 212	52 445	905 242	84 047	1 332 455
1998	30 400	430 584	15 629	207 287	137 720	945 334	183 749	1 583 205
1999	19 015	196 169	23 156	510 924	86 252	749 454	128 423	1 456 547
2000	12 963	332 251	31 298	809 055	47 621	660 512	91 882	1 801 818
2001	21 901	1 111 816	10 006	517 726	16 583	345 821	48 490	1 975 363
2002	20 986	1 595 912	14 125	671 371	25 093	282 312	60 204	2 549 595
2003	9095	988.320	23 587	1.142 001	24 899	1 078 813	57 581	3 209 134
2004	13 301	1 215 602	38 364	1.370 962	173 486	3 326 775	225 151	5 913 339
2005	13 657	1 487 607	22 605	988 430	531 557	4 223 037	567 819	6 699 074
Total	232 130	9 814 357	251 126	8 197 003	1 453 122	20 704 998	1 936 378	38 716 358

Note: Values updated by BTN and TR, in March 2005 prices.
Sources: Bank of Brazil, Bank of Amazon and Bank of Northeast reports.

Table 9.4   Contracted values/transfers from STN

Year	Fund			Total
	FCOa	FNO	FNE	
1994	85.0	135.4	81.2	92.8
1995	50.1	92.8	86.6	80.5
1996	67.5	56.6	115.5	94.1
1997	89.6	20.4	77.7	68.6
1998	109.1	52.5	79.8	80.2
1999	48.2	125.6	61.4	71.6
2000	73.2	178.3	48.5	79.4
2001	202.8	94.4	21.0	72.1
2002	253.2	106.5	14.9	80.9
2003	154.7	179.2	56.4	100.6
2004	168.1	189.6	153.4	163.6
2005	175.2	116.4	165.8	157.8
Annual Average				
1998/1995	79.1	55.6	89.9	80.9
2002/1999	144.3	126.2	36.5	76.0
2005/2003	166.0	161.8	125.2	140.7

Source: Ministry of National Integration

well below the values transferred annually by the National Treasury. This behaviour is the corollary of the defensive strategy adopted by public banks during FHC administration regarding the risks of credit. In fact, when lending to private borrowers, the public bank prefers to operate with public titles, which are more profitable and less risky. This strategy has huge consequences for the northeast region (the one that is the aim of the FNE), because of the weakness of its economy.

Therefore, there is an asymmetry between macroeconomic and regional development policies, and the search for better efficiency and less risk by banking institutions. As a consequence, there is a reduction in both credit supply and demand. The low dynamism of the local private sector, combined with a credit system which is not much articulated, generates problems in the effective demand, compelling both the public and banks to favour liquidity. Then a vicious circle of small volume of local credit (concentrated in more developed regions), low demand for resources and low economic dynamism is installed. Thus, the funds do not fulfil their central objective of supporting development projects to reduce regional inequalities. Hence, financing and credit are crucial for the success of regional development policy. More than merely a mirror of the inequalities, credit is fundamental in stimulating the effective demand.

From 2003 to 2005 the picture changes a little bit. As one can see, there is a trend showing an effort to increase the share of loans in relation to the amount of money transferred to the funds by the National Treasury. During the second term of the FHC administration, on average, only 76 per cent of the annual resources transferred to the funds were transformed in loans. In contrast, from 2003 to 2005, this relation increased to 140 per cent. This increase is most noted in the case of FNE. In the last year of the FHC administration only 14 per cent of the resources transferred by the National Treasury to FNE were transformed into loans. During Lula's administration these values are: 56.4 per cent, 153.4 per cent and 165.8 per cent.

The data discussed above show that during Lula's administration the public banks that administrated the constitutional funds for regional development changed their strategy related to these funds, looking more for increases in loans than on the pure and static efficiency.[7] Although it is impossible to say that this strategy will help to reduce regional disparities – to do this, it is necessary to analyse what projects this money is being utilized in – while no one can deny that it is a necessary step to achieve this objective.

We have tried to show that the financing funds have a central role in regional development policy. However, the results depend on the recuperation of state planning capacity as well as on the coordination between federal government, public and private banks, states and local authorities. As already mentioned in section 2, the asymmetric and conflicting character of the federalism in Brazil, along with the limitations imposed by the FRL, point to the need for more clarity and efficiency in the coordination of public and private agents. Thus, it is important to analyse the role of credit and financial concentration as the corollary of regional imbalances in Brazil. A study focusing on financing regional development must concentrate not only on the federative discussion and financing funds but also on the nature of financial inequalities in Brazil. This aspect is discussed in the next topic.

5 Credit and bank regional system

5.1 Bank system, credit and the centre–periphery relationship

One of the most common neglects in studies about regional imbalances is the role of money and credit. The theoretical discussion on the subject – including that which is strictly connected with the Keynesian tradition, for which the regional inequalities presuppose cumulative processes (Kaldor, 1994, Dixon and Thirlwall, 1975) – tends to disregard the role of money and credit in regional development. In this context, regional effects of the bank concentration process in Brazil after 1994 has not received adequate attention in the literature; Amado (1998) is one of the few exceptions.

As initially formulated by Dow (1982, 1987), the process of cumulative causation, much discussed theoretically and empirically by Kaldor and Myrdal, finds in the financial system an important instrument of intensification of regional imbalances. The region is a locus where the expectations are shaped and, as the levels of private investment are sensitive to these expectations, in some regions, identified as more risky, the economic agents tend to favour liquidity. Therefore, these regions may experience inadequate levels of effective demand. As the credit supply and demand are directly related not only to monetary policy, but also to borrowers' and banks' defensive attitudes, least developed regions tend to present, through the effects on monetary and income multiplier, less financial dynamism. As a result, there is a concentration of credit in more developed regions, since they are characterized by less uncertainty and less liquidity preference. Since this aspect is important to economic development, it is not possible to neglect the dynamic of the financial sector at the regional level. In fact, before reflecting the "real economy" at the regional level, this sector significantly influences the path of regional inequalities.

The peripheral economies are characterized by a stagnant economy, with under-developed markets predominating the primary sector and low technological content manufactures as well as an immature financial system.[8] Its dynamism is dictated by the volume of exports to the centre. All these characteristics generate uncertainty about the economic performance of the region leading to a higher liquidity preference. The uncertainty about the future leads economic agents to seek more liquid assets as a way of protection. Moreover, their investment decisions are delayed until a more favourable economic setting (Dow, 1993 and Dow and Rodríguez-Fuentes, 2003). Concerning credit supply, it is plausible to suppose that the banking system is under-developed in peripheral regions and consequently less able to supply credit. Besides, the residents' low levels of income in these regions restrict access to the banks, decreasing the amount of deposits (as a proportion of the income) and increasing the retention of paper-money by the public.

On the other hand, a central region is characterized by a prosperous economy and a sophisticated financial system. It is also a region with a productive system historically dominated by the industrial and services sector. Furthermore, it locates the financial institutions, making credit supply easier compared with peripheral regions. This entire picture increases security and confidence to invest in less liquid (and more profitable) assets leading to less liquidity preference in more prosperous regions. In effect, it is possible to infer that in central regions there will be higher proclivity towards demand as well as towards the supply of credit. As a result, the process of cumulative causation takes place such that a decrease in the centre's liquidity preference reduces even further the supply of credit at the periphery. This happens because the credit supply will move to places where there is a higher demand (Crocco, 2005).

In order to understand the dynamics of the regional financing system and its relationship with the economic dynamics it is important to figure out what is called by Ron Martin (1999, p. 9) 'a geographic circuit of the money'. This circuit can be characterized by two aspects. The first is the location structure of the financial system, which is directly connected with the urban structure and its centrality in a particular region. The urban hierarchy determines a financial hierarchy, in other words, an agglomeration of banking institutions in a more developed place would also offer more sophisticated services.

Another aspect is the so-called institutional geography of the financial system, which refers to the dissimilarities in the institutional models between countries. These differences affect banking development. There are several implications resulting from the difference between a model of regional banks (small banks, with headquarters acting only in the region), as in the United States and Italy, and a model composed by large national banks, as in England and Brazil.

Alessandrini and Zazzaro (1999) and Martin (1999), among others, affirm that local banks tend to be more involved with the local economy being more affected by its economic oscillations. On the other hand, national banks manage to protect themselves from local economic instability, compensating losses in these regions with profits in other localities. Banks of this type, with headquarters in the centre and acting also at the periphery, are more reticent concerning the extension of credit to the periphery. The reasons are the higher volatility in the dissemination of information. In this way, different institutional geographies can produce different processes of money circulation (savings, credit and applications).

It is also worth emphasizing that, in general, peripheral economies have an informal sector more important compared to the central regions. As a result, the banks' ratio of cash-deposits is higher, generating a smaller monetary multiplier and consequently difficulties in accessing credit. This vicious circle makes investment still more difficult in peripheral regions.

Brazil, as pointed out by Crocco (2004a), has strong regional financial disparities, which is a reflex of its economic inequality (*latu sensu*). Bank agencies are concentrated in most developed regions, so that these regions have a higher participation in the amount of deposits and credits. Taking as a starting point the relationship between centre–periphery and its credit and monetary characteristics we intend to analyse the regional dimension of financing in Brazil, demonstrating also the relevant role of credit concentration and enhanced liquidity on regional imbalances in Brazil.

5.2 Regional and financial inequalities in Brazil

To assess the regional influence of the financial variables, we extracted data from the SISBACEN (Central Bank System of Information) database. The database contains information on monthly statistics from 1988 to 2005 for all Federation Units. The data refers to main accounting items (assets and liabilities) of the financial system, with the aggregated monthly values for each operation for all local financial institutions. Through this database it is possible to evaluate the banking regional concentration and its effects on regional inequalities in Brazil.

By now we have already examined the financing funds for regional development; hereafter we focus on the role of the financial system, particularly private banks. To date there is no well-consolidated system to finance development in Brazil. An historical retrospect shows that the financial private sector, as states Alves Jr. (2002, p.332), *'was very competent to survive instability, but it did not appear able to produce the amount of credit and investment funding necessary to promote sustainable economic growth'*. It is from this perspective that we intend to seek ways to block this adverse trajectory. The state intervention, mainly in credit supply can open 'windows of opportunity' to increase private credit in less developed regions and, in this way, lessen the harmful effects of financial concentration from the perspective of reducing the regional disparities.

From the sum of two accounts from the balance available in the SISBACEN database, the Loans and Deducted Bonds account and the Financing account, we calculated an index of credit concentration by regions, taking as a basis the sum for the whole country. Table 9.5 shows the values for each region for 1991, 1997, 2003 and 2005.

It is clear, once more, there is a difference between FHC's administration and Lula's administration. First of all, it is important to stress the strong predominance of the southeast region and the growth of its concentration, varying from 66.87 per cent to 75.62 per cent until 2003. It is no surprise that São Paulo State concentrates most of the credit (more than 60 per cent of the total credit in 2003). It is worth noting that in high inflation periods (and this could be due to indexation problems), the credit concentration was much smaller than in the period following monetary stabilization. Maps of credit concentration can demonstrate the process of increasing concentration in the 1990s. To bank concentration, observed after the Real Plan (Alves Jr, 2002), we can add a concentration of credit supply. Secondly, it is important to note that the data for 2005, the third year of Lula's administration, shows an improvement in the regional distribution of credit compared to 2003. The southeast region had a decrease of 17 percentage points in its relative share. However, despite the fact that all others regions had shown an increase in their participation, especially the south region (from 10.4 per cent

Table 9.5   Index of credit concentration by regions unit – Brazil

| Region | Fund | | | |
	1991	1997	2003	2005
North	1.80	1.27	1.59	2.71
Northeast	10.94	7.13	6.95	8.83
Centre-West	9.95	4.54	5.13	9.65
South	10.44	9.46	10.41	20.16
Southeast	66.87	77.60	75.92	58.65

Sources: Laboratory of Studies in Money and Territory (LEMTe); Center for Regional Development and Planning – CEDEPLAR

to 20.2 per cent), the change in the north and northeast regions are low (from 1.6 per cent to 2.7 per cent in the north and from 6.8 per cent to 8.8 per cent in the northeast.

What is important is that a well articulated process of economic de-concentration and reduction of regional imbalances can only be possible concomitantly with a process of financial de-concentration. However, without the participation of public development banks in this process it is not likely that the attempts will be successful.

5.2.3 Financial intermediation and financial imbalances

Through the annual regional accounts, which are GNP indicators for each state and corresponding economic activity, it is possible to obtain data from 1998 to 2001 about the activities related to financial intermediation at the regional level. The concept of financial intermediation was introduced by the IBGE (Brazilian Institute of Geography and Statistics). Table 9.6 shows the participation of the regions in the economic activity as a whole and in financial intermediation.

We find remarkable the high participation of the centre-west in financial intermediation activity. However, this is due to the fact that many operations of the Central Bank, Federal Savings Bank and Bank of Brazil, as well as the National Treasury accounted for the Federal District – the capital of Brazil – which belongs to centre-west region. Consequently, the values for this region's participation are overestimated.

Table 9.6 also demonstrates that geographic concentration in financial activities is more important than concentration in economic activity. Besides, the degree of concentration of financial activities increased along the period of analysis. This happens because financial services tend to concentrate in large economic centres. The economic concentration in the southeast varied from 57.7 per cent in 1998 to 55.6 per cent in 2003 while the financial concentration

Table 9.6 Participation of regions on the added value of total activities and financial intermediation – Brazil

Region	Year					
	1998		2002		2003	
	All activities	Financial intermediation	All activities	Financial intermediation	All activities	Financial intermediation
Brazil	100.0	100.0	100.0	100.0	100.0	100.0
North	4.5	1.5	4.9	1.6	4.9	1.7
Northeast	13.1	7.3	13.4	9.1	13.6	7.9
Centre-West	7.1	17.9	7.6	9.6	7.5	8.8
South	17.6	11.6	17.8	14.7	18.6	13.6
Southeast	57.7	61.6	56.4	65.0	55.6	68.0

Source: IBGE

increased from 61.6 per cent to 68 per cent in the same period. In the northern region, the less representative at the national level, economic concentration varied from 4.5 per cent to 4.9 per cent and financial concentration from 1.5 per cent to 1.7 per cent in the same period. The Manaus Free-Trade Zone and the extractive activities in this region can explain these results. The small share of financial intermediation is explained, as for other less developed states, by the leaks of credit to more developed regions. In fact, although the production can take place in a particular region, as the financial system in Brazil is centralized and lacks regional banks (except the investment banks), part of the financing activities takes place in large centres like São Paulo. This fact corroborates the theoretical argument discussed above that the leaks in the financial sector tend to aggravate regional imbalances.

It is important to note that São Paulo is the state where the part of financial intermediation in the value added of productive activities and services is the largest, 10.1 per cent in 2003 (against 8.2 per cent in 1998). In the northern region we find the states where the relevance of financial intermediation in the economy is less important. In 2003 (the last data available), all states in this region, except for Tocantins (4.1 per cent in 2001), had participation of the financial activity below 3 per cent.

This behaviour corroborates the argument that peripheral regions tend to prefer liquidity and consequently experience less supply and demand for credit. At the same time they also under-use the bank sector in productive activities (less financial intermediation). The absence of a robust financial system to finance local economic activities supports the vicious circle of stagnation and informality in the least developed regions. This environment makes it harder to overcome regional inequalities.

Hence, the empirical evidence supports the hypothesis that a bank system based on large national banks as in Brazil, stimulates bank concentration. Nevertheless, because their headquarters are localized in the economic centres (the southeast, particularly São Paulo in Brazil), they feed and accentuate the industrial concentration process.

Owing to more stability and less uncertainty, the logic of the market leads to concentration of credit in the central region. Therefore, firms in that region are privileged with better access to credit and diversified bank services. However, in Brazil, there is an aggravating factor: the industrialization of the peripheral regions was stimulated by the government in such a way that activities in those places started mainly as branches of enterprises whose headquarters were in the centre. Thus, the credit operations happen mainly in the headquarters and the leaking of deposits is high. Again, there is a predominance of a vicious circle that, in the absence of intervention, tends to perpetuate itself.

6   Conclusions

Although it may seem simple at first sight, the relationship between regional imbalances and financial system is not trivial. In fact, if credit concentration is the corollary of regional imbalances in Brazil, the dynamics of public and banks' liquidity preference imposes more awareness in the formulation of regional development policies. The financing of regional development policy in Brazil cannot be understood without considering its connection to the fiscal mechanisms of public financing, to the Fiscal Responsibility Law and to the nature of the federalism.

In fact, the debate on regional development policies in Brazil must include broader issues, such as the articulation of the banking system (public and private), the characteristics of tax resources distribution, and the limitations of public expenses imposed by the FRL. The role of the State, despite its distortions, is crucial in this arrangement since financing policies for regional development depends on the government. Although it is not our purpose here to discuss this point, we must not forget that in Brazil the share of the state in policies for regional development led to huge distortions. It benefited the local elite and sustained the stagnation of the poor regions. These effects can be reduced through the institutionalization of financing policies based on targets and results, where the creation of new credit supply will depend on goals accomplished by the projects.

The results obtained in this research demonstrate the importance of rethinking the strategy of use of the constitutional and fiscal financing funds for regional development. These funds must be used in their entirety in order to avoid transfers from the National Treasury being kept in the public banks and used for operations of better efficiency, but inefficient from the point of view of being public instruments for increasing credit supply.

In the same way, the existence of a competitive federative system[9] as well as the requirements of the FRL goes against the most efficient policies of regional development. It would be naive to make the FRL responsible for the difficulties of increasing public expenses and rendering regional development policies not viable. The regional imbalances in Brazil are well known and certainly they have not worsened in recent years because of limitations imposed by the FRL. However, it is clear that fiscal policies preventing public investment, especially when combined with restraining monetary policies, produce harmful effects on economic growth in the short term and consequently, on long-term development.[10] This, plus an 'obsession for the fiscal balance' policy generates an amplification of the regional imbalances. The main reason for this is the fact that investments and augmentation of credits in less developed regions are risky and have a lower return rate.

Finally, it is worth emphasizing the effect of the credit system on regional disparities. Confirming the theoretical argument, the empirical results for Brazil, using the SISBACEN database, reveal the important role of the financial system as a component of those inequalities. In fact, the concentration of credit in more developed regions (mainly the southeast region and São Paulo State); the liquidity preference, both of banks and public in the northern and northeast regions – and its effects on credit supply and demand – and, finally, the relationship of these variables with the financial intermediation, demonstrate the importance of the financial system and credit for regional development.

From the connection between the three elements summarized above the policy proposals must recognize the importance of the financial system regulations, of the tax resources distribution and of the institutional arrangement for public expenses. In this way, this subject must be introduced in the regional debate instead of being treated only from the macroeconomic point of view.

Finally, the answer to the question in title of this chapter is yes: Lula's government has changed the way regional development policies and credit have been carried out in Brazil. Although economic policy in Lula's administration has not changed the orthodox prescriptions carried out by the FHC government, the analysis here shows some differences in 2003–06 period: on the one hand, the use of constitutional funds has improved during the Lula's administration. On the other hand, the distribution of credit by the bank sector continues to be concentrated in the most developed regions.

Notes

1   The authors would like to thank, without implications, Sueli Moro, Melissa Menezes, and João Romero for helpful comments.
2   The Fiscal Responsibility Law, from 5 May 2000, establishes the relationship among federal government, municipalities, and states in Brazil. It will be discussed in more detail below.
3   Database from the Brazilian Central Bank.
4   These data can be obtained in Jayme Jr and Santos (2004).
5   Besides these funds, there are indirect mechanisms of regional development financing spread by several institutions. As examples we mention the Codevasf, the Suframa, the DNOCS and the BNDES (Crocco, 2003, p.319).
6   It is worth noting that in the 1994–98 period, the GTB remained stable, so simple growth in the GNP could produce an elevation in the tax revenue and as a consequence, in the transfers to the funds. The probable explanations for the stagnation of federal transfers to the funds in this period are the low dynamics of the sectors responsible for collecting the tax revenues and the stagnation in the taxable income.
7   It is important to note that the interest rates charged in the loans using these Constitutional Funds are much lower than the market interest rate paid in the financial markets for public bounds. This implies that from the perspective of a pure and static concept of efficiency it is much better for banks to lend the Funds' resources to the government.
8   Even considering a national financing system without regional banks, its possible to believe that financial innovations implemented in central regions will only be available to peripheral regions after a time lag.
9   Competitive federalism stands for several federative sub-spheres trying to benefit from the possibilities to increase their own receipts while the federal government tries to create mechanisms to reduce tax transfers. Typical cases of federative competition are the fiscal war and the increase in the tax burden by the federal government through the creation of contributions not submitted to sharing as COFINS and CSLL.

10 About the mistaken mix of economic policies in Brazil in recent years, it is worth emphasizing that a restraining monetary policy base and high interest rates magnify fiscal imbalances through increasing public debt cost. Confronted with the necessity of reducing the debt/GDP ratio to obtain more credibility in financial markets, they find it impossible to operate with a balanced fiscal policy. In the attempt to reduce the operational deficit (and to guarantee larger primary surpluses) the National Treasury reduces investment and funding expenses. Consequently, the *'worst of the worlds'* takes place: monetary policy with high interest rates to keep inflation targets and a fiscal policy whose most significant expenses are the payment of interests and the amortization of internal debt. It is easy to observe the difficulty in using this type of policy mix to stimulate regional development policies.

References

Afonso, J.R.R. et al. (eds). 'Tributação no Brasil: Características Marcantes e Diretrizes para a Reforma'. 1998. mimeo.

Afonso, J.R.R. Brasil, um caso à parte. XVI Regional Seminar of Fiscal Policy. CEPAL/ILPES. Santiago, Chile. 2004.

Afonso, J.R. Responsabilidade fiscal – primeiros e próximos passos. 2002. Disponível em www.federativo.bndes.gov.br. Acess in 12/03/2004

Alessandrini, P. and Zazzaro, A. 'A "Possibilist" Approach to Local Financial System and Regional Development: The Italian Experience', in Martin, R. (ed.) *Money and the Space Economy*, 1999, John Wiley and Sons: New York.

Alves JR., Antônio José. 'Sistematização do debate sobre "Sistema de Financiamento do Desenvolvimento"' *in* Desenvolvimento em Debate: Novos Rumos dos Desenvolvimento no mundo, volume 2. Rio de Janeiro: BNDES, dezembro de 2002.

Amado, Adriana. 'A Questão Regional e o Sistema Financeiro no Brasil: Uma Interpretação Pós-Keynesiana'. São Paulo: *Estudos Econômicos*, 27(3), 417–40, Setembro–Dezembro, 1997.

Amado, Adriana. 'Moeda, financiamento, sistema financeiro e trajetórias de desenvolvimento regional desigual: a perspectiva pós-keynesiana'. *Revista de Economia Política*, 18(1), 69, janeiro—março, 1998.

BNDES, ÁREA PARA ASSUNTOS FISCAIS E DE EMPREGO. INFORME-SE: *edição n° 4. Janeiro 2000.*

Cavalcante, A. Crocco, M., e Jayme Jr, F. Preferência pela Liquidez, Sistema Bancário e Disponibilidade de Crédito Regional (*mimeo*). Belo Horizonte: CEDEPLAR, 2004.

Costa, A.J. Reforma Tributária: Uma Visão Histórica. USP, São Paulo. 1996.

Crocco, M. et al. 'Desenvolvimento Econômico, preferência pela liquidez e acesso bancário: um estudo de caso'. Texto para discussão n° 192. Belo Horizonte: UFMG/CEDEPLAR, 2003.

Crocco, M. 'O Financiamento do Desenvolvimento Regional no Brasil: diagnósticos e propostas'. *Agenda Brasil*, 297–332, 2004a.

Crocco, M. (et al.). 'Liquidity Preference of Banks and Public and Regional Development: the case of Brazil'. Texto para discussão, Belo Horizonte UFMG/CEDEPLAR, 2004b.

Dain, S. 'Impasses de um reforma tributária em tempos de crise'. In *Combate à inflação e reforma fiscal*, João P. Velloso (ed.). Rio de Janeiro, RJ, José Olympio. 1992, pp. 32–58.

Diniz, C.C. and Oliveira, F.A. 'Federalismo, Sistema tributário e a questão regional no Brasil'. In: Seminário Internacional sobre políticas regionais no Brasil. 1993. Belo Horizonte.

Dixon, R. and Thirlwall, A.P. 'A Model of Regional Growth-Rate Differences on Kaldorian Lines'. *Oxford Economic Papers*. July, 1975.

Dow, S.C. *Money and the Economic Process*. Edward Elgar, Cheltenham, 1993.

Dow, S.C and Rodríguez-Fuentes, C. 'Regional Finance: A Survey'. *Regional Studies*, 31(9), 903–20, 1997.

Dow, S.C and Rodríguez-Fuentes, C. 'EMU and the Regional Impact of Monetary Policy'. *Regional Studies*, 37(9), 969–80, December 2003.

Fernandes, Andréa Gomes. Sistemas de Crédito Local: o que ensinam as experiências internacionais. BNDES: Informe-SF, n° 13, maio 2000.

Giambiagi, F. A Condição de Equilíbrio da Trajetória do Endividamento Público: Algumas Simulações Para o Caso Brasileiro. Junho/1998 Disponível em www. bndes.gov.br/conhecimento/publicacoes. Acesso em 02/03/2004.

Greco, P.D. A Lei de Responsabilidade Fiscal e o Cadafalso Neoliberal. 2003 Disponível em www.mundo juridico.adv.br. Acesso em 29/03/2004.

IBGE. Contas Regionais do Brasil 2001 – contas regionais n°. 11. Rio de Janeiro: 2003. www.ibge.org.br

Jayme Jr, Frederico G. 'Crise fiscal, federalismo e endividamento estadual: um estudo das finanças públicas de Minas Gerais'. 1994. Tese dissertação de Mestrado. IE/UNI-CAMP, Campinas. 1994.

Jayme Jr, F.G. and Santos, V.C.V. Distribuição dos Recursos Tributários, Carga Tributária e Reforma Tributária: Impacto nos municípios. Belo Horizonte/Cedeplar: 2003 Texto para Discussão n. 205.

Kaldor, N. 'Causes of the Slow Rate of Economic Growth of the United Kingdom', in: King, J.E, *Economic Growth in Theory and Practice: a Kaldorian Perspective*. Cheltenham: Edward Elgar, pp. 279–318, 1994.

Martin, R. 'Introduction', in Martin, R. (ed.) *Money and the Space Economy*. London: Wiley, 1999.

Mora, Mônica. Federalismo e Dívida Estadual no Brasil. IPEA. 2002.

Oliveira, F.A. 'Crise, reforma e desordem do Sistema Tributário Nacional'. Tese de livre docência. UNICAMP, Campinas, 1992.

Oliveira, F.A. 'Sistema fiscal brasileiro: evolução e crise 1965/85'. Tese de doutora-mento.UNICAMP, Campinas, 1985.

Paula, L.F.R. et al. 'Ajuste Patrimonial e Padrão de Rentabilidade dos Bancos Privados no Brasil durante o Plano Real (1994/98)'. São Paulo: *Estudos Econômicos*, (2), 285–319, Abril–Junho 2001.

Prado, S. Aspectos Federativos do Investimento Estatal. 1995. Disponível em www. publicacoes.fundap.sp.gov.br/Federalismo. Acesso em 21/04/2004.

Serra, J. and Afonso, J.R.R. 'Finanças públicas municipais: trajetórias e mitos'. 1992. Disponível em federativo.bndes.gov.br/bf_bancos/estudos. Acesso em 21/04/2004.

Rezende, F. 'Modernização Tributária e Federalismo Fiscal'. In: Oliveira, F. and Rezende, F. 'Descentralização e federalismo fiscal: desafios da reforma tributária'. Rio de Janeiro, RJ. Editora Konrad Adenauer Stiftung. 2003, pp. 25–38.

Rezende, F. et al. 'A Tributação Brasileira e o Novo Ambiente Econômico: a reforma tributária inevitável e urgente'. Junho/2000 Disponível em www.bndes.gov.br/ conhecimento. Acesso em 03/02/04.

Tanzi, V. et al. *Brazil: Issues for Fundamental Tax Reform*, Washington, IMF, April 1992.

Willis, E. et al. 'The politics of decentralization in Latin America'. *Latin American Research Review*, 34(1), 1999.

10
Disentangling Policy and Politics: Non-Fiscal Implications of the Calculation of the PSBR in Brazil[1]

Lecio Morais
Câmara dos Deputados, Brasília – DF, Brazil

Alfredo Saad-Filho
Department of Development Studies, SOAS, University of London

1   Introduction

Controlling the public sector deficit is critically important for the formulation and implementation of macroeconomic policy in Brazil. At one level, the deficit[2] has become a key variable for the assessment of the stance and effectiveness of economic policy by international organizations, foreign lenders and investors and domestic agents. At another level, it is often claimed that lower deficits are essential for intertemporal macroeconomic stability in the country. In this context, the public sector borrowing requirement (PSBR) has become increasingly relevant.

This variable measures the fiscal balance of the central government (CG), including the federal government and the non-financial state-owned enterprises (SOEs). The PSBR is usually calculated through the variation in the net debt of the public sector, and it aims to measure the financial implications of fiscal policy. This is done in two ways: through its nominal level (public deficit, of PSBR as it is conventionally defined), and through the primary deficit (PSBR minus the net financial costs of the public sector debt). The PSBR was standardized internationally by the IMF in the 1980s, and it has become the most important measure of the public deficit in most countries (IMF, 1986 and Tanzi, 1999). Brazil has been using this concept with significant adjustments since 1983, but the methodology for the calculation of the PSBR was settled only in 1996.

This chapter shows that the methodology of calculation of the PSBR in Brazil is misleading. Although the PSBR presumably measures the difference between the consumption and investment expenditures of the CG and its tax revenues, its calculation is contaminated by several non-fiscal factors. These are due to the incorporation, into the calculation of the deficit, of the impact of exogenous shocks and the costs of monetary policy which are wholly unrelated to the government's fiscal policy stance. These non-fiscal factors are defined and explained below, and an example is provided through the calculation of the cost of the rediscount operations of the central bank.

Non-fiscal contamination in the calculation of the public deficit is especially important in Brazil because the PSBR has legally binding implications for fiscal policy.[3] Therefore, distortions in the calculation of the public deficit can not only create a misleading perception of the origins and magnitude of the deficit, but also trigger automatic policy adjustments which need not be scrutinized by the legislature.

This chapter has eight sections. This introduction is the first. The second explains the concept of fiscal balance (public sector deficit or fiscal deficit). The third distinguishes between fiscal and non-fiscal sources of the deficit, and demonstrates conceptually the potential for non-fiscal contamination of the deficit when it is measured through the conventional methodology. The fourth reviews the methodology of calculation of the PSBR in Brazil. The fifth explains the methodological and asset adjustments in the calculation of the PSBR in Brazil, and the impact of variations in the exchange rate for the measurement of the deficit. The sixth examines five non-fiscal factors that can affect the nominal balance of the central government in Brazil. The seventh estimates one of them, the cost of the rediscount operations of the central bank. The eighth is the conclusion. This chapter argues that contamination by non-fiscal factors in the calculation of the PSBR can generate significant distortions, but they could be at least recognized and publicly debated if the central bank made the impact of these variables explicit in the calculation of the deficit.[4] This chapter also claims that the conventional methodology of calculation of PSBR contributes to making fiscal policy an adjustment variable for structural economic problems in the economy, including the costs of monetary policy.

2   Fiscal and non-fiscal elements in the PSBR

In order to finance its expenditures (G), the government can tax (T), borrow from domestic or foreign banks, or sell securities, leading to the accumulation of a public sector debt (Dg). (A full list of all variables used is shown in the Appendix.) Therefore, the government's budget constraint is:

$$G = T + \Delta Dg \qquad (1)$$

There is a fiscal deficit if $G > T$:

$$G - T = \Delta Dg \qquad (2)$$

G comprises four types of expenditure: (a) consumption (Cg), which includes wages paid to civil servants and purchases of goods and services for current use;

(b) investment (Ig), including all modalities of capital expenditure; (c) transfers to the private sector (Tg), among them subsidies, pension payments, unemployment insurance and other monetary benefits, and (d) the service costs of the domestic public debt (iDg):

$$G = Cg + Ig + Tg + iDg \qquad (3)$$

From (2) and (3), and bearing in mind that Dg and iDg are net of the financial assets held by the government and the interest paid to the government, we have:

$$\Delta Dg = (Cg + Ig + Tg + iDg) - T \qquad (4)$$

The right-hand side of (4) is the budget deficit of the general government, which includes the central and subnational levels of government, government-owned agencies, trusts and decentralized bodies of public administration (such as the public universities), the social security system, and special funds financed through general taxation.

If we include the central bank and the non-financial SOEs, we arrive at the deficit of the consolidated public sector (PSBR). This requires two main adjustments. First, it is necessary to include the change in the value of the net monetary and financial assets of the non-financial SOEs (or the change of their net debt, ΔC), which is a potential source of finance for the public sector. Second, the same needs to be done for the central bank. In this case, the liabilities include the monetary base and the deposits of the financial institutions at the central bank. The assets include the domestic currency value of the international reserves (ER*, where E is the average exchange rate and R* is the stock of reserves; the asterisk indicates that the variable is measured in foreign currency), and the central bank loans to the financial institutions (rediscount).

Two further adjustments are needed. First, it is necessary to exclude the transactions between the general government and the central bank, which are internal to the consolidated public sector. In this case, Dg becomes the net public sector debt held by the public, excluding the public debt held by the central bank (Dbc), which is normally used in open market operations (OMOs). For the same reason, iDbc should also be excluded from iDg, which is the interest payments on this debt. Second, in order to avoid double-counting the government's external debt should be net of the external reserves of the central bank,[5] and ER becomes the domestic currency value of the net international reserves of the central bank. The interest revenue on ER* is given by Ei*R*, where i* is the international rate of interest.

Finally, the monetary base (M) includes the currency held by the public (m) and the compulsory and voluntary bank reserves deposited at the central bank (BR). Changes in the monetary base are due to five factors: (a) changes in the stock of currency held by the public; (b) changes in the central bank's holdings of public securities due to OMOs (ΔDbc); (c) changes in the international reserves (EΔR*);[6] (d) changes in the credit supplied by the central bank to the commercial banks (rediscount, ΔL), and (e) changes in bank deposits (ΔD), which affect BR through the ratio r(BR) (see (8) below):

$$\Delta M = \Delta m + \Delta BR = \Delta m + [\Delta Dbc + E\Delta R^* + \Delta L + r(BR)] \tag{5}$$

It is now possible to define the deficit of the consolidated public sector (PSBR), including the general government, the central bank and the non-financial SOEs, as:

$$PSBR = \Delta M + \Delta Dg + E\Delta R^* + \Delta C \tag{6}$$

3   Non-fiscal factors and the calculation of the public sector deficit

Identities (4) and (6) measure different types of deficit. In (4), only fiscal factors are included: T, the components of G, and the interest paid on the domestic public debt. In contrast, (6) includes the monetary authority. This leads to the inclusion of three types of non-fiscal variables into the calculation of the public sector deficit.

First, the interest received on the net external reserves (which is included in EΔR*). This is determined by the difference between the interest rate on the currency reserves held by the central bank and the interest rate on the external debt (i*). They are determined in the international financial markets, and they include two components: the basic interest rate i** (such as the libor or the prime rate), which is fully exogenous, and the country risk. In mainstream economics, this risk depends on the solvency of the country and the credibility of government policy and, therefore, it is partly determined by the public deficit.

Second, the relationship between the domestic interest rate (i) and the basic international interest rate (i**). If the country follows a floating exchange rate regime with free capital movements, the relationship between these rates of interest is given by the covered interest parity condition:

$$i = f(Dg, i^{**}, \hat{E}) \tag{7}$$

where $\hat{E}$ is the expected exchange rate. In this case, two non-fiscal variables, i** and $\hat{E}$, influence directly the domestic interest rate and, therefore, the public sector deficit in (4) and (6).[7] Specifically, exogenous changes in the international interest rate will affect the public sector deficit.

Third, bank behaviour also influences the monetary base. Starting from (5), we know that BR is a fraction of the bank deposits (D), and that BR includes both compulsory (BRc) and voluntary (BRv) reserves:

$$r = \frac{BRc}{D} + \frac{BRv}{D} \tag{8}$$

The ratio BRc/D is determined by the monetary authority, but BRv/D is chosen by the banks, and it depends on macroeconomic variables and the preferences of individual banks, including their target liquidity and rate of return, and their credit strategy. Moreover, although BRc/D is discretionary, D is partly determined by the level of national income and the domestic interest rate.[8]

In the three cases examined above, non-fiscal variables will affect the fiscal deficit, if the monetary authority is included in the definition of public sector. This implies that OMOs are ambiguous. These operations finance government spending and regulate the supply of money in line with the central bank's policy objectives. In the latter case, they are heavily influenced by the behaviour of the banks and the level of economic activity. In other words, monetary policy can respond to non-fiscal imperatives, for example, short-term changes in bank strategy.

This section has shown that non-fiscal factors can influence the calculation of the public deficit, whether it is defined as deficit of the general government or deficit of the consolidated public sector. These non-fiscal factors can affect the deficit directly, through changes in stocks (M or Dg) or, indirectly, through changes in flows (interest on R* or service costs on Dg).

In neoclassical theory, persistent public sector deficits invariably have adverse implications for the economy. They tend to raise aggregate demand to unsustainable levels, increase the public sector debt, induce inflation and currency devaluation, raise interest rates and crowd out private investment (Tanzi, 1999). This will bring down the rate of growth of productivity and, with it, the GDP growth rate. If the fiscal deficit can have such strongly adverse implications, it is essential to measure it adequately in order to provide useful guidelines for the economic agents, analysts and policymakers. It was shown above that contamination by non-fiscal factors can affect the calculation of the public sector deficit. Even from a strictly neoclassical point of view, the calculation of the deficit should make these factors explicit, in order to facilitate the analysis of their macroeconomic implications.

4   Calculation of the PSBR in Brazil

It was shown above that the calculation of the fiscal deficit can be adapted to different definitions of the public sector. For example, the CGBR include the national and subnational levels of the public administration, autonomous agencies, public trusts and the social security system. In contrast, the borrowing requirements of the consolidated non-financial public sector (PSBR) include, in addition to the CGBR, the balance of the non-financial SOEs and the central bank.

In practice, the nominal PSBR is calculated by the change of the net debt stock of the public sector (NDPS) in a given period:

$$PSBR_t = NDPS_t - NDPS_{t-1} \qquad (9)$$

The NDPS includes the monetary and financial assets and liabilities of the public sector,[9] including the payments made and the revenues due in the period (regardless of whether or not they were actually made).[10] Typically, the NDPS is calculated analogously to the consolidated public sector deficit, in (6):

$$NDPS = M + Dg + ER^* + C \qquad (10)$$

Dg can be disaggregated into a large set of financial assets and liabilities, including the domestic government debt held by the public (Bgp), the bank balances of the government and the SOEs (d), financial funds (such as the Worker's Assistance Fund, *Fundo de Amparo ao Trabalhador*) (fn), and the debt of the subnational levels of government (dgp):

$$Dg = Bgp + d + fn + dgp \qquad (11)$$

From (10) and (11):

$$NDPS = M + Bgp + d + fn + dgp + ER^* + C \qquad (12)$$

The NDPS of the general government (NDPSg) excludes the monetary authority, but includes the domestic currency value of the external debt of the general government (EBg*):

$$NDPSg = Bgp + d + fn + dgp + EBg^* + C \qquad (13)$$

Changes of the NDPSg are commonly used to gauge the fiscal deficit (see, for example, BCB, 2000, p. 89).[11]

The nominal balance (borrowing requirements) of the general government (GGBR) measures the change of the net domestic and external debt (Dgp) of the GG during the period. From (4) and (6):

$$GGBR = \Delta Dgp = (Cg + Ig + Tg + iDgp) - T \qquad (14)$$

Subtracting the interest paid on the net debt of the general government (iDgp), we obtain the primary deficit of the GG (Pg). Pg measures the difference between the non-financial expenditures and the non-financial revenues of the general government:

$$Pg = GGBR - iDgp = (Cg + Ig + Tg) - T \qquad (15)$$

The primary deficit is an important indicator of the solvency of the government. A primary deficit implies that government revenues are insufficient to pay even the interest on its debt which, in extreme situations, may suggest that the government is entangled in a Ponzi scheme. Alternatively, if the government runs a primary surplus it has not only been paying the interest on the public sector debt, but also the principal. Even if there is still a nominal deficit, a primary surplus suggests that the public sector debt is sustainable. In this sense, the primary deficit is a proxy for the risk of lending to the government (Freitas, 1999, p. 65).

The calculation of the public deficit includes several methodological adjustments, some of which are discussed below. In addition to these adjustments, the calculation of the PSBR in Brazil has changed significantly since the early 1980s.[12] In what follows, this study refers only to the borrowing requirements of the consolidated non-financial public sector and, specifically, to the CGBR.

The CGBR includes the non-financial federal enterprises and 'the assets and liabilities of the central bank, and, therefore, the monetary base' (BCB, 2000, p. 89). Consequently, the NDPS also includes such central bank assets as the credits to the financial institutions (rediscount)[13] and the international reserves (R*). The central bank of Brazil argues that its accounts should be included into the NDPS because the central bank 'transfers its profits automatically to the Treasury, and ... it is the institution that collects the inflation tax' (BCB, 2000, p. 89).[14]

This is partly due to Brazil's long experience with high inflation, which has led several observers and financial institutions to question the government's commitment to monetary stability. It is also partly due to the central bank practice of financing the Treasury. This chapter cannot review the arguments for and against the inclusion of the accounts of the monetary authority into the public sector deficit. However, the non-fiscal implications of their inclusion should be made explicit. Take, for instance, the rediscount operations (L), including the loans to restructure financial institutions. It was shown above that L is included in the asset side of the net public debt. If the rediscount operations are sterilized there is no immediate change in the net debt, because $\Delta L = \Delta M + \Delta Dg$. However, the ensuing repayments will affect the monetary base. Even more significantly, the difference between the asset and liability interest rates on the rediscount operations will have an impact on the public deficit. This is because the interest rate charged by the central bank (i^L) is usually *lower* than the rate of return obtained by the banks with these resources (iBg). This difference is the net cost (implicit subsidy) of the rediscount loans. This subsidy has an unwarranted impact on the Brazilian public sector deficit because of a methodological inconsistency in its calculation (see below).

Another specificity of the calculation of the fiscal deficit in Brazil is due to the definition of the deposits of the federal government at the central bank (the government's 'single account') as a liability of the monetary authority. Since the balances of the federal government are held outside the banking system, all public sector expenditures, tax revenues and domestic public debt flows have a direct impact on the monetary base (they are undistinguishable from the creation or destruction of high-powered money):

$$\Delta M = (G - T) + \Delta Bgp \qquad (16)$$

Since these changes in the monetary base are due to changes in the bank reserves (BR), identity (5) can be expanded to include the government's single account:

$$\Delta M = \Delta m + [\Delta Dbc + E\Delta R^* + \Delta L + r(BR) + [(G - T) + \Delta Bgp] \qquad (17)$$

Identity (17) has important implications for the deficit of the Brazilian central government. In theory, the Brazilian government finances its deficits through the sale of securities, and these deficits can lead to money creation only through triangular operations in which the central bank purchases securities in the open market. However, since the single account is outside the banking system, in practice the central government can *also* monetize its deficit by running an overdraft. By the same token, since fiscal surpluses contract the monetary base, the PSBR falls whenever the government hoards resources in the single account.

The calculation of the NDPS in Brazil departs from (12), which refers to the consolidated public sector. With the inclusion of the net debt held by the public and other central bank accounts including M, L, and the other accounts of the central bank (k), Dgp is given by:

$$Dgp = Bgp + d + fn + dgp + L + k \qquad (18)$$

Consequently, the Brazilian NDPS is:

$$NDPS = Bgp + d + fn + dgp + L + k + M + ER^* \qquad (19)$$

Given this expanded definition of Dgp, the nominal balance of the central government is:

$$CGBR = \Delta Dgp + \Delta M + E\Delta R^* \qquad (20)$$

But the primary balance (P) is still determined by (15): it is the nominal balance minus the financial expenditures and revenues of the CG or, alternatively, the non-financial expenditures minus the tax revenues:

$$P = CGBR - (iDgp + i^*R^*) = (Cg + Ig + Tg) - T \qquad (21)$$

It was shown above that (20) includes non-fiscal factors in the definition of the public deficit. It will be shown below that this non-fiscal contagion tends to increase when the accounts of the monetary authority are included, as is the case in (21).

5 Adjustments and the impact of exchange rate fluctuations

The PSBR distinguishes between two types of debt of the Brazilian CG: its total debt and its net fiscal debt, which includes several adjustments. As was shown above, the nominal balance of the CG is given by the variation of its net debt during the period. The central bank of Brazil (BCB, 2000, p. 90) defines two methodological adjustments in the calculation of the NDPS. Both refer to the net external debt:

- The *stock-flow adjustment* compensates the difference between the use of end-of-period exchange rates to calculate the domestic currency value of the net external debt, and the use of average exchange rates to calculate the currency flows in the period.
- The *adjustment to variations in the exchange rate* (Av) compensates the impact of changes in the exchange rate on the net external debt during the period:

$$Av_t = (R^* - R^*_{t-1}) - \left(\frac{R^*}{E_t} - \frac{R^*_{t-1}}{E_{t-1}}\right) E \qquad (22)$$

where E_t and E_{t-1} are the end-of-period exchange rates and E is the average exchange rate.

The central bank of Brazil (2000, p. 90) rightly argues that:

> In general, when they obtain external finance governments do so in the currency of the lending country, or in another unit of account valid for such contracts (US dollar, SDR, euros, and so on). Therefore, fluctuations in the exchange rate between these currencies, or between the Brazilian real and the US dollar, do not affect the public sector deficit, because they do not affect the external debt in the currency in which the loan was contracted.

Changes in the exchange rate can have problematic implications, because the domestic public debt is calculated according to the due date of its service commitments, regardless of the payments actually made, while the external debt is measured according to the actual monetary flows (see Brazil and IMF, 2002, A.4 and A.6).[15] This can make their values difficult to ascertain, especially if the value of the currency changes suddenly. The only way to address this problem is through an alternative form of presentation, which makes explicit the impact of the variations of the exchange rate on the NDPS.[16]

Another type of adjustment refers to the exclusion of the proceeds of privatizations from the NDPS, which is defensible for both fiscal and operational reasons, but it applies only to the value of the sale but not to the corresponding net debt. Finally, the exclusion of the so-called 'skeletons' from the government's accounts cannot be examined here because of the widely diverse sources of these liabilities.

This section has shown that the variables excluded from the nominal balance are deeply heterogeneous. In general, the adjustments in the calculation of the fiscal deficit are due to practical or political convenience (rather than conceptual coherence), and they do not address the non-fiscal contamination identified previously.

6   Non-fiscal contamination of the PSBR in Brazil

This section examines five non-fiscal factors affecting the nominal balance of the central government in Brazil. They have two sources: first, the mismatch between the interest rates accruing to certain government assets and its most significant liability, the domestic public debt and, second, monetary authority decisions, for example, OMOs or changes in the compulsory bank reserves. These factors can also affect the primary balance, if they trigger pressures for fiscal retrenchment.

(a) Cost of the external reserves: The interest flow on the net reserves of the central bank (R*) can change because of variations in the basic international interest rate (i**). Their impact on the PSBR is:[17]

$$I^1 = \Delta i^{**}(ER^*) \tag{23}$$

(b) Open market operations: OMOs change the stock of government securities held by the public (Bgp). These are short-term operations, and they should not affect the NDPS.

(c) External transactions: These transactions affect the monetary base and, therefore, the NDPS, especially through their impact on the bank reserves. If the variations in the base are sterilised the debt held by the public changes, and the additional interest flows will put pressure on the fiscal balance.

(d) Changes in the value of the net international reserves due to variations in the exchange rate: Exchange rate fluctuations affect the nominal balance both directly and through the change in the stock of public securities indexed to the dollar. The methodological adjustment explained in the previous section eliminates the former but not the latter (the central bank or Brazil has been calculating both balances since October 2001). In spite of its obvious importance for the nominal balance, it is difficult to estimate the non-fiscal impact of the changes in the exchange rate.

(e) Net cost of the rediscount: Rediscount operations can affect the nominal balance in two cases. First, if they lead to changes in M and, second, if they change Bgp (supposing that the interest paid to the holders of securities, i^B, is different from the interest rate charged to the financial institutions taking rediscount loans, i^L). In this case, the central bank grants a non-fiscal subsidy which expands the nominal deficit. The net cost of the rediscount is given by the difference between these two interest rates:

$$I^R = \left(\frac{1 + i^B}{1 + i^L}\right) L \tag{24}$$

The potential impact on the net debt of the Brazilian central government of the non-fiscal elements identified above shows that the concepts of NDPS and primary and nominal deficits are *contaminated*. As they are currently calculated, they present a misleading picture of the public sector deficit and the fiscal policy stance.

7 Estimate of the net cost of the rediscount

Identity (24) indicates how the net cost of the rediscount can be calculated. The relevant interest rates are available only between July 1997 and December 2002, and they lead to the results presented in Table 10.1. This table shows that the BCB subsidized the financial institutions during the entire period, except the second semester of 1997. Table 10.2 shows the significance of this subsidy vis-à-vis the nominal deficit of the central government.

The subsidy implicit in the rediscount operations is only one of the non-fiscal elements influencing the conventional calculation of the public sector deficit. Its magnitude and analytical importance (and, potentially, its influence over economic policy) suggest that it is important to take these variables into account explicitly in the calculation of the public deficit. This is essential in order to address the distortions that currently influence the formulation of fiscal and monetary policy in Brazil.

Table 10.1 Impact of the net cost of the rediscount of the BCB on the central government deficit

	Nominal deficit of the central government* % GDP	Cost of the rediscount (+ = subsidy)	
		% GDP	% deficit
Jul–Dec 1997	3.17	−0.42	−13.39
Jan–Dec 1998	4.93	0.55	11.14
Jan–Dec 1999	2.73	0.07	2.59
Jan–Dec 2000	2.30	0.49	21.26
Jan–Dec 2001	2.11	0.09	4.33
Jan–Dec 2002	0.70	0.05	7.62

* Excluding changes in the exchange rate; + = deficit.
Source: Bulletin of the BCB, several issues.

Table 10.2   Net cost of the rediscount of the BCB and primary surplus

	Primary surplus of the central government* % GDP	Cost of the rediscount (+ = subsidy)	
		% GDP	% result
Jul–Dec 1997	−0.47	−0.42	–
Jan–Dec 1998	−0.55	0.55	−99.57
Jan–Dec 1999	−2.36	0.07	−2.99
Jan–Dec 2000	−1.88	0.49	−26.02
Jan–Dec 2001	−1.83	0.09	−4.98
Jan–Dec 2002	−2.42	0.05	−2.21

* Negative = surplus.
Note: the result in 1997 is nil because, in the absence of a subsidy, the revenue is financial and not included in the primary surplus.
Source: Bulletin of the BCB, several issues.

8   Conclusion

This chapter has demonstrated the importance of non-fiscal factors in the calculation of the PSBR in Brazil. This has been done conceptually, and through the estimation of the impact of one of these elements, the cost of the rediscount operations of the BCB.

It was shown that the conventional calculation of the PSBR (according to the IMF methodology) incorporates several non-fiscal factors, among them the net interest on the international reserves and the interest rates on the public sector debt. In the Brazilian case, institutional and political peculiarities have broadened the concept of central government deficit through the inclusion of the accounts of the monetary authority (among them the monetary base and the rediscount operations), which have expanded further the contagion of non-fiscal factors in the calculation of the deficit. Most of this contagion represents the costs of central bank policy. Although this contamination is implicit in the calculation of the PSBR, its impact is not normally evident, and the relevant variables are not readily available. It is essential to increase the transparency of the calculation of the PSBR in Brazil, initially by making these variables explicit.

The priority attributed to inflation stabilization by successive governments, including the Lula administration, has increased the importance of the fiscal balance and, therefore, the methodology surrounding its calculation.[18] The contamination of the deficit by non-fiscal elements can distort the perception of the economic agents, and the government itself. Moreover, lack of clarity about the costs of monetary policy and the costs of the external shocks can transfer these costs to fiscal policy. In practice, this can make fiscal policy an adjustment variable for the structural problems of the economy. This is probably unwarranted and, at the very least, it deserves careful public debate.

Notes

1 This is a revised and updated version of Morais and Saad-Filho (2005).

2 In this chapter, 'public sector deficit', 'public deficit' and 'fiscal deficit' are synonymous.

3 Complementary Law 101 (2000) (the so-called 'fiscal responsibility law', FRL), and the annual budget laws (*leis de diretrizes orçamentárias*, LDO) limit government spending according to quarterly primary surplus targets. If they are not achieved, the government must either raise taxes or cut its non-financial expenditures.

4 As is already done for the monetary base (table II.1 in the monthly bulletin of the central bank of Brazil).

5 There would be double counting because the external debt is contained in the international reserves (when they are borrowed abroad) and, subsequently, in the monetary base, when the foreign currency inflows are converted into domestic currency. The external debt also counts as part of the domestic public debt.

6 Since M is a liability, this change appears with the opposite sign of the corresponding operation in ER*.

7 If the exchange rate is fixed, it is determined exogenously by the central bank. If it is floating, its variation is influenced by the fiscal deficit. In either case, i** is a non-fiscal component, while Ê depends on the circumstances.

8 It can be argued that the commercial banks exercise little or no influence on the monetary base, because the central bank can manipulate BRc/D and the interest rates. However, this would merely transfer the impact of changes in the monetary base to other components of the public sector deficit, for example, the stock of securities held by the public, the rediscount operations, or their cost.

9 This is the typical form of calculation of the PSBR. It is called 'below the line' because it is not measured by the accounts of the state institutions but by the balances of their creditors.

10 For the central bank of Brazil (BCB, 2000, p. 89), states that 'the appropriation of charges is accounted for *pro rata*, independently of the payments made during the period'.

11 Evidently, each country adjusts the calculation of the NDPS to its own accounting conventions and institutional features.

12 The analysis in this chapter is based on the NDPS data published in the monthly bulletin of the BCB and the methodology available in the Manual of Public Finances (BCB, 2000). Unfortunately, the BCB has not published methodology of calculation of the PSBR in Brazil, the criteria for the selection of the accounts included in the NDPS, the method of calculation of the accrued interest or the methodological and asset adjustments.

13 This account includes the traditional rediscount operations (for liquidity support), and loans linked to financial restructuring programmes, such as PROER. PROES, the programme for restructuring state-owned banks, is included in a separate account, 'Renegotiation (law 9496/1997 and PROES)'. This account also includes the renegotiation of state government debt since 1997, which can also be a source of subsidies to the financial sector.

14 The real peculiarity of the relationship between the BCB and the Treasury is the automatic transfer to the Treasury not only of the *profits*, but also of the *losses* of

the central bank. This has been done since 1998 (and, retroactively, since 1994), following the Provisional Law (*medida provisória*) 1789/1998 (later 2179-36/2001), and article 7 of the FRL.

15   Although the methodology was preserved in the Letter of Intent of 15 December 2003, the technical memorandum including the detailed performance targets, assessment criteria and methodology of calculation of the relevant variables was not released.

16   After the exchange rate crisis of 1999, the BCB started calculating the NDPS both with and without the impact of the devaluation on the stock of public securities indexed to the dollar (see Bulletin of the BCB from volume 35 (4), April 1999).

17   In the calculation of the PSBR in Brazil, all stocks are measured at end of period. However, the difference between stocks and flows during the period is compensated through (22).

18   The Bulletin of the BCB publishes the tables of uses and sources of the public sector accounts (Tables IV.18 and IV.19, available at http://www.bcb.gov.br/ ?BULLETIN), which identify the 'conditioning factors' of the variation of the PSBR. However, the available data is restricted to the main NDPS accounts and their impact on the PSBR, and they do not explain the sources of their impact.

References

Banco Central do Brazil (BCB) (2000) *Manual de Finanças Públicas*, Brasília: BCB.

Brazil and IMF (2002) *Memorando de Entendimento Técnico*, http://www.fazenda.gov. br/portugues/fmi/fmimte12.pdf.

Freitas, C.E. (1999) *A Reavaliação da Dívida Pública Federal Brasileira*. Brasília: Editora FGV-EPGE.

Giambiagi, F. (1997) *Necessidade de Financiamento do Setor Público: Bases para a Discussão do Ajuste Fiscal no Brasil – 1991/96*. Textos para Discussão BNDES no. 53, Rio de Janeiro.

International Monetary Fund (IMF) (1986) *A Manual of Government Financial Statistics*. Washington: IMF.

Morais, L. and Saad-Filho, A. (2005) 'Impactos Não-Fiscais no Cálculo da Necessidade de Financiamento do Setor Público no Brazil', *Ensaios FEE* 26 (1), 2005, 415–40.

Saad-Filho, A. and Morais, L. (2000) *The Costs of Neomonetarism: The Brazilian Economy in the 1990s*. London: South Bank University Business School.

Tanzi, V. (1999) 'Mensuração do Déficit Público', in: M. Blejer and A. Cheasty (eds.) *Como Medir a Inflação: Questões Analíticas e Metodológicas*. Brasília: Secretaria do Tesouro Nacional.

Appendix: List of variables

Av: adjustment of the variations of the exchange rate.
Bg*: external debt of the general government.
Bgp: domestic public debt held by the public.
BR: bank reserves deposited at the central bank.
BRc: compulsory bank reserves.
BRv: voluntary bank reserves.
C: net debt of the non-financial state-owned enterprises.
CG: central government (federal government and non-financial state-owned enterprises).

Cg: government consumption.

CGBR: Central government borrowing requirements.

d: bank balances of the government and state enterprises.

D: deposits held in commercial banks.

Dbc: public debt held by the central bank.

Dg: public debt of the general government, or domestic net debt of the consolidated public sector.

dgp: bank debt of subnational levels of government.

Dgp: net domestic and external debt of the general government.

E: averate exchange rate.

Ê: expected exchange rate.

EBg*: domestic currency value of the external debt of the general government.

ER*: domestic currency value of the net international reserves.

fn: financial funds (such as the Workers' Support Fund, *Fundo de Amparo ao Trabalhador*).

FRL: fiscal responsibility law.

G: government expenditures.

GG:general government (central government, subnational governments, specialist public agencies, trusts and decentralised bodies (such as the public universities)) and the social security, and the funds financed through taxation.

GGBR: general government borrowing requirements.

i^{**}: basic international interest rate (e.g., libor or prime rate).

i^*: international rate of interest.

i: interest rate on the domestic public debt.

i^B: interest rate paid to the holders of public securities.

iBg: interest accrued by the financial institutions with their rediscount loans.

iDbc: interest paid by the government, net of that paid to the central bank.

iDg: interest paid by the general government and other costs of the domestic public debt, or interest on the net domestic debt of the consolidated public sector.

iDgp: interest on the net debt of the general government.

Ig: government investment.

i^L: interest rate charged by the central bank on the rediscount loans.

I^R: non-fiscal impact (net cost) of the rediscount.

k: other accounts of the central bank.

L: central bank loans to the financial institutions (rediscount).

LDO: *lei de diretrizes orçamentárias*, annual budget law.

m: currency held by the public.

M: monetary base.

NDPS: net debt of the public sector.

NDPSg: net debt of the general government.

OMOs: open market operations.

P: primary balance (deficit) of the central government.

Pg: primary deficit of the general government.

PSBR: public sector borrowing requirements, or deficit of the consolidated public sector (general government, central bank and non-financial state enterprises).

R*: net international reserves.

SOEs: state-owned enterprises.

T: taxes paid to the government.

Tg: government transfers to the private sector.

11
The Interest Rate During the Lula Government: A Research Agenda

Carlos Vidotto
Universidade Federal Fluminense, Brazil

João Sicsú
Universidade Federal do Rio de Janeiro, Brazil

1   Introduction

Brazilian interest rates have been consistently high, despite their downward trend in 2006. The real interest rate has rarely been below ten per cent for several years, which seems to be its floor level. Several explanations have been offered for this phenomenon, with important implications to the economy. High interest rates are allegedly used to tame inflation and/or regulate the exchange rate. However, one might argue that high interest rates induce a permanent fiscal imbalance, because of the heavy burden of the domestic public debt, and do not allow the rate of unemployment to fall, due to the restrictions imposed on demand.

This chapter reviews the evolution of the Brazilian economy in recent years, in order to suggest a research agenda regarding the causes and consequences of the path of the interest rates during this period. The chapter is divided into three sections. The first focuses on the relationship between interest rates and the exchange rate. The second focuses on the links between the interest rate and the fiscal imbalances, and the third analyses the influence of the interest rate on the rate of inflation, and the social costs related to it.

2   The interest rate and the exchange rate

The liberalization of the capital account of the balance of payments in the last 15 years, along with the adoption of a floating exchange rate regime in 1999, has established a strong relationship between the exchange and the interest rates in the Brazilian economy. This economy can be regarded as *small*, since even a modest flow of capital can change the exchange rate, sometimes significantly and abruptly. The exchange rate has been highly volatile since January 1999. Also, since then, the Brazilian economy has faced episodes of currency overvaluation and financial turbulence, beyond the crisis of 1998–99, as was the case in 2001 and 2002.

The crisis of 1998–99 originated in the domestic economy. Low international reserves, large current account deficits, and the pegged exchange rate regime with an overvalued currency fed expectations that this economic policy regime was unsustainable. The consequences of these economic imbalances were huge capital flight, a dramatic loss of reserves and, finally, an abrupt devaluation of the Real. The Central Bank of Brazil (BCB) reacted by increasing the interest rate and allowing the Real to float since January 1999. In that month, the exchange rate devaluation reached 41.6 per cent, and the basic interest rate was raised from 19 per cent per year in November 1998, to 45 per cent in March 1999.

During 2001, several factors – the electricity rationing imposed by the government, the Argentinean financial crisis, the financial scandals in the US (for example, the episodes involving Enron and Arthur Andersen) and the terrorist attacks in the United States – contributed to the capital flight. The BCB reacted, again, by increasing the interest rate. Between February and July, the basic interest rate rose from 15.25 per cent to 19 per cent per year, a period in which the Real suffered a devaluation of 16 per cent.

In the following year, presidential elections were scheduled for October and the opposition candidate Luiz Inácio Lula da Silva promised significant changes to the existing economic model. His lead in the polls contributed to capital flight during that year. The consequence was another strong devaluation of the Real, and the BCB increased the interest rate again. Between July and December the exchange rate declined 33.1 per cent, and the basic interest rate increased from 18 to 25 per cent.

This suggests that the BCB was targeting the exchange rate, and using the interest rate to achieve this goal. Whenever the exchange rate showed signs of volatility and tended to decline, the BCB raised the interest rates. Capital flows, so to speak, *drove* the interest rate. The interest rate was an endogenous variable, determined by the exchange rate, while the exchange rate was determined by the capital movements.[1]

During 2000, and between early 2003 and June 2004, the exchange rate was less volatile and tended to become overvalued. In both periods the BCB reduced the interest rate. When the exchange rate became less volatile and tended to decline, the BCB reduced the interest rates. This positive correlation between the exchange rate and the interest rate can be seen in Figure 11.1, as well as the precedence of the former's movements over the latter's.

Although there was a floating exchange rate regime between 1999 and 2004, the BCB reacted against movements of the domestic currency. This suggests that the policy regime adopted until mid-2004 was an *exchange rate regime managed by the interest rate* and, partially, by the use of reserves and/or the sale of Treasury bills indexed to the exchange rate. Yet the interest rate seemed to be the main instrument used to control the exchange rate: the regime was characterized by 'fear of floating'. The BCB did not have a significant degree

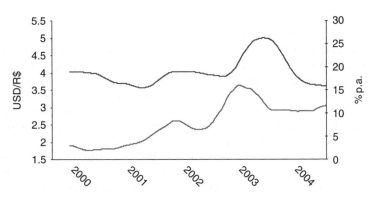

Figure 11.1   Brazil: Exchange rate and interest rate (Jan 2000–Jul 2004)
80-day moving average series.
Source: BCB *apud* IPEADATA.

of freedom to set the interest rate but, instead, followed a feedback rule. Therefore, and in reference to the Mundell–Fleming model,[2] there was no 'possible trinity', that is, the co-existence of free capital movements, a floating exchange rate regime and the monetary policy autonomy, because the real world was characterized by 'fear of floating'.

If a central bank suffers from fear of floating and wishes, at the same time, to increase its monetary policy autonomy, it should reduce the degree of mobility of capital and/or keep a large amount of reserves. Brazil did not do either of them. As a result, it lost autonomy to determine the interest rate. This strategy, which rested upon the intense use of high interest rates, and could not resort to reserves (because they were insufficient), was unsuccessful, because the exchange rate remained volatile. In fact, given the inefficacy of high interest rates to stem the currency crisis, the Brazilian government had to resort to the usual lending programme of the International Monetary Fund, with their well-known conditionalities.[3]

Tranquility was restored in the international front in August 2004, and capital flows returned to the developing countries. At that point, the BCB decided to raise interest rates again in order to tame inflation. That signalled a change in BCB policy. The basic interest rate (Selic) rose from 16 per cent to 19.75 per cent, in May 2005. This attracted substantial capital inflows, which added to the inflows due to the country's trade surplus. The outcome was the revaluation of the Real by 22 per cent in that period. The close connection between the interest rate and the exchange rate was maintained, but the direction of causation was reversed. Under the new policies, high interest rates cause the capital inflows and the revaluation of the exchange rate. In contrast, until July 2004 it was the exchange rate that determined the interest rate.

In the new context, it is correct to say that the BCB reaction function aims to control inflation, as it is officially stated by the authorities. Since the exchange rate is negatively correlated with the interest rate, it has also been used to achieve inflation control. In sum, the current policy framework is characterized by autonomous monetary policy, floating exchange rates and liberalized capital flows.

Figure 11.2 shows the higher interest rates leading the revaluation of the exchange rate. Since mid-2005 the decline in the interest rate was not followed by the devaluation of the Real. Although they fell, the interest rates remained high (13.75 per cent in November), which helped to support the inflows of foreign capital. There was no devaluation because the BCB intensified its accumulation of reserves, see Figure 11.3 (in December 2005 the Brazilian government paid in advance the rest of its debt to the IMF).

Traditionally, several countries, especially in Asia (for example, China, Malaysia and India) have employed the exchange rate as an instrument for regulating international competitiveness in order to achieve commercial surpluses. Brazil is not following the same strategy. The (overvalued) exchange

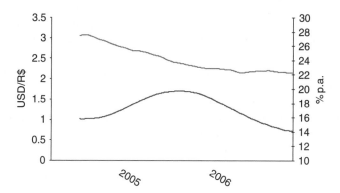

Figure 11.2 Brazil: Exchange rate and interest rate (Aug 2004–Oct 2006)
80-day moving average series.
Source: BCB *apud* IPEADATA.

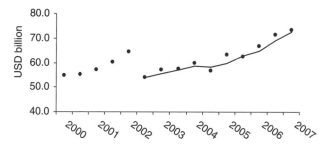

Figure 11.3 Brazil: International reserves
Source: BCB *apud* IPEADATA.

rate is a supplementary tool for inflation control. This operates through two channels: it reduces exports, especially manufactures, in order to restrict domestic demand (along with the interest rates), and it fosters competition between imported and domestic goods.

Starting from the indications mentioned above, several questions are worth investigating in further detail. First, can Brazilian monetary policy be characterized as endogenous until July–August 2004 and, later, as exogenous (when it started to determine the exchange rate)? Second, to what extent are the interest rates and the trade surplus the main reasons explaining the overvaluation of the Real since July 2004? Third, to what extent does the overvalued exchange rate help to maintain inflation under control?

3   The interest rate and the fiscal administration

When examining Brazilian fiscal policy, it is easy to confirm that financial market agents and policymakers, under both F.H. Cardoso and Lula, share a common approach: the absolute emphasis on the stabilization of the public debt and the debt–output ratio (D/Y). The term 'stabilization' in the Brazilian context only means that this indicator is expected to show a declining trend. When stressing this meaning of the term as a key reference for the formation of expectations, the policy makers impose an important restriction on the fiscal policy stance.

From the point of view of a fiscal policy stance focusing on full employment, the term stabilization would suggest the need to achieve a given rate of output growth, taking into account, at the same time, the importance of maintaining the solvency of the domestic public debt. Therefore, the formation of expectations of demand, that is, the prospects of economic growth and the entrepreneurs' expectations for their investment projects should be important components of this conception of fiscal policy. The essence of a counter-cyclical fiscal policy should be public spending strategy, which by fostering optimistic demand expectations, would stimulate private investment spending the economic downturn.

However, in Cardoso and Lula's administrations, the term stabilization applied in the context of fiscal policy has been limited to indicating the government's capacity to service its debt. As a consequence, the possibility of implementing an activist fiscal policy, which could stabilize the rate of GDP growth at high levels, is discarded. In fact, even the expression 'fiscal policy' has been virtually excluded from the official vocabulary. Its meaning has been replaced by the need for a sound debt administration in order to demonstrate its solvency.

Even if assessed from the government's perspective, fiscal management has shown poor results in the recent period. The fact that D/Y was stable around 51.5 per cent between October 2004 and February 2006 offers strong evidence in support of this statement. The main reason for this outcome is that, by narrowing the horizon of fiscal management, the recent Brazilian administrations have sacrificed the goal of maintaining a high level of output. They have sacrificed full employment, making a long-lasting fiscal adjustment less likely – which would be easier to achieve in an expanding economy, with growing public revenues and lower public spending associated with social programmes (because of the lower level of unemployment). One example of this potential outcome is the brief upturn initiated at the end of 2003, and aborted by monetary policy in 2004, which allowed the debt/GDP ratio to fall from 58 to 51 per cent in less than a year. In Figure 11.4, it can be seen that variations in the interest rate can explain the changes in D/Y.

The evidence strongly suggests that the current fiscal policy is self-defeating. The high interest rates under which the Brazilian economy has been operating for over a decade have inflated the financial burden of the public sector debt.[4] Fiscal adjustment has become entirely dependent on a rising primary budget surplus.[5] Not only has fiscal stabilization not been achieved, but the pursuit of primary surpluses rests on a combination of higher average tax rates and public expenditure restrictions, resulting in the deterioration of the country's infrastructure and, the declining coverage of the existing social programmes. As a result, this type of fiscal management constantly reintroduces suspicions of fiscal fragility, which affects the expectations of debt solvency.

Given the low rate of output growth in the recent years, the growth of tax revenues has depended largely on the rising efficiency of collection and (consequently) on the increase in the fiscal burden. The latter rose, as a proportion of GDP, from 28 per cent in 1994 to 34 per cent in 2003. Primary surpluses have been achieved through the restriction of both public investment and public social spending. In turn, the high interest rates on the public debt have caused a remarkable growth in its costs. Therefore, despite the government's efforts to achieve higher primary surpluses, it has never been able to eliminate the nominal public deficit (which includes interest payments). In the last

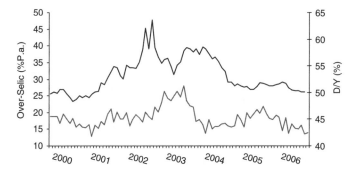

Figure 11.4   Brazil: Debt/GDP and over-Selic interest rate (2000–06)
Source: BCB *apud* IPEADATA.

three years of the Cardoso administration, and in the first three years of Lula, the nominal deficit has been around 3.6 per cent of GDP, even though the primary surplus target increased from 3.75 to 4.25 per cent of GDP. Table 11.1 below shows the conditioning factors of the growth of D/Y; the shaded lines indicate that the nominal interest rate has been the main explanatory factor for the nominal public deficit and the high D/Y ratio, despite the achievement of significant primary surpluses.

The diagnosis underlying the 1994 stabilization programme, the Real Plan, emphasized the establishment of a fiscal regime compatible with monetary stability – that is, a regime that could produce a balanced budget in the short run – as a critical requirement for success. Several events have made it impossible to achieve this goal. From the start, the implementation of the plan suffered from the type of insertion of the Brazilian economy into the global financial environment. The increasing inflows of capital induced by high domestic interest rates reduced the country's net external debt, as the BCB accumulated reserves. However, this process led to the simultaneous expansion of the domestic debt due to the sterilization of the domestic equivalent of these inflows of foreign capital. Thus, the BCB swapped (cheap) foreign debt for (much more expensive) domestic debt.

Table 11.1   Brazil: Net debt evolution

	2	20	2
Total net debt balance	5	51	5
Net debt-growth[1]	2	–	–
Conditioning factors:	1	2	2
Public sector	3	2	3
Primary	–	–	–
Nominal interest	7	6	8
Exchange adjustment [2]	9	–	–
Domestic security. debt	4	–	–
External debt	4	–	–
External debt	0	0	–
Acknowledgement of	0	0	0
Privatizations	–	0	0
GDP growth effect[3]	–	–	–

1) Net accumulated debt-growth as percentage of GDP when considering all factors taken together GDP, divided by the current GDP accumulated in the last 12-month period valuated, calculated by the formula: Conditioning Factors/GDPAccumulated In 12Months)*100, not reflecting debt growth as percentage of GDP.
2) Indicates the sum of the monthly impacts up to the reference month.
3) It takes into account the change in the ratio debt/GDP due to growth observed in GDP, calculated by the formula: Dt-1/(GDPcurrent month/ GDP base month)-Dt-1.
Source: BCB Monthly Bulletin, November 2006.

The structural reforms implemented during the Real Plan also help to explain the almost continuous expansion of the Brazilian public debt. They included the renegotiation of state and local government debts, the recognition of contested public sector debt certificates ('skeletons'; see below), and the privatization programme. The attempt to control state and local government debt culminated with several agreements to fund their existing debt. These agreements involved, on the one hand, exchanging the existing debts for lower-cost securities issued by the federal government. On the other hand, the federal government imposed, among other conditions, the privatization of the assets owned by these institutions – especially the state banks. This operation caused an expansion of approximately R$ 103 billion in the public debt. The 'skeletons' consisted of public sector liabilities not previously registered in the public sector accounts. Their impact on the public debt between 1994 and 2001 reached R$ 63 billion.[6] In the same period, the privatization programme contributed R$ 59 billion to curb the growth of the debt.

The launch of the Real Plan coincided with the moment when financial globalization showed its instability, which imposed a high cost on the Brazilian economy because of its external vulnerability. International financial crises were addressed through a higher spread between the domestic and international interest rates, and through the offer of hedge instruments for financial investors. For example, the BCB not only sold foreign reserves, but also sold bonds indexed to the exchange rate in order to mitigate the capital flight. The costs of these responses to international instability were among the factors leading to the expansion of the public debt: the devaluation of the exchange rate, along with the rise of the interest rate, explains the expansion of the debt during currency crises (for example, 1999 and 2000).

Another aspect of the evolution of the debt helps to illustrate the high degree of its subordination to the interest rate policy and, secondarily, the behaviour of the exchange rate. The debt not only increased from 29.2 to 42.6 per cent of GDP; its composition and valuation criteria also changed significantly. First, most of the debt had been securitized, with the share of debt in the form of bonds increasing from 11.5 to 35.4 per cent of GDP.[7] Second, the swap of non-financial for securitized debt was followed by an increase in the relative weight of bonds indexed to the interest (Selic) rate. Third, and in close connection with these movements, there was a tendency for shortening the maturity structure of this debt. Since an increasing portion of the debt was financed on an almost daily basis, any change in the basic interest rate was immediately reflected in the interest paid to the creditors.

In the first two years after the introduction of the inflation targeting regime, there was an improvement in the composition of the debt. The percentage of the debt indexed to the Selic and the exchange rate fell. However, this happened in parallel with a significant growth in the securitized D/Y ratio, after the 1998–99 currency crisis. Furthermore, since 2001 even the improvement in the composition of the debt ended, following the deterioration in confidence and another episode of capital flight, which intensified the creditors' demand for bonds indexed to the exchange rate.

In 2002, Cardoso's last year in office, a further worsening of expectations followed the growth of the opposition candidate Lula da Silva in the polls. The government imposed several measures to attenuate the capital flight and the dollarization of the financial assets. There was initially an abrupt rise of the Selic rate, and a change in the required reserve ratio on demand deposits, which were meant to increase the opportunity cost of carrying exchange rate indexed assets. Moreover, the Brazilian government borrowed US$ 10 billion from the IMF. In the fiscal area, the primary surplus target rose from 3.5 per cent to 3.88 per cent of GDP.[8] The significance of these 'market friendly' signals coming from Lula da Silva should not be underestimated. Even more explicitly, he also indicated the continuation of the prevailing economic policies by promising 'not to break contracts'.

This was the fiscal legacy left by Cardoso to his successor. The D/Y ratio rose from 42.6 per cent to 55.5 per cent of GDP between 1998 and 2002. The profile of the debt deteriorated: the share of Selic-indexed bonds tripled when compared with the period immediately before the 1998–99 crisis, reaching 60.3 per cent of the federal securitized bonds. In summary, the monetary policy changes associated with the introduction of the inflation targeting regime, the floating exchange rate regime and the liberalization of the capital account of the balance of payments have consolidated a policy hierarchy. At the top stands monetary policy, and fiscal policy is slotted in a subordinate position.

Given this legacy, the Lula government has selected credibility as its main priority. This required maintaining the same macroeconomic model, but with greater intensity of implementation of fiscal and monetary policy. The neoliberal agenda of the previous government was revitalized, and the contractionary fiscal policy framework was preserved, which implies that the decrease of D/Y remains the sole objective. For instance, the reform of the public pension fund system, which was blocked by the Workers' Party during the Cardoso administration, was immediately resumed by Lula da Silva.[9]

The Lula government initially raised the target for the primary surplus to 4.25 per cent of the GDP. However, fiscal management has been even tighter. In 2003, the actual surplus was 4.32 per cent of GDP, in the following year it reached 4.59 per cent and, in 2005, 4.84 per cent of GDP. This additional effort to achieve credibility was insufficient to make D/Y decline to under 50 per cent – the target agreed with the IMF in 2002, when it was supposed to be achievable simply through a primary surplus of 3.75 per cent.[10] The 55.5 per cent debt/GDP ratio inherited from Cardoso increased to 57.2 per cent at the end of 2003, and quickly fell to 51.7 per cent in 2004 – the only year when there was an acceptable growth rate during the Lula government. Since then, it has remained stable at this level.

Initially, the Lula administration tried to convince the IMF to accept a so-called 'counter cyclical primary surplus', which would allow the reduction of the fiscal target when output growth was below target. However, the government moved from this proposal to launch a fiscal adjustment programme which would commit it by law to an even tighter fiscal stance until 2010. This proposal was defeated within the government.[11]

To escape the logic underlying the conventional diagnosis of debt sustainability, which focuses only on D/Y and huge primary surpluses, it is essential to take into account the nominal deficit as a whole: that is, to analyse the composition of fiscal spending. This will reveal, once again, the nature of the current Brazilian macroeconomic policy regime – the subordination of fiscal to monetary policy, which is also shown by the financial burden of the public debt. Debt interest payments increased from an annual average of 6.7 per cent of GDP in 1996–2002, to 8.0 per cent in 2003–05, after Lula took office.

The evolution of the debt burden in the recent period was not homogeneous. In 2003, when the interest rate was rising most of the time, D/Y increased around 200 base points. In 2005, in a similar scenario and with an even larger primary surplus, that ratio remained stable. In contrast, D/Y fell significantly in 2004, when the interest rate was relatively low and output growth was strong (4.9 per cent).

Having examined the evidence, an important question never asked in orthodox studies, arises: what are the criteria for choosing the most favorable macroeconomic environment for fiscal adjustment, including a countercyclical fiscal policy? Any macroeconometric application after this suggestion should consider a theoretical step to develop models whose causality can be the opposite of the orthodox, which goes from the fiscal fundamentals to the determination of interest rates. It was suggested above that the opposite is also conceivable: high interest rates cause the (nominal) deficit and the expansion of the public debt.

4   Interest rates and inflation control

In Brazil, the interest rate has been employed as an effective instrument to control inflation at least since mid-2004. The interest rate has been generally high for several years, leading the wealth holders to make their portfolio as liquid as possible. The investment rate has not increased because of the simple Keynesian rule: it is generally more convenient to hold government bonds than to purchase fixed capital assets. The former generate high profits at a relatively low risk. Since the monetary conditions in Brazil imply a permanent situation of weak demand, a large number of investment projects yields low returns and suffers from high risk. This dynamics explains, to a large extent, why the investment rate gravitates around only 19 per cent of the GDP, and why the annual average growth rate of the Brazilian economy in 2003–06 was only 2.6 per cent.

The oscillations of the interest rate affect future demand. When facing an increase in interest rates, ongoing investment projects are not abandoned, but the new ones, which were at planning stage, are discarded. Therefore, it is future (rather than current) demand that has depressed higher interest rates. This time lag between the action and its effect, that was described by Friedman (1968), has been estimated for the Brazilian economy by the BCB (see Bogdanski et al., 2000). Another process also requires careful study. It was shown in that paper that, when the interest rate rises, inflation falls only after 6–9 months. In the first six months, inflation rises. What is probably happening is that, as firms have financial costs and current demand is not weakened by the higher interest rates, firms have scope to pass these additional costs on to prices. This would explain why an increase in the interest rate has an initial inflationary impact.

After six months, profit margins become incompatible with a reduced demand. Each firm tries to reduce costs in order to preserve its profit margin. Programmes for reducing waste are put into place, which cuts current demand. Workers are fired, while others are employed to do the same jobs at lower wages, which causes a further reduction in demand. Workers are also hired and 'employed' again as outsourced suppliers of services at lower wages, which also reduces demand. In conclusion, higher interest rates not only disarm future investment, but also reduce future consumption through unemployment and/or the reduction in remunerations.

Many critics of this monetary policy regime state that, if the inflationary pressures result from supply-side shocks, then demand-constraining instruments (such as the interest rate) should not be used: the interest rate is only effective against demand inflation, rather than cost inflation. These critics are wrong. The interest rate is effective in controlling any type of inflation. Inflation is always due to the disequilibrium between supply and demand, which can be eliminated by acting on the supply side as well the demand side – the interest rate works on the latter, while incomes policies work on the supply side.

A more consistent criticism could be addressed to the use of the interest rates against inflation. This is not based on its ineffectiveness, since it has been proved to be effective, but on its undesirable impact on demand and employment. This would be a critique of both the intensity with which this instrument is used, and its theoretical underpinnings. It is necessary to attach a less critical role to the interest rate as an instrument to control inflation, and to try to avoid using it entirely.

One can accept that the interest rate should be employed as an anti-inflation instrument among others, but this should be widely and intensely supported by instruments capable of avoiding a supply shock. In this arrangement, the interest rate would be low, since inflation control would be basically secured by other instruments. The interest rates rise only to offset the malfunctioning of the other instruments. These instruments could include, for example, the adjustment of profit margins and a wage policy based on the growth of productivity.

In this arrangement, higher interest rates would signal a fall in future demand. This expectation would prevent firms from passing the entire impact of higher costs (which could not be avoided by the supply-side instruments) to prices, because this would probably lead to difficulties selling their output. However, this difficulty would never really come true because the interest rate is already relatively low. In turn, the entrepreneurs would not notice that there was no real demand decrease, and would think that they have sold their output because they did not adjust their prices. This framework would keep inflation under control without causing unemployment, since the entrepreneurs believe that the signals, generated from small increases in the interest rate, would have a real impact on demand.

In this arrangement, firms would slowly pass on higher costs to prices, as supply shocks are absorbed by prices when only the interest rate is used as an anti-inflationary instrument. Naturally, this arrangement would depend on the entrepreneurs' belief that small increases in the interest rate (which is assumed to be low) could lead to demand reductions creating difficulties to their future sales. Otherwise, the interest rate would have to be raised to a point where it would reduce demand to keep prices under control, causing unemployment – which is exactly the undesirable effect of the orthodox approach.

This macroeconomic architecture could be adopted as a regime of transition to abandon the inflation targeting regime currently in operation in Brazil. In other words, the interest rate would be kept as an instrument to control inflation, side by side with several other instruments. The better these instruments, the lower the interest rate would be and, gradually, its anti-inflation function would fade away.

Finally, let us mention some examples of supply-side instruments that can help keep prices under control in Brazil. Utilities prices, for example electricity, public transport and petrol, have given a significant contribution to inflation in the recent period. The electricity rates are indexed to the general price index, when they should be adjusted by taking in account costs, productivity and planned investments. The productivity of public transport has decreased steadily due to traffic jams, which have also been responsible for the large increase in transportation fares and the deterioration in the quality of the services. In order to raise the productivity of the transport system, it would be necessary to introduce a large investment programme to build subways and ring-roads. Finally, the price of petrol in Brazil varies with the international oil price, even though Brazil is self-sufficient in production. Breaking this link would allow the price of petrol to be determined by domestic supply and demand, which would isolate the Brazilian economy from international oil price shocks.

Additional questions to be examined statistically are, first, whether the rise of the interest rate in Brazil causes, in fact, an increase in the rate of inflation in the subsequent period. Second, what are the social (unemployment) costs of inflation control, in a monetary regime that uses only the interest rate to achieve this goal? Third, what is the capacity of the interest rate to control inflation?

5   Concluding remarks

The development of a research agenda on the behaviour of the interest rate in Brazil can provide more accurate answers to the questions listed below, all of them essential to compile a 'dossier' on the interest rate. This chapter has justified these questions in several ways. The questions are: (i) is the interest rate an endogenous or exogenous variable?; (ii) does the exchange rate lead the interest rate, or is it the other way around? (iii) is the overvaluation of the exchange rate in Brazil primarily determined by the trade surplus or by the high interest rate, which induces a large capital inflow? (iv) should the interest rate be reduced to achieve a balanced public budget? (v) alternatively, should the public budget be balanced in order to allow the interest rate to fall? (vi) does an increase in the interest rate immediately cause an increase in the rate of inflation? (vii) what is the lag between an increase in the interest rate and a reduction of inflation? (viii) what is the cost of raising the interest rate in terms of unemployment, and (ix) what is the relationship between the interest rate and the rate of inflation?

Notes

1 The positive correlation between the exchange rate and the interest rate is discussed in Sicsú (2002).
2 See Mundell (1962) and Fleming (1962).
3 The first US$ 18 billion stand-by agreement was initially established for the period 1998–2001 (36 months), as a part of a US$ 41.5 billion rescue package involving other multilateral financial institutions. A new stand-by was established for September 2001–December 2002, including US$ 15 billion as a supplementary reserve facility. A new stand-by was signed in September 2002 for the following 15 months, reaching US$ 30 billion.
4 The rise of the basic interest rate, in Brazil, causes an expansion of the public debt service, since that rate represents the return on most of this debt.
5 The primary surplus equals receipts less non-interest payments, while the nominal deficit includes the financial expenditures.
6 Estimates from Nascimento and Gerardo (s.d.)
7 Data from the Monthly Bulletin of the Central Bank of Brazil and related to the net public debt.
8 The target of 3.75 per cent of GDP was imposed in June. By September 2002 the Brazilian government negotiated a new stand-by agreement with the IMF, with a new target of 3.88 per cent of GDP. In the Letter from the Minister of Finance to the Director General of the IMF, the Brazilian government states that the presidential candidates were aware of the document and agreed with its terms.

9 The consolidated non-financial public sector budget includes the fiscal budget in a strict sense and the social security budget. The latter includes the general pension system, embracing the private sector workers, and the public sector workers' system. The reform included a new contribution (tax) on the retired workers (11 per cent of their pensions, after a certain level) and, for new public sector workers, the change to a capitalization regime.

10 According to the technical memorandum attached to the stand-by agreement of September 2002.

11 The ministers of planning and finance were defeated by the minister of civil administration. Some analysts saw a presidential decision behind this victory.

References

Bogdanski, J., Tombini, A.A. and Werlang, S.R.C., 'Implementing Inflation Targeting in Brazil', Working Paper no. 1, Banco Central do Brasil, 2000.

Cardim de Carvalho, F. and Sicsú, J., 'Controvérsias Recentes sobre Controles de Capitais'. *Revista de Economia Política*, 24(2), 2005.

Mundell, R., 'The Appropriate Use of Monetary and Fiscal Policy for Internal and External Stability'. *IMF Staff Papers*, vol. 9, 1962.

Fleming, J.M., 'Domestic Financial Policies under Fixed and Floating Exchange Rates'. *IMF Staff Papers*, vol. 9, 1962.

Friedman, M., 'The Role of the Monetary Policy'. *American Economic Review*, March, 1968, 1–17.

Nascimento, E.R. and Gerardo, J.C., Lei Complementar 101/2000: dois anos de Responsabilidade Fiscal (versão atualizada) s.d., available at www.tesouro.fazenda. gov.br/hp/downloads/LRF2Ed.pdf

Sicsú, J., 'Flutuação Cambial e Taxa de Juros no Brasil'. *Revista de Economia Política*, 22(3), 2002.

12
Fixed Income Debt Management and Uncertainty in the Lula Administration, 2002–2005[1]

Rogério Sobreira[2]
Brazilian School of Public and Business Administration, Getulio Vargas Foundation

Paulo Gaya[3]
Brazilian Central Bank

1 Introduction

In November 1999, the National Treasury and the Brazilian Central Bank started a programme to change the maturity and profile of the domestic public debt (BACEN/STN, 1999). The aim of this programme was to extend the maturity of the domestic debt and increase the share of fixed income debt in the total debt. These outcomes were achieved only in part. Between early 2000 and late 2001, the maturity of the fixed income debt was extended from 8.5 months to 26 months. The percentage of fixed income debt also increased, in 2000, from 10.2 per cent in January 2000 to 14.8 per cent in December. However, the adverse shocks experienced by the Brazilian economy during 2002 – the devaluation of the Argentine peso, the mark-to-market crisis of Brazilian mutual funds, and the electoral crisis, with the fear of victory of Luiz Inácio Lula da Silva – increased uncertainty and led to a reduced maturity of the domestic debt. They also led to an increase of the interest rate-indexed securities, which reached 60.8 per cent at the end of 2002, while the share of fixed income bonds decreased sharply to 1.9 per cent in January 2003. After that, good fundamentals helped to restore investor confidence, leading to a recovery of the share of fixed income bonds in the total debt. As a consequence, the share of these bonds increased to 27.9 per cent in December 2005, and 35 per cent in November 2006.

The uncertainty mentioned above is related to the movements of the rate of interest, as a consequence of peaks of the inflation rate experienced by the Brazilian economy during 2002. The inflation targeting regime was introduced in 2000 and, consequently, the interest rate should follow the path needed to achieve the year's inflation target.

The volatility of the rate of interest inevitably raises the volatility of the profits of the fixed-income bonds negotiated in the secondary market. This leads to a corresponding increase in the variance of the bids, and the required premium for this type of bond also tends to increase. This volatility, in turn, helps to check the demand for fixed income bonds.

The chapter examines the management of the fixed income debt and the behaviour of the auctions for fixed income bonds in the Brazilian economy in 2002–05. It attempts to explain how the uncertainties surrounding a 'left' government impacted upon the management of the public debt in general, and of the fixed income debt in particular, and the factors responsible for the dispersion of bids. Economic theory (Cammak, 1991; Milgrom and Weber, 1982; Umlauf, 1993) suggests that the more uncertain the environment, the higher should be the variance of the bids. Consequently, in times of intense uncertainty, it becomes harder for the Treasury to sell fixed income bonds.

The chapter is organized as follows. In the next section we review debt management in Brazil during the Lula administration, especially the change in the debt profile anticipated by the *'Plano Anual de Financiamento'* (Annual Finance Plan).[4] The following section describes the characteristics and behaviour of the auctions for fixed-income bonds (LTN and NTN-F) in Brazil during this period. In the sequel, the behaviour of the auctions in the period is examined in more detail, and some econometric results are provided, in order to explain the determinants of the variance of bids for the period. The final section concludes this chapter.

2 Debt management and debt behaviour in the Lula administration

According to the *'Plano Anual de Financiamento'* of 2002 (PAF, 2002), the main objectives of the Treasury for the domestic public debt were to increase the average maturity and the percentage of fixed income debt in the domestic public debt. In spite of the fact that the average maturity of the domestic debt had increased monotonically since 1999, this trajectory was interrupted in 2002. The uncertainty due to the election of a left-wing candidate has helped to shorten the maturity of the domestic public debt since mid-2002, as can be seen from Figure 12.1.

The analysis of the maturity behaviour during the period, however, shows that the shortened maturity cannot be explained only as a consequence of the uncertainties surrounding the economic policy of the Lula administration. It can also be a consequence of the attempt to increase the percentage of the fixed income bonds in the total domestic debt.

The main problem related to the increase of fixed income debt refers to the behaviour of the rate of interest. The longer the maturity of the fixed income bonds, the higher the interest rate risk, that is, the risk of loss as the interest rate increases. In Brazil, the pattern of the prime (Selic) rate is quite volatile (Figure 12.2). Consequently, the interest rate risk is quite high for the holders of fixed income bonds.

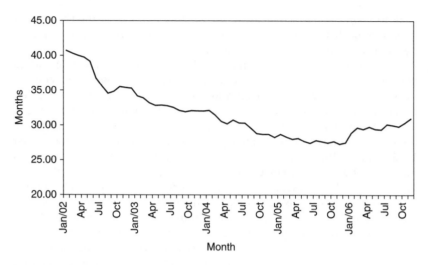

Figure 12.1   Brazil: public debt: average maturity, 2002–06
Source: National Treasury.

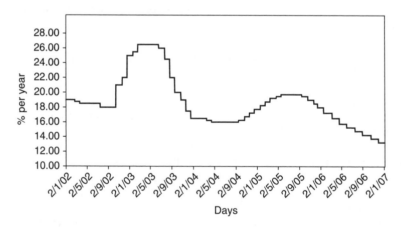

Figure 12.2   Brazil: Selic rate, 2002–07
Source: Brazilian Central Bank.

In spite of the shortened maturity, the profile of the debt changed substantially in this period, as can be seen from Figure 12.3. The percentage of fixed income bonds increased, and the percentage of interest-rate linked bonds decreased substantially. The good news about this change is the fact that the interest rate risk has been carried more and more by the bond-holders, and the cost of the debt has declined. This gives us another explanation for the behaviour of the maturity of domestic debt. In order to avoid the interest

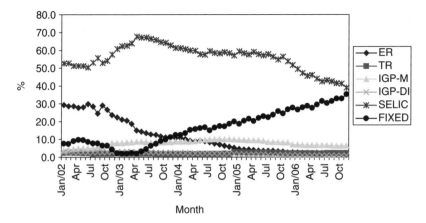

Figure 12.3 Brazil: public debt by type, 2002–06
Source: Brazilian Central Bank.

rate risk, the holders of fixed income bonds typically demand a higher interest rate in the auctions. Thus, the longer the maturity of the bond, the higher is the rate demanded. To avoid the ensuing costs, the Treasury prefers to reduce the maturity of the bonds. In this respect, it is important to mention the fact that the Selic rate was very volatile during this period. Accordingly, the risk of loss due to holding fixed income debt is high. Clearly, if the behaviour of the Selic rate was more benign, the task of the Treasury would be easier.

It is important to mention that the debt management related to the main aim – that is, to increase the participation of the fixed income bond – in the first Lula administration was very successful. Nowadays, the percentage of the fixed income debt is around 35 per cent, and the share of interest-rate linked debt is around 39 per cent. The increase in the participation of fixed income debt is important not only because the costs of a higher interest rate is transferred to the holder, but also because of the efficiency of monetary policy. In an environment in which the participation of interest rate-linked debt is very large, the efficiency of monetary policy is lower because the wealth effect is positive. In other words, the gains of the increase in the rate of interest are transferred to the holders, who face a higher budget constraint and, therefore, can increase their consumption levels. Under these circumstances, it is difficult to convince the holders to buy long-term fixed income bonds. Thus, the Treasury had to face the shortened maturity of the domestic public debt as a price to pay for a more favourable debt profile.

When we look at the maturity according to the type of bond issued, we can have a more detailed view of the effects of the debt management related to the fixed income bonds implemented in this period. Until the end of 2003, the LTN – the National Treasury Bill – was the only fixed income bond issued by

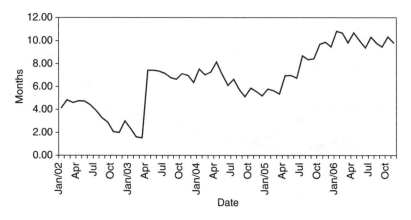

Figure 12.4   LTN maturity, 2002–06
Source: Brazilian National Treasury.

the Treasury. This bill is a typical zero-coupon bond (or discount bond). The Treasury decided to increase the proportion of fixed income bond issuing more LTN. Typically, this kind of bond does not allow long maturities – typically, its maturity is one year – so the Treasury had to change its strategy and started issuing coupon bonds.

This limitation aside, the Treasury was successful in extending the maturity of these bonds, as can be seen in Figure 12.4. This gave the Treasury the ability to issue coupon bonds.[5]

In spite of this benign environment, the ability of the Treasury to increase the proportion of coupon bonds was quite limited. The evolution of the public debt in Brazil since 2002 shows several significant features in comparison to the previous years.[6] The proportion of NTN-F in the total fixed income debt was very insignificant – less than 1 per cent (Figure 12.5). Nowadays, this partici-pation is much higher than in the previous years. However, it is very thin in international terms (in comparison with US and UK, for instance) – in spite of its increase in the last year, this proportion is less than 5 per cent of the total debt. One of the reasons for this is the fact that the liquidity of this bond is very low; therefore, the willingness of the holders to buy this type of bond is low.

We also must bear in mind another feature of this bond that, combined with its low liquidity, helps to understand the low demand for this bond, which is, that the maturity of the NTN-F is typically higher than the maturity of the LTN. Since its liquidity is low, the holders of fixed income bonds do not accept keeping this bond in their portfolios for long periods. The only way to solve this problem in the short term is to increase the remuneration of the bond. That was precisely what the Treasury undertook. Nowadays, the rate paid by the NTN-F is much higher than the rate of the LTN.

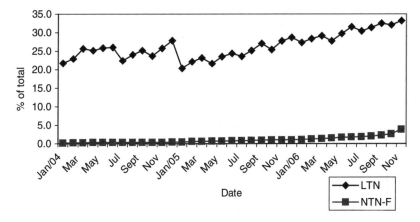

Figure 12.5   Fixed income debt in the market by type of bond, 2004–06
Source: Brazilian National Treasury.

We can, therefore, conclude that the strategy of increasing the proportion of fixed income debt and reducing the interest-rate linked debt followed by the Treasury in the Lula years has been sustained mainly through LTN. The Treasury, thus, needs to increase the proportion of NTN-F in order to change effectively the profile of the fixed income debt.

To achieve this goal it is necessary to change drastically the macroeconomic policy environment, in order to diminish the volatility and uncertainty surrounding the evolution of the interest rate. In this respect, it is important to pursue a fiscal policy stance including a significant primary surplus and control of current spending. The fiscal policy in the first Lula administration was characterized by high fiscal surplus and a certain control of spending. However, in the last year of the first administration these controls were reduced, and the market started to have doubts about the ability and willingness of the government to keep the fiscal stance that characterized the first half of the administration.

It is important to mention (PAF, 2003; PAF, 2004; PAF, 2005) that the increase in the fixed income debt was possible only because the macroeconomic environment was favourable. Figures 12.3 and 12.5 show that the increase in the share of fixed income debt started in 2003, when the Selic rate began to decline. The same happened to the maturity of the LTN. In this respect, it is important to notice that the LTN maturity decreased in 2005 because of the increase in the Selic rate. It is also important to notice that the proportion of NTN-F started to increase effectively only when the Selic rate began to fall in the last quarter of 2005. Thus, only when the government can signal an effective decrease in the rate of interest will agents demand longer term fixed income bonds. This is precisely what is expected in the second Lula administration.

Table 12.1   Days of LTN auctions

Day	% of total auctions
Monday	15
Tuesday	258
Wednesday	12
Thursday	82
Friday	8

Source: Brazilian Central Bank.

3   The Treasury bill auctions

In the period under analysis, the most important fixed income security issued by the Treasury to increase the share of fixed income debt was the LTN. After 2003, the Treasury started issuing National Treasury Notes series F (NTN-F) in competitive auctions. As was mentioned in the previous section, the NTN-F is a typical coupon bond – the coupons are paid semi-annually – and the LTN is a zero-coupon bond. The Brazilian Central Bank used to issue fixed income securities but, since 2000, the Fiscal Responsibility Law prevented the Central Bank from issuing securities. Nowadays, only the Treasury is allowed to issue them.

The face value of the LTN is R\$ 1000, and the interest is paid as a discount of the face value. Its maturity is variable, but the bills are issued in a way their maturities always fall in the first day of a quarter (January, April, July and October). The face value of the NTN-F is also equal to R\$ 1000. The coupon rate is 10 per cent per year, and it is paid semi-annually. The average maturity of the NTN-F is higher than that of the LTN. The maturity date of all the NTN-F issued until now is 1 January. The LTN and NTN-F are sold at a discriminatory price auction. The auction is announced one day in advance. Each bidder can submit up to five bids, and the bids include the price the bidder is willing to pay and the quantity the bidder is willing to buy at that price. There are no quantitative restrictions on the amount a bidder can buy in the auction, and one bidder can buy all the securities on offer. The settlement date is typically the day after the auction. After the auction, the securities can be negotiated in the secondary market. The auctions are typically run on Tuesdays. However, in the weeks when the Monetary Policy Committee meets the auctions are postponed, generally to Thursday.

In our study, we analysed 375 LTN auctions that took place in 2002–05. Table 12.1 shows the distribution of the days of occurrence of the auctions in this period. As can be seen, Tuesday is the most frequent day of occurrence of LTN auctions.

We also analysed 102 competitive auctions of NTN-F during this period. The distribution of the days of these auctions can be found in Table 12.2.

Table 12.2   Days of NTN-F auctions

Day	% of total auctions
Monday	9
Tuesday	61
Wednesday	3
Thursday	29
Friday	0

Source: Brazilian Central Bank.

Tuesday is also the most frequent day of occurrence of the auction of NTN-F. In this respect, it is important to notice that the National Treasury decided to concentrate the auctions of both bonds – and not only the fixed income bonds, but all securities issued by the Treasury – in the same day in order to have a better result in the auctions since the dispersion of the bids is typically lower in this situation. The bonds were also issued in order to mature on the same day, in order to increase the degree of fungibility of the bonds and help price formation in the secondary market.

Only the institutions registered in the settlement and custody system for operations involving Treasury securities (Selic) can participate in the auctions. In this system, institutions can bid until one hour after the beginning of the auction. Since the bids are analysed individually, a participant can have more than one bid accepted by the Treasury.

It is important to notice a change in the rules of the LTN auctions that occurred in the second semester of 2002. In that period, probably as a consequence of the increase in the variance of the auctions, the Treasury decided to change the kind of auction from discriminatory to uniform price auction. As can be seen from Figure 12.6, the weighted variance[7] of the interest rate of the LTN auctions increased substantially in the second semester of 2002, in contrast with the first semester of that year. Accordingly, the degree of acceptance of bids declined and the interest rate premium increased. In such circumstances, the Central Bank decided to change the rules of the auctions. In the discriminatory price auction adopted by the Central Bank, the cut-off price is the lowest price of the competitive bids. After the determination of the cut-off price, the Central Bank distributes the supply of LTN in descending order of price.

In spite of the change in the auction rules, the number of bids declined, possibly reflecting the uncertainties associated to the presidential elections and the conduct of public debt management if the left candidate were to win. The average maturity of the LTNs auctioned also declined, as can be seen from Figure 12.4. The longest LTN issued in this period had a maturity of only 82 working days. The number of auctions also declined, reflecting the difficulty of

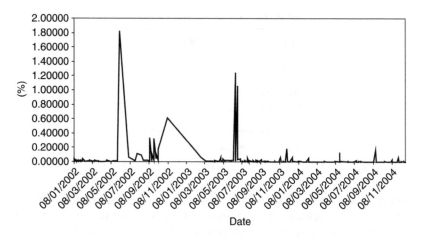

Figure 12.6   Weighted variance of the rate of LTN auctions, 2002–04
Source: Brazilian Central Bank.

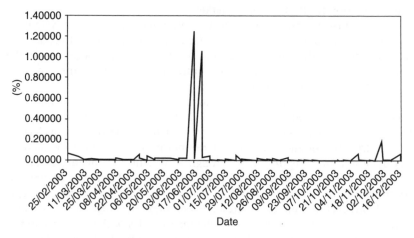

Figure 12.7   Weighted variance of the rate of LTN auctions, 2003
Source: Brazilian Central Bank.

price formation in the auctions. As a consequence, at the beginning of November the LTN auctions ceased until the inauguration of the new administration. The auctions were reinitiated only at the end of February 2003.

In comparison with the previous period, 2003 was a year of low disturbances at the LTN auctions. The weighted variance declined sharply, and the maturities and the number of bids increased (see Figure 12.7). The number of auctions increased gradually from the beginning of the year until the 'historical' average of eight auctions per month had been achieved. By contrast, 2004 was a year of great volatility in the LTN auctions. The weighted variance rose, but the average maturity of LTN auctioned continued to increase. The monthly number of auctions also increased, reaching almost ten per month. This number reflects the increased difficulty of the Central Bank to reach the market consensus in terms of the price – and interest rate – of LTN.

In this case, the lack of consensus was probably related to the uncertainty regarding the trajectory of the rate of interest and the behaviour of inflation (cf. BACEN, 2004). As a consequence of the threat of inflation, the Central Bank started to increase the rate of interest. Since October, this rate increased 0.5 percentage points per month until December, reaching 17.75 per cent per year at the end of 2004, against 16 per cent at the end of August.

The market started to anticipate the behaviour in the prime rate by the middle of 2004. Accordingly, on 20–21 May the Central Bank realized 13 LTN auctions, selling only a small part of the total supply. The average rate of interest also changed, moving from 17 per cent at the end of April to more than 19 per cent in May.

It is also important to notice the change in the variance of the auctions, especially for the LTN of longer maturities. By April, this variance (for LTN maturing in 400 working days) was around 0.003. In early May it had reached 0.005, and 0.08 on 20 May. As a consequence, this type of LTN was supplied again only in October.

4 Econometric results: what are the determinants of the variance of the bids of LTN and NTN-F auctions during the Lula administration?

One of the aims of this chapter is to analyse empirically the determinants of the variance of the interest rate in the LTN auctions. The hypothesis being tested is that the volatility of the various markets are related since they reflect the same basic uncertainty. The variance of the auctions is, then, the dependent variable in our model. As independent variables we selected the variances of the rate of interest of interbank operations maturing in one day (CDI), the variance of the interest rate futures contracts (DIFUT) and the variance of the secondary market of LTN (Selic).

As for the variance of the rate of interest of interbank operations maturing in one day – which, according to Garcia and Rezende (2000), can be seen as a proxy for the confidence of the agents in the future behaviour of the rate of interest – we took the variances of operations realised up to three days before the date of the LTN auction. The volume of the operations weighted the variances. As a proxy for the variance of the interest rate of the secondary market of LTN, we also took the variance of operations realised up to three days before the date of the LTN auction.

Table 12.3   Regressors and expected signal

Regressor	Expected signal
Variance of interbank market (VCDI)	$B_1 > 0$
Variance of futures market (VDIFUT)	$B_2 > 0$
Variance of secondary market of LTN (VSELIC)	$B_3 > 0$
Maturity (VMATU)	$B_6 > 0$

4.1   LTN auctions

Between 1 January 2002 and 31 December 2005, the Treasury realized 375 LTN auctions with 26 maturity dates. Until 2002, the typical maturity date for this bond was the first Wednesday of the month. At the beginning of 2003, the Treasury decided to change the maturity date, creating a pattern where the bond would mature always at the beginning of the quarter. This pattern was implemented in order to improve the price formation process of the bond.

It was observed that the futures contract of the one day interbank rate (DI Futuro) transacted in the Brazilian Futures and Mercantile Exchange (BM&F) allows the design of a financial operation with a fixed interest rate which matures at the beginning of the quarter. More specifically, the maturity of this operation is the first working day of the month of maturity. This operation helps the price formation of fixed income bonds, since it is referred in the price formation of this futures operation. Therefore, the Treasury decided to change the maturity dates of the auctioned bonds in order to make the linkage between the futures and the spot market for the rate of interest more explicit. Thus, since 2003, the maturity date of the LTN was changed to the first working day of the quarters (January, April, July, and October). The bond holders, thus, can pay attention to the futures market of interest rate in order to bid the rate in the LTN auctions.

Considering this aspect of the maturity date of LTNs, we decided to reject the older auctions in which maturity dates were different from those determined by the new pattern, keeping 16 from the 26 mature bonds. Our sample, thus, included 282 LTN auctions realized since 25 February 2003. In this respect, it is important to mention that the price formation criteria were different in the rejected auctions. Thus, to homogenize the sample we took into account only auctions with the same price formation criteria. It is also important to mention that the link between the futures interest rate market and the spot market was an aspect that we decided to incorporate explicitly in the regressions through the variable DIFUT.[8]

We tested the variance of the bids in the LTN auctions against the following variables: MSEC, DIFUT, CDI, and DU. The result of this regression can be found in Table 12.4.

Table 12.4   Regression for the LTN auctions

Dependent Variable: VAR
Method: Least squares
Sample: 1282
Included observations: 282

Variable	Coefficient	Std. Error	t-Statistic	Prob.
C	0.007248	0.005999	1.208286	0.2280
MSEC	−0.003062	0.019363	−0.158116	0.8745
DIFUT	0.012920	0.086393	0.149551	0.8812
CDI	0.107296	0.059847	1.792841	0.0741
DU	−1.01E-05	1.73E-05	−0.587035	0.5577

R-squared	0.016806	Mean dependent var	0.006520
Adjusted R-squared	0.002608	S.D. dependent var	0.036940
S.E. of regression	0.036892	Akaike info criterion	−3.744075
Sum squared resid	0.377002	Schwarz criterion	−3.679502
Log likelihood	532.9146	F-statistic	1.183681
Durbin-Watson stat	2.056504	Prob(F-statistic)	0.318188

As can be seen in Table 12.4, the R-squared is very low (only 1.6 per cent), which implies a very low predictive power. Moreover, the coefficients were non-significant and the signals of some of the variables were different from the expected. Since this model did not fit our expectations, we move on to examine another model with a higher predictive power.

Following Garcia and Rezende (2000), we utilize the logarithm of the variables to mitigate those variables whose values were significant far away from the average, reducing their weight in the regression. Our result was much closer from what theory would expect.

The new regression included a sample with 229 LTN auctions, since 53 auctions presented a value of MSEC equal to zero, which made impossible the calculation of the logarithm. The new regression is presented in the Table 12.5.

As can be seen in Table 12.5, the log of the variance of the Selic rate in the secondary market, of the variance of the futures rate of interest, of the variance of the interbank rate (CDI), and of the maturity date (in working days) presented a predictive power of the behaviour of the variance of the rate of the LTN equal to 36 per cent. We also tested different models, combining the four regressors, but they had a lower R-squared. Thus, the best model was the one presented in the Table 12.5. The Akaike and Schwarz criteria also pointed to this model as the best one. It is also important to notice that all the regressors are significant at the 1% level.

We used the Breusch–Godfrey test for serial correlation to check for the existence of serial autocorrelation in the residuals, instead of the Durbin–Watson test. The reason is that the Durbin–Watson test is more limited and allows for

Table 12.5   LTN auctions: new regression

Dependent Variable: LOG(VAR)
Method: Least squares
Sample (adjusted): 2281
Included observations: 229 after adjustments

Variable	Coefficient	Std. Error	t-Statistic	Prob.
C	−5.307391	1.134891	−4.676566	0.0000
LOG(MSEC)	0.138887	0.050293	2.761578	0.0062
LOG(DIFUT)	0.149969	0.041497	3.613945	0.0004
LOG(CDI)	0.808110	0.104195	7.755719	0.0000
LOG(DU)	0.666437	0.195916	3.401644	0.0008
R-squared	0.361260	Mean dependent var		−7.090029
Adjusted R-squared	0.349854	S.D. dependent var		1.555537
S.E. of regression	1.254256	Akaike info criterion		3.312554
Sum squared resid	352.3872	Schwarz criterion		3.387526
Log likelihood	−374.2874	F-statistic		31.67256
Durbin-Watson stat	1.969794	Prob(F-statistic)		0.000000

the verification of only one lag. We ran the Breusch–Godfrey test for 5 lags. The test gives a probability of 0.139962, implying that we cannot reject the null hypothesis of serial autocorrelation at the 5% level. We can also observe that none of the regressor coefficients are significant (see Table 12.6).

We used the White test to check for heteroskedasticity. This test is good because it does not require any previous hypothesis about the heteroskedasticity. In this test, the null hypothesis is the existence of the homoskedasticity. The test indicated a probability of 46% and, therefore, we cannot reject the null hypothesis at the 5% level. Table 12.7 presents the result of this test.

Finally, we tested the model for the existence of some form of dynamic heteroskedasticity using the Auto Regressive Conditional Heteroskedasticity (ARCH) test (Wooldridge, 2003). In this test, the null hypothesis is the absence of ARCH. We ran the test with 5 lags, and the results are presented in Table 12.8. As can be seen, at the 5% level we cannot reject the null hypothesis, since the probability is 64 per cent.

Our model, thus, has the following form:

$$LOG(VAR) = -5.31 + 0.14 * LOG(MSEC) + 0.15 * LOG(DIFUT) \\ + 0.81 * LOG(CDI) + 0.67 * LOG(DU)$$

In the log-log model, a small change in one regressor has an impact in the dependent variable near the value of the coefficient of the regressor. Thus, *ceteris paribus*, if MSEC increases by 1 per cent, the variance of the bids in LTN auctions increases by approximately 0.14 per cent; if DIFUT increases by

Table 12.6   Serial autocorrelation test for LTN auctions

Breusch–Godfrey Serial Correlation LM Test:

F-statistic	1.649258	Probability	0.148163
Obs*R-squared	8.309930	Probability	0.139962

Test Equation:
Dependent Variable: RESID
Method: Least squares
Presample and interior missing value lagged residuals set to zero.

Variable	Coefficient	Std. Error	t-Statistic	Prob.
C	0.129778	1.129210	0.114928	0.9086
LOG(MSEC)	−0.012163	0.050245	−0.242075	0.8089
LOG(DIFUT)	0.008946	0.041505	0.215545	0.8295
LOG(CDI)	−0.019146	0.104421	−0.183353	0.8547
LOG(DU)	−0.044357	0.195213	−0.227222	0.8205
RESID(−1)	−0.071097	0.076395	−0.930657	0.3531
RESID(−2)	0.135675	0.074270	1.826795	0.0691
RESID(−3)	0.103164	0.077747	1.326925	0.1859
RESID(−4)	0.082935	0.074663	1.110794	0.2679
RESID(−5)	0.105391	0.074116	1.421969	0.1565

R-squared	0.036288	Mean dependent var	−3.88E-16
Adjusted R-squared	−0.003317	S.D. dependent var	1.243205
S.E. of regression	1.245265	Akaike info criterion	3.319259
Sum squared resid	339.5998	Schwarz criterion	3.469203
Log likelihood	−370.0552	F-statistic	0.916255
Durbin-Watson stat	1.844625	Prob(F-statistic)	0.511813

1 per cent the variance increases by 0.15 per cent; if CDI increases by 1 per cent the variance increases by 0.81 per cent, and if DU increases by 1 per cent the variance increases by 0.67 per cent. Thus, all regressors are significant and they are positively correlated with the variance of the bids in the LTN auctions. The volatilities of the various interest rate markets move together with the volatility of the LTN auctions, reflecting the same uncertainty regarding the future behaviour of the interest rate.

After studying the determinants of the variance of the bids in the LTN auctions, we took a subset of auctions – the auctions of the bonds whose maturity dates were different from the maturity dates of LTN traded in the secondary market. We created a dummy variable called PRIMEMIS, which is equal to 1 when the LTN sold had a maturity date different from the LTNs traded in the secondary market, and 0 otherwise. In this case, we cannot use MSEC as an independent variable since there was no similar LTN being traded in the

Table 12.7   White test for LTN auctions

White heteroskedasticity test:

F-statistic	0.987349	Probability	0.467277
Obs*R-squared	13.89431	Probability	0.457614

Test Equation:
Dependent Variable: RESID^2
Method: Least squares
Sample: 2281
Included observations: 229

Variable	Coefficient	Std. Error	t-Statistic	Prob.
C	−42.65801	34.25418	−1.245337	0.2144
LOG(MSEC)	0.253752	1.760747	0.144116	0.8855
(LOG(MSEC))^2	0.039746	0.043589	0.911841	0.3629
(LOG(MSEC))*(LOG(DIFUT))	0.058209	0.060103	0.968494	0.3339
(LOG(MSEC))*(LOG(CDI))	−0.045992	0.164975	−0.278781	0.7807
(LOG(MSEC))*(LOG(DU))	0.111144	0.317752	0.349782	0.7268
LOG(DIFUT)	−1.682012	1.745852	−0.963434	0.3364
(LOG(DIFUT))^2	−0.010650	0.018268	−0.582990	0.5605
(LOG(DIFUT))*(LOG(CDI))	−0.228107	0.166877	−1.366911	0.1731
(LOG(DIFUT))*(LOG(DU))	0.169678	0.300324	0.564983	0.5727
LOG(CDI)	−2.955148	3.855564	−0.766463	0.4442
(LOG(CDI))^2	0.251597	0.259692	0.968829	0.3337
(LOG(CDI))*(LOG(DU))	0.704130	0.740163	0.951317	0.3425
LOG(DU)	11.73808	11.95768	0.981635	0.3274
(LOG(DU))^2	−0.537187	1.069474	−0.502291	0.6160

R-squared	0.060674	Mean dependent var	1.538809
Adjusted R-squared	−0.000777	S.D. dependent var	2.868552
S.E. of regression	2.869667	Akaike info criterion	5.009527
Sum squared resid	1762.287	Schwarz criterion	5.234444
Log likelihood	−558.5909	F-statistic	0.987349
Durbin-Watson stat	2.077748	Prob(F-statistic)	0.467277

secondary market. The number of observations is thin, only 16, and, consequently, the robustness of the regression is low. Our aim in studying this situation was to try and understand what is behind the variance of the bids of LTN when there is no secondary market reference; that is, when the uncertainty is typically higher than in other LTN auctions.

We ran a log-log regression for this model. Initially, we tried to use the variance of the Selic rate, the variance of the futures interbank rate, the variance of the spot interbank rate, and the maturity date in working days. However, they did not perform well. We then tested various combinations of regressors. The

Table 12.8   ARCH test for LTN auctions

ARCH Test:

F-statistic	0.660316	Probability	0.654384
Obs*R-squared	3.389525	Probability	0.640166

Test Equation:
Dependent Variable: RESID^2
Method: Least squares
Sample (adjusted): 7271
Included observations: 104 after adjustments

Variable	Coefficient	Std. Error	t-Statistic	Prob.
C	1.254004	0.400512	3.131004	0.0023
RESID^2(−1)	−0.046185	0.104311	−0.442761	0.6589
RESID^2(−2)	0.101489	0.090969	1.115637	0.2673
RESID^2(−3)	−0.061360	0.103800	−0.591141	0.5558
RESID^2(−4)	0.083527	0.104043	0.802811	0.4240
RESID^2(−5)	−0.020141	0.091317	−0.220563	0.8259

R-squared	0.032592	Mean dependent var	1.346021
Adjusted R-squared	−0.016766	S.D. dependent var	2.880488
S.E. of regression	2.904534	Akaike info criterion	5.026384
Sum squared resid	826.7594	Schwarz criterion	5.178945
Log likelihood	−255.3720	F-statistic	0.660316
Durbin–Watson stat	2.077873	Prob(F-statistic)	0.654384

best model was the one presented in Table 12.9, where the independent variable is only the variance of the spot interbank rate. In this case, the R-squared was almost 53 per cent. The model was not rejected by the Breusch–Godfrey test for serial correlation with a lag, nor by the White heteroskedasticity test. The number of observations prevented us to test for ARCH.

The form of this model is:

$$LOG(VAR) = -0.72 + 1.27 * LOG(CDI)$$

We expected that the variance of the logarithm of the futures interbank rate and the maturity date would also be significant. However, the small number of observations did not lead to a robust result. Since there are only four maturity dates per year, it will be necessary to collect more observations to have a more conclusive result. In the future, we will not be able to perform a more robust regression since the evolution of the secondary market for the LTNs with maturity dates according to the pattern adopted by the Treasury at the beginning of 2003 will create a very different situation from the one analysed

Table 12.9   Regression for the LTN auctions without secondary market

Dependent Variable: LOG(VAR)
Method: Least squares
Date: 20/04/06 Time: 12:55
Sample: 1282 IF PRIMEMIS = 1
Included observations: 16

Variable	Coefficient	Std. Error	t-Statistic	Prob.
C	−0.722236	1.387204	−0.520641	0.6108
LOG(CDI)	1.267585	0.319204	3.971086	0.0014
R-squared	0.529720	Mean dependent var		−6.100769
Adjusted R-squared	0.496129	S.D. dependent var		1.689321
S.E. of regression	1.199145	Akaike info criterion		3.317564
Sum squared resid	20.13129	Schwarz criterion		3.414137
Log likelihood	−24.54051	F-statistic		15.76952
Durbin-Watson stat	1.654791	Prob(F-statistic)		0.001393

in this chapter. This exercise tried to capture the market sentiment when the change of pattern occurred.

4.2   NTN-F auctions

After testing for the determinants of the variance of the bids in the LTN auctions, we tried to apply the same model for the NTN-F. Our sample included 102 auctions between December 2003 and December 2005. It includes all NTN-F auctions since this bond started to be offered by the Treasury.

Our first problem related to the implementation of the LTN model was the fact that the secondary market of NTN-F was very thin during this period. There were only 147 transactions involving this bond in the secondary market during this time, which amount to an average of one transaction per week. In terms of comparison, the number of transactions of LTN in the secondary market in this period was 140.5. These numbers give a good idea of the difference in liquidity between these bonds.

Thus, the regressors of our log-log model were reduced to three variables: the logarithm of the maturity date (in workind days) (DU), the logarithm of the spot interbank rate (CDI), and the logarithm of the futures interbank rate (DIFUT).

The result of the model is presented in Table 12.10. We can see that the coefficients are not significant, except for the maturity date. As a consequence, we made several changes in order to make the model more robust.

We tested various combinations between the regressors. The only variable that performed well was the maturity date, as can be seen in Table 12.11.

At the 5% level, this model was not rejected by the Breusch-Godfrey test for serial correlation, as can be seen in Table 12.12.

Table 12.10 Regression for NTN-F auctions

Dependent Variable: LOG(VAR)
Method: Least squares
Sample: 1102
Included observations: 91

Variable	Coefficient	Std. Error	t-Statistic	Prob.
C	−23.41925	3.856028	−6.073412	0.0000
LOG(DU)	2.579763	0.531647	4.852401	0.0000
LOG(CDI)	0.036107	0.289451	0.124743	0.9010
LOG(DIFUT)	0.022008	0.092894	0.236918	0.8133
R-squared	0.220909	Mean dependent var		−5.723741
Adjusted R-squared	0.194044	S.D. dependent var		1.624269
S.E. of regression	1.458189	Akaike info criterion		3.635228
Sum squared resid	184.9893	Schwarz criterion		3.745595
Log likelihood	−161.4029	F-statistic		8.222877
Durbin–Watson stat	2.026589	Prob(F-statistic)		0.000070

Table 12.11 New regression for NTN-F auctions

Dependent variable: LOG(VAR)
Method: Least squares
Date: 21/08/06 Time: 00:58
Sample: 1102
Included observations: 95

Variable	Coefficient	Std. Error	t-Statistic	Prob.
C	−22.15138	3.438571	−6.442032	0.0000
LOG(DU)	2.349865	0.491526	4.780752	0.0000
R-squared	0.197277	Mean dependent var		−5.727530
Adjusted R-squared	0.188645	S.D. dependent var		1.594486
S.E. of regression	1.436237	Akaike info criterion		3.582757
Sum squared resid	191.8382	Schwarz criterion		3.636523
Log likelihood	−168.1810	F-statistic		22.85559
Durbin–Watson stat	1.913335	Prob(F-statistic)		0.000007

The White heteroskedasticity test was also significant, that is, it did not reject the null hypothesis, as can be seen from Table 12.13.

The ARCH test with 5 lags also did not reject the null hypothesis (Table 12.14). Thus, the model was not rejected by any one of the three tests we ran.

The R-Squared of this model is 20 per cent. It has the following form:

$$LOG(VAR) = -22.15 + 2.35 * LOG(DU)$$

Table 12.12 Serial correlation test for NTN-F auctions

Breusch–Godfrey Serial Correlation LM Test:

F-statistic	2.119470	Probability	0.070450
Obs*R-squared	10.21070	Probability	0.069481

Test equation:
Dependent variable: RESID
Method: Least squares
Presample and interior missing value lagged residuals set to zero.

Variable	Coefficient	Std. Error	t-Statistic	Prob.
C	−0.156494	3.421157	−0.045743	0.9636
LOG(DU)	0.022580	0.489039	0.046172	0.9633
RESID(−1)	0.037424	0.109296	0.342410	0.7329
RESID(−2)	−0.002211	0.110065	−0.020085	0.9840
RESID(−3)	−0.120225	0.104232	−1.153439	0.2519
RESID(−4)	−0.207617	0.105572	−1.966599	0.0524
RESID(−5)	0.232890	0.111161	2.095073	0.0390

R-squared	0.107481	Mean dependent var		1.45E-15
Adjusted R-squared	0.046628	S.D. dependent var		1.428577
S.E. of regression	1.394874	Akaike info criterion		3.574313
Sum squared resid	171.2192	Schwarz criterion		3.762493
Log likelihood	−162.7799	F-statistic		1.766225
Durbin–Watson stat	1.848885	Prob(F-statistic)		0.115301

The explanation for this result can be found in the absence of liquidity of the NTN-F in the period under analysis. The main effect of this lack of liquidity is the absence of a secondary market where the participants in the auction could trade their bonds. Therefore, the holders must keep their bonds until maturity. The lack of a secondary market reduces the importance of the volatility of the spot rate of interest, and increases the uncertainty due to the holding period of the bond. That is why the maturity date is so important in the determination of the variance of the bids in the NTN-F auctions, as expressed by our model. It is also important to notice that these bonds do not embody a higher interest rate risk precisely because of the absence of a secondary market. However, the reinvestment risk is high in an environment featuring declining interest rates. In contrast, the default risk is perceived to be higher in comparison with the LTN, because the holders cannot easily sell their bonds. Finally, the liquidity risk is high because the secondary market is very thin. Thus, when the holders want to sell their bonds, they find this difficult because there are no buyers. It is not a matter of price; it is a matter of absence of a market for these bonds. When the holders decide to buy, they need to take these risks into account. That is why the maturity date is so important in the determination of the variance of the bids.

Table 12.13 White heteroskedasticity test for NTN-F auctions

White Heteroskedasticity Test:

F-statistic	2.318704	Probability	0.104126
Obs*R-squared	4.558832	Probability	0.102344

Test equation:
Dependent variable: RESID^2
Method: Least squares
Sample: 1102
Included observations: 95

Variable	Coefficient	Std. Error	t-Statistic	Prob.
C	264.1539	193.9708	1.361823	0.1766
LOG(DU)	−73.52439	55.75462	−1.318714	0.1905
(LOG(DU))^2	5.144023	4.000547	1.285830	0.2017

R-squared	0.047988	Mean dependent var	2.019349
Adjusted R-squared	0.027292	S.D. dependent var	3.167078
S.E. of regression	3.123562	Akaike info criterion	5.146895
Sum squared resid	897.6107	Schwarz criterion	5.227543
Log likelihood	−241.4775	F-statistic	2.318704
Durbin–Watson stat	2.093533	Prob(F-statistic)	0.104126

Table 12.14 ARCH Test for NTN-F auctions

ARCH Test:

F-statistic	1.237908	Probability	0.302567
Obs*R-squared	6.172078	Probability	0.289833

Test equation:
Dependent variable: RESID^2
Method: Least squares
Sample (adjusted): 6100
Included observations: 67 after adjustments

Variable	Coefficient	Std. Error	t-Statistic	Prob.
C	1.427335	0.683677	2.087733	0.0410
RESID^2(−1)	−0.043018	0.122851	−0.350163	0.7274
RESID^2(−2)	0.083506	0.128830	0.648188	0.5193
RESID^2(−3)	−0.065081	0.129300	−0.503334	0.6165
RESID^2(−4)	0.018979	0.120227	0.157860	0.8751
RESID^2(−5)	0.274939	0.117066	2.348589	0.0221

(*Continued*)

Table 12.14 (Continued)

R-squared	0.092121	Mean dependent var	2.023367
Adjusted R-squared	0.017704	S.D. dependent var	3.247543
S.E. of regression	3.218667	Akaike info criterion	5.261097
Sum squared resid	631.9488	Schwarz criterion	5.458532
Log likelihood	−170.2468	F-statistic	1.237908
Durbin–Watson stat	1.539064	Prob(F-statistic)	0.302567

Finally, it is important to mention the fact that the liquidity of the futures contracts whose maturity dates are similar to the maturity dates of the NTN-F is also very low. This helps to blur the price formation of these bonds, since there is no clue as to the behaviour of the interest rate in the distant future.

5   Summary and conclusions

The chapter has discussed the management of the domestic debt in the first Lula administration. It has examined especially closely the fixed income bonds, because the Treasury explicitly pursues a strategy of increasing the average maturity of the public domestic debt, and raising the share of fixed income debt.

The chapter showed that the first Lula administration was largely successful on both fronts. However, when we examined the share of fixed income debt, we saw that the largest part of this share includes short-term zero coupon bonds (LTN), instead of coupon bonds whose typical maturity is higher than the maturity of the zero coupon bonds. This result can be explained by two factors. First, the great uncertainty surrounding the future behaviour of the rate of interest (Selic) and, more specifically, the uncertainty surrounding fiscal policy. Consequently, the interest rate risk is perceived as being too high, and the bond holders prefer to buy short-term bonds. Second, the absence of a deep secondary market for the NTN-F, which prevents the bond holders from selling the bond easily. Clearly, those explanations are closely correlated, since the uncertainties affecting the interest rate lead bond holders to prefer LTN rather than NTN-F. In this situation, the Treasury has gradually decreased the supply of LTN, and increased the supply of NTN-F. Of course, it should be pointed out that, during this process of change of profile of the fixed income debt, the average maturity of this debt declined, and it tended to increase later, when the uncertainties fell.

This strategy started to be adopted at the end of the first Lula administration. It was shown above that the proportion of NTN-F started to increase more rapidly at the end of 2005 (and early 2006). In the second Lula administration, it is expected that the proportion of NTN-F should continue to increase. In this respect, it is important to mention the fact that the Treasury issued for the first time a ten-year NTN-F at the beginning of 2007.

The chapter also discussed in more detail the role of the uncertainties around the behaviour of the rate of interest in both LTN and NTN-F auctions. The main objective was to understand the difficulties faced by the Treasury to achieve its objectives in terms of debt management. We showed that the uncertainty in the various markets for interest rates are correlated with the maturities of the auctioned bonds. Both the spot rate of interest and the futures rate of interest appeared to be good indicators of the market expectations for the future behaviour of the interest rate.

The role performed by the secondary market in the determination of the dispersion of bids was made clear when we tested the model for the LTN without secondary market. In spite of the small number of observations, the model showed that only the spot interbank rate was significant in explaining the dispersion of the bids in these auctions. The absence of a futures market can be explained by the fact that, when there is no secondary market, the future behaviour of the rate of interest is meaningless. The absence of the maturity dates can be explained by the fact that the market did not have any reference in terms of the behaviour of the rate of interest at the maturity date, simply because the maturity of these LTNs was different from the maturity of the interest rate futures contracts. When we tested our model for the NTN-F auctions, the absence of the secondary market was more critical in the definition of the form of the model.

The absence of the secondary market is critical because it prevents the market participants from forming expectations about the future behaviour of the rate of interest, since there is no price (and interest rate) history related to this bond. In the case of the NTN-F auctions, only the maturity date was significant as a regressor. It was shown in the previous section that this variable embodies both the liquidity risk and the default risk of the bond. Again, the absence of a secondary market prevents even the futures market from properly forming the price (and the rate of interest).

This chapter, thus, has also examined the role of the uncertainty – as represented by the dispersion of the bids – in the bondholder's decisions. It also features the importance of liquidity in the willingness of these agents to buy long-term fixed income bonds. In this respect, any strategy to extend the maturity of the domestic public debt and to change its profile, increasing the proportion of fixed income debt, requires a reduction in the volatility of the rate of interest, the implementation of a more stable macroeconomic environment (that is, an environment less subject to structural breaks), a better fiscal stance and the development of the secondary markets for coupon bonds. That is precisely what the new Lula administration needs to do in order to improve even more its domestic debt management.

Notes

1 We would like to acknowledge the superb research assistance of Viviane Santos Vivian. Jaime de Jesus Filho also provided very important econometric assistance.
2 Associate Professor of Economics and Finance, Brazilian School of Public and Business Administration, Getulio Vargas Foundation (EBAPE/FGV). Member of the Money

and Financial Markets Study Group at the Institute of Economics, Federal University of Rio de Janeiro (IE-UFRJ). Researcher of Pronex (FAPERJ/MCT). Correspondence to sobreira@fgv.br.

3 Master in Public Administration, Brazilian School of Public and Business Administration (EBAPE/FGV) and Brazilian Central Bank. The opinions here do not reflect those of the Brazilian Central Bank.

4 The *'Plano Anual de Financiamento'* is a yearly report in which the Treasury describes its strategy for the debt management in the year to come.

5 As can be seen in the next section, the extended maturity of LTN was followed by a decrease in the variance in the auctions of this bond, which can be seen as an increase in the confidence of the bond holders.

6 The year 2002 was chosen because it is the borderline between the end of the Cardoso administration and the beginning of the Lula administration. As a consequence, this year has some implications for the debt management in the years to come.

7 This is the variance adjusted by the maturity of the securities auctioned.

8 Our calculations were made with E-Views 5.0.

References

Araújo Carlos Hamilton Vasconcelos. Mercado de títulos públicos e operações de mercado aberto no Brasil – aspectos históricos e operacionais. *Notas Técnicas do Banco Central do Brazil*. N. 12. Brasília: Banco Central do Brasil, 2002.

Bacen. Annual Report. Brasília: Bacen, 2004.

Bacen/STN. 'Mudanças nos mercados primário e secundário da dívida pública mobiliária federal interna'. Mimeo. Brasília, 1999.

Bikhchandani, Sushil and Huang, Chi-Fu 'Auctions with resale markets: A model of treasury bill auctions'. *Review of Financial Studies*. 2(3), 311–40, 1989.

Bogdanski, Joel, Tombini, Alexandre Antonio and Werlang, Sérgio Ribeiro da Costa. Implementing Inflation Targeting in Brazil. Working Papers Series. No. 1. Brasília: Banco Central do Brasil, 2000.

Cammack, Elizabeth. 'Evidence on bidding strategies and the information contained in treasury bill auctions'. *Journal of Political Economy*. 99, 100–30, 1991.

Garcia, Márcio G.P. and Rezende, Leonardo B. 'Leilões de títulos da dívida pública pelo Banco Central do Brasil: Um estudo dos fatores condicionantes da dispersão das propostas para os BBCs'. *Revista de Economia Política*. 20(4), 8–25. São Paulo, 2000.

Milgrom, Paul and Weber, Robert. 'A theory of auctions and competitive bidding'. *Econometrica*. 50(5), 1089–22, Sep. 1982.

Mills, Terence C. *The Econometric Modeling of Financial Time Series*. Cambridge: Cambridge University Press, 1993.

PAF (2002). *Plano Anual de Financiamento*. Brasília: Tesouro Nacional.

PAF (2003). *Plano Anual de Financiamento*. Brasília: Tesouro Nacional.

PAF (2004). *Plano Anual de Financiamento*. Brasília: Tesouro Nacional.

PAF (2005). *Plano Anual de Financiamento*. Brasília: Tesouro Nacional.

PAF (2006). *Plano Anual de Financiamento*. Brasília: Tesouro Nacional.

Silva, Anderson Caputo. Bidding strategies in the Brazilian treasury auctions. Série de textos para discussão. N. 265. Brasília: Universidade de Brasília, 2002.

Umlauf, Steven R. 'An empirical study of the Mexican treasury bill auctions'. *Journal of Financial Economics*. 33, 313–40, June. Rochester: University of Rochester, 1993.

Wooldridge, Jeffrey M. *Introductory Econometrics: A Modern Approach*. 2nd edn, Mason: Thomson, 2003.

Index